BOWMAN LIBRARY
MENLO SCHOOL AND MENLO COLLEGE

P9-CKT-811

Pushkin Threefold

WALTER ARNDT, translator of Pushkin's *Eugene Onegin*, the present anthology, and Goethe's *Faust*, was born at Constantinople in 1916 as a citizen of the Free and Hanseatic City of Hamburg. He had nine years of classical schooling at Breslau, Silesia (now restored to Poland as Wroclaw), and in 1934 moved to Oxford, where in the intervals of rowing for Oriel College he read Economics and Political Science.

After Oxford, Mr. Arndt went to Poland for graduate study at Warsaw, and after learning Polish began his study of Russian. In 1939 he resigned his German citizenship and volunteered for the Polish army. After the peripatetic campaign of 1939 he escaped from a German POW camp, spent a year in the Polish underground at Warsaw forging Nazi documents, and made his way to Istanbul by way of Berlin in 1940. Here, in an enforced civilian interlude, he took a degree in mechanical engineering at Robert College and resumed intensive study of Russian language and literature.

Between 1942 and 1945, Mr. Arndt was active in political, military, and war-economic intelligence with the U.S. Office of Strategic Services and, later, O.W.I. in the Aegean theatre. He taught at Robert College and worked in U.N. refugee resettlement between 1944 and 1949, when he emigrated to the United States. There he taught Classics and modern languages (French, German, and Russian) at Guilford College in North Carolina until 1956, when he received his doctorate in Comparative Linguistics and Classics at the University of North Carolina.

After Ford fellowships at Ann Arbor and Harvard, Mr. Arndt held successive appointments in linguistics and Slavic languages and literatures at Chapel Hill. He left in 1966 as Chairman of the Department of Linguistics, Slavic, and Oriental Languages to take up a professorship and, later, the chairmanship in Russian at Dartmouth.

Mr. Arndt's verse translation of Pushkin's *Eugene Onegin* was published in 1963 and awarded a Bollingen Prize that year. His verse translation of Goethe's *Faust* in the metric forms of the original will be published in 1972. He has also translated from Lermontov, Tyutchev, Fet, Pasternak, Evtushenko, Heine, Wilhelm Busch, Morgenstern, and Rilke, and published books on linguistic theory and glottochronology.

Pushkin Threefold

NARRATIVE, LYRIC, POLEMIC, AND RIBALD VERSE

The Originals with Linear and Metric Translations by

WALTER ARNDT

NEW YORK ✛ E. P. DUTTON & CO., INC.
1972

Copyright © 1972 by Walter Arndt
All rights reserved. Printed in the U.S.A.

FIRST EDITION

No part of this book may be reproduced or transmitted in any form or
by any means, electronic or mechanical, including photocopy, recording,
or any information storage and retrieval system now known or to be
invented, without permission in writing from the publisher, except by
a reviewer who wishes to quote brief passages in connection with a
review written for inclusion in a magazine, newspaper or broadcast.

Published simultaneously in Canada by
Clarke, Irwin & Company Limited, Toronto and Vancouver

Library of Congress Catalog Card Number: 69-17218

SBN 0-525-18652-2 (Cloth)   SBN 0-525-47260-6 (DP)

To my casual critics,
Miriam, Robby, Dave, Prue, and Corinne,
indulgent providers and consumers, one and all,
of poetry and patience

Acknowledgments

The author and publishers express their gratitude to the following for permission granted to reprint, adapt, or otherwise make use of materials previously published:

The South Atlantic Modern Language Association and the Northwestern University Press for introductory passages first published, respectively, in the *South Atlantic Bulletin,* Vol. XXIX, No. 3 (May, 1964), and the *Tri-Quarterly,* No. 8 (Winter, 1967).

To Dimitri von Mohrenschildt for eleven verse translations of poems by Pushkin, first published in the *Russian Review,* Vol. XXIV, No. 1 (January, 1965).

The American Association for the Advancement of Slavic Studies for the verse translation of *The Gypsies,* first published in a slightly different version in the *Slavic Review,* Vol. XXIV, No. 2 (June, 1965).

HMH Publishing Co. Inc., holders of the copyright, © 1965, for *Tsar Nikita,* originally published in a slightly different version as "Czar Nikita and His Forty Daughters" in *Playboy* magazine (December, 1965).

Grateful acknowledgment is due to the American Philosophical Society for a travel and research grant awarded the author in the autumn of 1966, which enabled him to work on Pushkin's library and original Pushkin manuscripts in the *Puškinskij Dom* of the Soviet Academy of Sciences in Leningrad and on the materials held by the Pushkin Museum in Moscow.

The author further expresses his warm sense of obligation to Edmund Wilson, George Steiner, Vsevolod Setchkarev of Harvard University, and his colleagues Professors Richard Sheldon, Nathan Rosen, and Guy de Mallac-Sauzier, for thoughtful criticism and stimulating suggestions in relation to the verse translations of *The Bronze Horseman* and *Tsar Saltan*.

Contents

Introduction   xxv

METRIC TRANSLATIONS

Shorter Poems

[1817]   Liberty   3
[1818]   To Chaadaev   6
                To the Author of *History of the
                    Russian State*   6

                History of a Versifier   7

[1819]   In the Country   7
                Seclusion   9
[1821]   The Dagger   10
[1822]   Epigram on
                    A. A. Davydova   11
                To a Foreign Girl   11
[1823]   A Little Bird   12
                Night   12
                "As freedom's sower in the
                    wasteland"   13
[1824]   On Count Vorontsov   13
                To the Sea   13
                "Rose-maiden, no, I do not
                    quarrel"   15
                The Grape   16

THE ORIGINALS WITH LINEAR TRANSLATIONS

Стихотворения

Вольность   164

К Чаадаеву   170

Автору «История
  Государства
  Российского   170

История
  стихотворца   172

Деревня   172

Уединение   176

Кинжал   176

На А. А. Давыдову   180

Иностранке   180

Птичка   180

Ночь   182

«Свободы сеятель
  пустынный...»   182

На Воронцова   184

К морю   184

«О дева-роза, я в
  оковах...»   188

Виноград   188

Shorter Poems

Liberty   165

To Chaadaev   171

To the Author of *History of the
  Russian State*   171

History of a Versifier   173

In the Country   173

Seclusion   177

The Dagger   177

On A. A. Davydova   181

To a Foreign Girl   181

A Little Bird   181

Night   183

"Freedom's sower in wilderness,"
  183

To Vorontsov   185

To the Sea   185

"Oh rose maiden, I am in fetters;"
  189

The Grape   189

[1824]   "Liza is afraid to love."   16

[1825]   "When first the roses wither,"
                              16
                            Ex Ungue Leonem   17
                            André Chénier   17
                            To . . .   18
                            Winter Evening   19
                            "What if life deceives and baits
                              you,"   20
                            Bacchic Song   20
                            "The season's final blossoms
                              bring"   20
                            Tempest   21
                            To Friends   21
                            Prose and Poetry   22
                            "You're the kind that always
                              loses,"   22
                            "Oh, Muse of satire, breathing
                              fire!"   22
                            On Alexander I   23

[1826]   "Beneath the azure heaven of her
                              native land"   23

                            To Vyazemsky   24
                            To Yazykov   24
                            Confession   25
                            To I. I. Pushchin   26
                            Stanzas   26

«Лизе страшно полюбить...» 190

«Лишь розы увядают...» 190

Ex Ungue Leonem 190

Андрей Шенье 192

К*** 192

Зимний вечер 194

«Если жизнь тебя обманет...» 196

Вакхическая песня 198

«Цветы последние милей...» 198

Буря 198

Приятелям 200

Прозаик и поэт 200

«Нет ни в чем вам благодати...» 202

«О муза пламенной сатиры!...» 202

На Александра I 202

«Под небом голубым страны своей родной...» 204

К Вяземскому 204

К Языкову 206

Признание 206

И. И. Пущину 210

Стансы 210

"Lisa is afraid to love." 191

"So soon as roses wilt," 191

Ex Ungue Leonem 191

André Chénier 193

To . . . 193

Winter Evening 195

If life deceives you," 197

Bacchic Song 199

"The last flowers are dearer" 199

Tempest 199

To Friends 201

Prose-Writer and Poet 201

"Grace in anything eludes you;" 203

"Oh, Muse of flaming satire!" 203

On Alexander I 203

"Beneath the blue sky of her native land" 205

To Vyazemsky 205

To Yazykov 207

Confession 207

To I. I. Pushchin 211

Stanzas 211

[1826?] To the Emperor Nicholas I 27

[1826] Winter Journey 27
[1827] Three Springs 28
          Arion 29
          The Poet 29
          The Talisman 30
[1828] To Dawe, Esq. 31
          Remembrance 31
          Thou and You 32
          Young Mare 32

          Foreboding 33
          "Raven doth to raven fly," 34

          "Capital of pomp and squalor," 34
          The Upas Tree 35
          "The dreary day is spent, and dreary night has soon" 36

          "Blest he who at your fancy's pleasure" 36
[1829] "I loved you: and the feeling, why deceive you," 37

          "As down the noisy streets I wander" 37
          At the Bust of a Conqueror 38

Императору
    Николаю 212

Зимняя дорога 212

Три ключа 214

Арион 216

Поэт 216

Талисман 218

To Dawe, Esqr 220

Воспоминание 220

Ты и вы 222

«Кобылица
    молодая...» 222

Предчувствие 224

«Ворон к ворону
    летит...» 224

«Город пышный, город
    бедный...» 226

Анчар 226

«Ненастный день потух;
    ненастной ночи
    мгла...» 230

«Счастлив, кто избран
    своенравно...» 230

«Я вас любил:
    любовь еще, быть
    может....» 232

«Брожу ли я вдоль
    улиц шумных...» 232

К бюсту завоевателя 234

To the Emperor Nicholas I 213

Winter Road 213

Three Springs 215

Arion 217

The Poet 217

The Talisman 219

To Dawe, Esq. 221

Remembrance 221

Thou and You 223

"Young mare," 223

Foreboding 225

"Raven to raven flies," 225

"Gorgeous city, wretched city,"
    227

The Upas Tree 227

"The dismal day has flickered out;
    the dismal night's mist" 231

"Blest he who wantonly was
    chosen" 231

"I used to love you: love has still,
    it may be," 233

"When I wander along noisy
    streets" 233

At the Bust of a Conqueror 235

[1829]   The Monastery on Mt. Kazbek
39

The Snowslide   39

[1830]   "What use my name to you, what
good?"   40

"At moments when your graceful
form"   41

Fountain at Tsarskoe Selo   41

Conjury   42

[1830]   "Bound for the distant coast that
bore you,"   42

[1831]   At Kutuzov's Grave   43

To the Slanderers of Russia   44

Echo   46

[1832]   In a Beauty's Album   46

Album Verse   47

[1833]   "But for my soul's obscurely
asking"   47

"Don't let me lose my mind, oh,
God;"   47

[1835]   "Bitterly sobbing, the maid chid
the youth with jealous
reproaches;"   48

"I was assured my heart had
rested"   49

[Between 1827   "She looks at you with such soft
and 1836]   feeling,"   49

Монастырь на Казбеке 236

Обвал 236

«Что в имени тебе моем?...» 238

«Когда в объятия мои...» 240

Царскосельская статуя 240

Заклинание 242

«Для берегов отчизны дальной...» 242

«Перед гробницею святой...» 244

Клеветникам России 246

Эхо 250

Красавица 250

В альбом 252

«Когда б не смутное влеченье...» 252

«Не дай мне Бог сойти с ума...» 252

«Юношу, горько рыдая, ревнивая дева бранила...» 254

«Я думал, сердце позабыло...» 256

«Она глядит на вас так нежно...» 256

The Monastery on Mt. Kazbek 237

The Snowslide 237

"What is there for you in my name?" 239

"When into my embraces" 241

Fountain at Tsarskoe Selo 241

Conjury 243

"For the shores of your distant country" 243

"Before the sacred sepulcher" 245

To the Slanderers of Russia 247

Echo 251

A Beauty 251

Album Verse 253

"Were it not for the troubled urging" 253

"God grant that I not lose my mind." 253

"Bitterly sobbing, the jealous maiden was chiding the youth;" 255

"I thought my heart had quite forgotten" 257

"She gazes at you so tenderly," 257

[1836]   From Pindemonte   49

                  Narrative Poems, Fairy Tales,
                  and Ballads

[1822]   Tsar Nikita and His Forty
                       Daughters   52
[1824]   The Gypsies   59
[1825]   The Bridegroom   81
                  Count Nulin   88
[1831]   Tsar Saltan   100

[1833]   The Bronze Horseman   128

                  Selected Stanzas from
                  Eugene Onegin:
[1823–1831]   A NOVEL IN VERSE   146

(Из Пиндемонти)   256

From Pindemonte   257

*Поэмы, Сказки
и Баллады*

*Narrative Poems, Fairy Tales,
and Ballads*

Царь Никита и сорок его
   дочерей   260

Tsar Nikita and His Forty
   Daughters   261

Цыганы   274

The Gypsies   275

Жених   314

The Bridegroom   315

Граф Нулин   326

Count Nulin   327

Сказка о Царе Салтане, о
   сыне его славном и
   могучем богатыре князе
   Гвидоне Салтановиче
   и о прекрасной
   Царевне Лебеди   348

Tsar Saltan   349

Медный Всадник   400

The Bronze Horseman   401

Избранные Строфы из
Евгения Онегина:
РОМАН В СТИХАХ   428

Selected Stanzas from
Eugene Onegin:
A NOVEL IN VERSE   429

Illustrations

Notebook page inscribed on May 27, 1822, showing
    Pushkin's signature in French and Russian   xxix

An early manuscript page of THE GYPSIES   60

One of Pushkin's notebooks, opened to the first stanza
    of EUGENE ONEGIN   147

A notebook page showing rough drafts of stanzas II, 29,
    30 of EUGENE ONEGIN   148

Introduction

Pushkin enjoys in his country a veneration comparable to that accorded to Goethe in Germany and Mickiewicz in Poland—with the immense difference that, generation after generation, young people read him spontaneously and quote him with love and pride—and at great length. I have yet to meet the schoolboy in the U.S.S.R. who would lump Pushkin together with trig and M-L (Marxism-Leninism) among the "ughs" of the school curriculum. It is doubly pleasant, therefore, to assume that a new collection of translations from Pushkin no longer needs an elaborate biographical-critical send-off to introduce the author to an American public.

To the extent that this is true, we are indebted for it, first of all, to the progress achieved in a scant twenty years of Slavonic studies at American universities, starting from the early pioneering efforts of a handful of senior scholars,[1] most of whom are fortunately still living and active; to some degree, perhaps, we owe it to the late-blooming prominence attained in other fields by one of the foremost Pushkin disciples anywhere in the world, Vladimir Nabokov; and of late, to the patient and often exemplary work of a younger generation of students and devotees of Russian literature in the academic and publishing worlds. Those who still find it difficult, owing perhaps in part to a popular vodka advertisement, to "place" Pushkin—in this group may be the editors of several unjustly revered encyclopedias—are referred to the Pushkin biographies by Simmons, Troyat, Mirsky, and Setchkarev, to name only the more accessible ones; and if their time is too short, to John Fennell's ad-

[1] Like Samuel Cross, Leo Wiener, Leonid Strakhovsky, Albert Parry, and A. P. Coleman, Ernest Simmons, René Wellek, and Roman Jakobson, Michael Karpovich, Renato Poggioli, and Wiktor Weintraub, Isaiah Berlin, Gleb Struve, Dimitri von Mohrenschildt, and Wacław Lednicki.

mirable introduction to the 1964 Pushkin anthology in the Penguin Poets series.

There are to my knowledge no more than three sizable Pushkin anthologies for English readers, of which two closely resemble each other in purpose and design, do not contain Russian originals, and show considerable overlap of contents. The older and more voluminous of the latter is Avram Yarmolinsky's collection of 1936,[2] which has gone through several editions and revisions. The more recent and compact one is the Dell paperback volume edited and introduced by Ernest Simmons, which appeared twenty-five years later. Each of these contains forty-odd shorter poems; *Eugene Onegin* in full or in part; *The Bronze Horseman* and one of the rhymed fairy tales in the familiar Oliver Elton translations; one or two of the dramatic works; and a more or less extensive sampling of Pushkin's prose. Close to one-half of the contents of the two are quantitatively the same. In the Yarmolinsky volume, the translations of the short poems selected are almost all by Babette Deutsch. Professor Simmons sampled a greater variety of translators for the lyrics and ballads he selected, drawing, for instance, on the artists, chiefly English, who had contributed Pushkin translations to the two *Books of Russian Verse* issued by Macmillan of London some twenty years ago, like Baring, Bowra, Elton, Jerrold, V. de S. Pinto.

The latest volume preceding the present one, confined to metric works and featuring the Russian originals with fine, accurate prose translations in small print below them, was edited and magisterially introduced by John Fennell of Oxford for the Penguin Poets series in 1964. The selections of shorter verse forms are about equal in number, but on balance more interesting and representative in their variety, than those of the two predecessors, avoiding, as they do, the better-known poems already chosen for the earlier *Penguin Book of Russian Verse.*

---

[2] *The Works of Alexander Pushkin: Lyrics, Narrative Poems, Folktales, Plays, Prose.* Selected and edited, with an introduction, by Avram Yarmolinsky (New York: Random House, 1936). Reissued later as a "Borzoi" volume under the title *The Poems, Plays, and Prose of Pushkin.*

The present collection is limited to rhymed verse. It is designed to be accessible and useful, for one thing, to a reader with little or no knowledge of Russian. To him it offers, by juxtaposing line-by-line prose versions with verse translations by one and the same hand, a fairer chance to assess the textual, though hardly the emotional and atmospheric, fidelity of the final product, the English imitation, and to make up his mind which he would rather follow if one or the other jars on him. At worst, or in a sense at best, it may become an incentive to take up Russian or learn it better. To those versed in Russian, on the other hand, it will afford an opportunity not merely to have originals and English imitations close together, but also, for what this may be worth to them, to follow the reconstitution process (which of course cannot aim or stop at a decent "literal" version in prose and deserve the name of translation) through two of its many interacting states or suspensions. Admittedly, this nonsequential and ultimately untraceable process is here somewhat artificially presented as though it consisted essentially of two stages. Actually, the creator of a verse translation generally would not interpose a full, or perhaps even a partial, prose version between the original and the English poem—*pace* the absurd postulate of "literalness"— any more than, say, an artist copying in tempera a painting in oils would necessarily make or want an intermediate etching such as Millet made of his *Reapers*. Nor is the translator's end product often likely to remain final in his mind. In fact, my contention is (as may be deducible from the foregoing and will be obvious by the end of this introduction) that the final version in verse is not a further departure from the original, exacted by technical difficulties, than that represented by a "literal prose" version, but a difficult journey *back* toward the full impact of the original, toward the integral sound-rhythm-sense aggregate experienced in it or through it by the native reader or hearer. The point at which this journey starts is not a "literal prose" version at all, but a sort of colloidal suspension of the elements in a bilingual mind, from which the new poem ultimately precipitates into its new medium and idiom.

However this may be, at least the public of this new sort of verse reader is no longer a wholly captive one, as was true in the all-

English anthologies enumerated, where Pushkin was more helplessly at the uncertain mercies of his translators; nor is it deprived entirely of the virtues and graces, such as they may be, of the metric form in English, as is the case with presentations like the Fennell volume, not to mention the sad ritual murder performed for the purposes of an ever more insatiable lexical necrophilia in the first volume of Nabokov's otherwise peerless commentary on *Onegin.*

In order to make my lineal prose versions somewhat more faithful I decided to understand "literal" to imply the desirability of preserving the rhythm and length, though not the rhyme, of a line if possible. Accordingly, "natural" word order at times took second place to fidelity of this sort, and the choice of synonyms was somewhat influenced by it too, within the proper limits of semantic accuracy. Square brackets were used, not wholly consistently I am sure, where English syntax seemed to demand an insertion; parentheses where it seemed to call for an omission. Pushkin's punctuation, with its distinct penchant for commas, semicolons, dashes, and dots, was retained as far as reasonably possible. Trying to reflect the economy and syntactic accentuation of Pushkin's poetic diction and the accuracy of his lexical choices, I have taken more liberties not only with the word order of Anglo-American prose conventions but also occasionally with its lexical tolerance than may seem justifiable to some. I certainly favored the original word order, as poetically more significant and potent, over expository English syntax where the two were in conflict, substituting, for example, an English passive for a Russian active in the case of an emphatic antecedent Russian direct object. On the other hand, Pushkin's rather facile recourse to *i . . . i* for metric convenience in his numerous "both . . . and" passages was not usually imitated where it would have become an embarrassment to English diction in a passage like "outdoors there raged 'both' storm and rain."

The Russian text of the poems, though not necessarily their often conjectural sequence within a given year, or the typeface, was taken from the Soviet edition, *A. S. Puškin, Sobranie Sočinenij, Gosudarstvennoe izdatel'stvo xudožestvennoj literatury* (Moskva, 1959–62).

The arrangement of the selections is chronological by years within

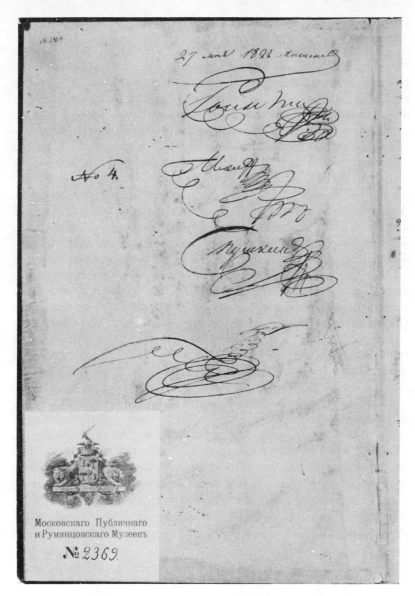

Московскаго Публичнаго
и Румянцовскаго Музеевъ
№ 2369.

Notebook page inscribed on May 27, 1822, at Kishinev in Bessarabia, showing Pushkin's signature in French and Russian.

each section, without consistent regard, however, for sequence within each year, which is often impossible to establish. Nor was any attempt made, despite strong temptation, to assign the shorter poems to "genres" such as those strung together in the subtitle, or others that might be descernible in the opulent tapestry of Pushkin's total *oeuvre*. Among the major Pushkinian glories not represented is the delicately burlesque mock-epic in fairy-tale form, *Ruslan and Ljudmila*, which established Pushkin's fame in 1820, unless the artistic folktale, playfully romantic, parodic, or bawdy, here sampled by *Tsar Nikita* and *Tsar Saltan*, sufficiently adumbrates this form. Another, less important, omission is the cycle of lyrics innocently adapted from Mérimée's pseudo-Yugoslav anthology, *Songs of the Western Slavs*, and the charming proto-Formalist conceit in octaves, *The Cottage in Kolomna*, which is *sui generis* and has been offered in a different context. Despite some hesitancy over presenting again some of the contents of my *Eugene Onegin* translation of 1963, I have included here a small selection of sequential stanzas from each chapter, simply because an anthology of Pushkin's rhymed poetry cannot well ignore the novel in verse altogether. The duplication is somewhat redeemed by the emendations introduced in the course of a current revision of the whole translation.

I have exercised considerable restraint in footnoting, for too much of it deprives the reader of some of the mystery and zest of discovery, and tends to leave the instructor who may use the book feeling underemployed and thwarted. It is fun, for instance, to try and find out for oneself why the bountifully cunniferous witch in *Tsar Nikita* is rewarded with, of all things, some candle-ends in spirits among less homely bits of grisliness. This sort of passage enables the instructor to drop the hard-earned information into a pause in his exposé with a smooth "of course" and a properly Nabokovean air of masterful casualness.

I am calling this book *Pushkin Threefold*, then, because it represents an attempt, not previously made to my knowledge for any poet, to present in a single volume three versions, each useful in its way and, one hopes, triply useful in conjunction: the original works;

rather meticulous translations into plain or occasionally "rhythmic" prose; and verse translations reproducing as faithfully as possible the form, the spirit, and the flavor of the originals. Fennell and Obolensky in the Pushkin volumes of the Penguin series did the first two of these with distinction; many translators have achieved intermittent success with the third. I have felt for some time that complete fairness to a variety of readers demanded all three simultaneously. The ensuing musings on verse translation, eminently omissible for anyone not particularly interested in that art or craft, may shed some light on my reasons.

Traduttore, traditore—"translator, traitor"—mocks the Italian pun like a malicious echo; and it implies no question mark, but rather an exclamation point of *Schadenfreude,* a snigger of wicked enjoyment. From the safe port of criticism the expert who needs no translation hugs himself over the discomfiture of the wretch who set out to dismount a poetic artifact cast in an alien medium, and to reassemble it into a new poem of his own, calling the two the same—or seeming to. But as far as this Introduction is concerned, the added question mark is the point of the citation, which one could translate, punning back etymologically at the Italian, "translator, traducer." To me the translators-traducers are (as Pushkin says of his fellow poets) "a brotherhood I can't condemn, because, you see, I'm one of them."

In using this occasion to examine some selected modes and dilemmas of poetic translation, my motive is not merely personal experience and involvement. It is the evident truth that all of us who acknowledge an emotional stake in literature are ultimately at the mercy of the brotherhood of traitors or traducers; quite directly when we wish to look beyond our own linguistic boundaries; indirectly if we wish to savor fully almost any of the major pieces of our own national literatures, which are invariably impregnated with a supranational tradition reaching back into untraceable antiquity. We cannot read Pope's translation of the *Iliad* or much of Dryden simply as English poems without shortly confronting the question of how much of this poetry is Homer or Vergil, even how much of

Vergil is Homer again. The massive borrowing by Milton from Salandra in the theme, characters, and structure of *Paradise Lost* was assuredly only the last and most wholesale of a series of loans. We cannot escape inquiry into the nature of the process of creative metamorphosis, when at its inception lies not an intricate blend of contemporary personal experience, but the already transmuted experience of another mind in an antecedent work of art, often continents and ages removed, and moving within its own associative and linguistic code. In such a case we find ourselves witnesses, to a degree proportionate to our linguistic sophistication, at both ends of the creative process. We are able, and tempted, to tell the artist "you cannot say this—you misrepresent your experience," for much of his experience is there for us to compare with his final product.

The poet is not so helplessly exposed to privileged eavesdropping as the translator; nor, on the other hand, is he a power behind someone else's throne. The translator is both of these—a gray eminence deciding what will reach the oligoglot public, and in what form; and a poor relation at the margin of letters, poorly regarded despite the fact that his handicaps are in some ways more stringent than the poet's: he must be a poet, if not a great one, and one who will put what light he has under a bushel.

Those aware of this constant admixture of translingual experience in seemingly "national" writing of caliber are bound to wonder about the ambiguous likenesses-unlikenesses, as teasing as an elusive family resemblance, between any work and its partial matrix. When such a matrix is not only acknowledged but explicitly claimed as a nearly congruent and equivalent model, more searching scrutiny, on the part of both artist and reader, must attend the process of transmutation or carrying-across—the *trans-lation*.

The store of images and emotions unlocked by words in intricate conjunction, the secret world of associative relays that are set to operate on each other in an instantaneous, yet almost infinite chain reaction—this whole complex system exists, for anyone, only in his own, at most in two or three languages. And *it* is the medium of poetic experience, it cannot be synthesized piecemeal by affirmation, description, and persuasion through a commentator's already interpretive diction in another language. Hence, even an inferior associative orchestration, resembling it, in the hearer's language is superior to mere aural or visual reproduction of the original plus exegesis—"the cold way." This reproduction simply does not reproduce—it describes, analyzes, exhorts—it tries to teach rather than to transport the reader.

The central problem, surely, is that of accuracy; or more basically, the problem of what constitutes accuracy. Within it are contained many others, such as that of the proper *unit of translation*—word, phrase, stanza, poem; that of the alleged enmity between form and content, which, it is claimed, makes verse translation resemble a constant arithmetical product of two factors, rhyme and reason. If you increase one, the other diminishes, the product remains constant —a constant of inadequacy. Then, to name another problem within the realm of accuracy, there is the dilemma of allusiveness or associative authenticity of a special sort.

A particular blend of these, where accuracy assumes a more fundamental dimension of meaning, may be labeled the problem of simplicity—one of the most disheartening in verse translation into English. It is posed by a certain frugality and calm—lexical and metaphorical—in the original that to the English mind borders on triteness; an intractable quality that in the long poetic run, through some magic of craftsmanship, by way of a rejuvenation of the reader's imagination, turns into a haunting inevitability, a disarming utter rightness. Verse translators into English from such media as Chinese, Greek, Russian, and at times German verse encounter this dilemma with especial force. Gilbert Murray's renderings or adaptations from the Greek, Oliver Elton's from Pushkin, Heine translations, have all suffered, consciously or otherwise, from the fundamental contrast in poetic instrumentation, as well as in the nature of the aesthetic hearer-response labeled "poetic," between those verse traditions and the English, or at any rate the nineteenth-century English one. Edmund Wilson in his perceptive centenary essay on *Eugene Onegin* (1937) speaks to this problem in a vein similar to that of Maurice Baring's Introduction to the *Oxford Book of Russian Verse:*

. . . the poetry of Pushkin is particularly difficult to translate. It is difficult for the same reason that Dante is difficult: because it says so much in so few words, so clearly and yet so concisely, and the words themselves and their place in the line have become so much more important than in the case of more facile or rhetorical writers. It would require a translator himself a poet of the first order to re-produce Pushkin's peculiar combination of intensity, compression, and perfect ease. A writer like Pushkin may easily sound "flat," as he did to Flaubert in French, just as Cary's translation of Dante sounds flat. Furthermore, the Russian language, which is highly inflected and able to dispense with pronouns and prepositions in many cases where we have to use them, and which does without the article altogether, makes it possible for Pushkin to pack his lines (separating modifiers from substantives, if need be) in a way which renders the problem of translating him closer to that of translating a tightly articulated Latin poet like Horace than any modern poet that we know. Such a poet in translation may sound trivial just as many of the translations of Horace sound trivial—because the weight of the words and the force of their relation has been lost with the inflections and the syntax.

Gilbert Murray was reduced to well-tempered despair by the re-fusal of his Greek originals to get excited, or to erupt into stylistic shock effects of the kind that his English-trained poetic sense kept demanding. This mildest of men could become almost exasperated on the subject; and even in print he has ventured this mannerly half-complaint:

I have often used a more elaborate diction than Euripides did because I found that, Greek being a very simple language and English an ornate one, a direct translation produced an effect of baldness which was quite unlike the original.

Maurice Baring, the anthologist of the *Oxford Book of Russian Verse,* was struck forcibly by a similar difference in climate and orchestration between Russian and English. Edith Hamilton has analyzed with a wealth of illustration the striking contrast in the very stuff and temper of poetry between Greek and English. Both she and Baring emphasized the seemingly inbred need for expressive hyperbole in English—understood by everyone as not merely "poetic license" but part of the poetic essential of a verbally fresh view, the most conventional variety of estrangement (*ostranenie*). Greek appears to abhor this device as cheap and needless. Our response mechanisms, says Edith Hamilton, are conditioned to "caverns measureless to man, down to a sunless sea," to "magic casements opening on the foam of perilous seas." To which anyone can add uncounted examples: rose-red cities half as old as time, skylarks that are, all in the same poem, blithe spirits, clouds of fire, poets hidden in the light of thought, highborn maidens in a palace tower, glowworms golden in a dell of dew. Intoxicating stuff, but as the poet says himself: "bird thou never wert. . . ."

In the calmer realms of Greek, Russian, and much German poetry, such exuberant music of the spheres, still quiring to the young-eyed cherubins, takes on a dubious aroma of the over-ripe and overrich. A skylark is a skylark over there, the ocean may be wine-colored, but it is still recognizably the ocean; no slimy things do crawl with legs upon the slimy sea. Fancy is tight-reined: milk is white and good to drink, girls are *dulce ridentes, dulce loquentes,* wide-eyed, dark-lashed, ivory-browed even: but their faces launch no ships, let alone a thousand; they are never fairer than the evening air, clad in the beauty of a thousand stars, splendid angels, newly dressed, save wings, for heaven. . . . Consider how Pushkin, not insensitive to beauty, but like Pericles' Athenians, lover of beauty *with economy,* evokes the seasons with a sparing stanza of calm shorthand here and there in *Eugene Onegin.* The following is a passage that Edmund Wilson preferred to render in prose in his essay; and it may be verified in the present volume that in verse translation some of the English verbal decoration has already accrued to it:

> Autumn was in the air already;
> The sun's gay sparkle grew unsteady,
> The heedless day became more brief:
> The forest, long in darkling leaf,
> Unclothed itself with mournful rustle;
> The fields were wrapped in misty fleece;

> A caravan of raucous geese
> Winged southward; after summer's bustle
> A duller season was at hand:
> November hovered overland.

And then he turns to sharp little genre pictures, all seen truly and calmly, never doped to overcharge the poetic nerve with imagery:

> Through frigid haze the dawn resurges;
> Abroad the harvest sounds abate;
> And soon the hungry wolf emerges
> Upon the highway with his mate.
> The scent scares into snorting flurry
> The trudging horse, and travelers hurry
> Their uphill way in wary haste.
> No longer are the cattle chased
> Out of the stalls at dawn, the ringing
> Horn-notes of shepherds do not sound
> Their noontime summons all around.
> Indoors the maiden spins, with singing,
> Before the crackling pine-flare light—
> Companion of the winter night.

Compare Byron, describing a high mountain:

> . . . the monarch of mountains.
> They crowned him long ago
> On a throne of rocks, in a robe of clouds,
> With a diadem of snow.

By way of more detailed illustration, one may select one of many short pieces by Heinrich Heine and despair over the mysterious alchemy of obscurely relevant irrelevancies, rhythmic mutations, and pivotal silences that transmutes commonplace lexical and semantic material into a memorable lyric evocation:

> Es ragt ins Meer der Runenstein,
> Da sitz ich mit meinen Träumen.
> Es pfeift der Wind, die Möwen schrein,
> Die Wellen, die wandern und schäumen.

Ich habe geliebt manch schönes Kind
Und manchen guten Gesellen.
Wo sind sie hin? Es pfeift der Wind,
Es schäumen und wandern die Wellen.

Here is the most hackneyed *Weltschmerz,* one is bound to say, in diction of well-worn pocket change, seemingly powerless to stab with any novelty of vision or insight. The poet sits on the seashore, musing on bygone love and friendship, as the wind whistles about his ears and the waves break and ebb below. The words for the most part are the most obvious at hand: *sea, wind, love, waves, sit;* the *schönes Kind* is quite faceless, and so are the *gute Gesellen.* There are, to be sure, three or four words of "big magic," which carry what may be termed a suprasemantic charge of associations: *ragt, Runenstein, Träumen, wandern;* but at least two of these had long worked overtime for the romantic poets. They contrive to radiate diffuse associations all about them, but they neither ravish the imagination with metaphor nor dope the nerves with hyperbole; they transcend, yet do not upset the surface boundaries of reason and syntax. It is by their very lack of display, their refusal to stun or transport, that they imperceptibly draw the reader more deeply into the creative process itself, as part of the fresh vision or mood of the instant of experience regenerates itself within him as his own. And this precisely is the must of highest poetic effect: not a passive gaping at verbal fireworks, not a vicarious orgasm, but the incomparable excitement of creative experience. How exactly is it brought about?

Of the charged words, the remotest from rational context, the most willful (though still fitting the contextual frame) is of course the *runestone.* Its enigma presides over the first line, and subtly over the whole poem, like one of the three wrinkled hags that spin out our fate, like the dead sailor over a certain passage in Eliot. This runestone need not be there so far as the cognitive content of the poem is concerned. And yet, it adds something, precisely the something which, with some formal elements, is essential to save the two quatrains from triteness: it casts a note of inscrutability and despair over all that transpires there. Runes denote what is indecipherable, fateful, and ancient, and the irrelevant presence of the runestone reinforces from a subconscious realm two suggestions already contained in the body of the poem: the idea of an aloof inanimate environment, and the helpless questioning plaint of human transience, powerless to cope with the riddle of existence. Beyond this, the associative connection between *Runen* and *raunen,* that mystery-charged word for "secretly whispering," adds its subterranean force to the tritely foaming waves and the tritely whistling seawind. On the surface, obvious agents do expected things: the wind whistles, the waves foam, the seagulls scream, the pretty flappers are loved, and so are the good companions. But all is estranged and newly charged under the secret auspices of the runestone's obscure despair; the stark loom (*ragen*) of its jutting into the sea; the "roving" of the waves (not aimless so much as "of unfathomed and unshareable purpose"), suggested in *wandern,* so banal a word in other contexts. The soothing and drugging effect of sea and wind, conjured up from everyone's childhood, draws fresh magic even from the worn surface of *Träumen.* When I tackled Heine's provocative bit of sorcery for the sake of demonstration, I came up, rather bruised, with this:

> The runestone juts into the brine,
> I sit beside it dreaming.
> The seawinds hiss, the seamews whine,
> The waves, they go foaming and streaming.
>
> I have loved many a pretty miss
> And some of the best lads roaming.
> Where have they gone? The seawinds hiss,
> The waves go streaming and foaming.

I felt constrained to respect the three charged words as best I could; to render the surface lexical triteness of much of the rest; and most confining of all, to preserve the marvelously simple syntactic reversal of that keyline of the pulsing waves, which occurs in one order in line 4, in reversed order in line 8. It interrupts with its dreamy dactyls the iambic beat of the rest: first, *Die Wellen, die wandern und schäumen*—simple setting of the scene; and then, denying participation in the pathetic human query with a powerful echo of mocking repetition—*Es schäumen und wandern die Wellen.* This effect brings the poetic consummation—suddenly there is real ache, real poignancy. But for the translator, at once there begins the winding path of painful compromise: there is no simple English term the equal of *ragen,* with its joint connotation of vertical looming and sharp cragginess. One has to settle for "jut." Because the subdued jingle of end rhyme is needed for the artful *Folklorelei* of the little piece, one may try "brine" for sea, despite its obnoxious Viking flavor, for the seamews cannot well "cry" or "scream" in English for reasons of rhyme and/or semantics. Only "whine/brine" lies at hand. Similarly with the "pretty miss" here brought in—she is far too pert for the dreamy, artless archetype of *schönes Kind,* but in response to "miss" the wind can "hiss," just as in response to "foaming," "many a good lad" has to yield to "some of the best lads roaming." Or is one to choose the more literal "many a good young fellow," and make the waves "bellow" indecently in the parting line—in which case they would duly have to bellow also in line 4, rudely bursting into the elegiac murmur that pervades the whole? The gray eminence of the translator may contrive to release an echo of the wistful music of the whole; but usually at a painful price.

It may now be clearer what a dragon there is to slay in the deceptive jejuneness of simplicity. Centuries of sophisticated English, stately, baroquely jeweled, evocatively obscure, rear up in revolt against perpetrating anything as flat and bland as "there I sit with my dreams" or "I have loved many a pretty maid." Remember Mr. Huxley's pathetic painter-poet, Lypiatt, who was laughed to scorn for using that inadmissible word, *dream—le rêve*—no really, it is far too late for that! Housman dared something similar, but his is after all a very special product, and he was steeped in classical simplicity himself. Yet when we try to translate, do we dare to go back to the very witches' caldron of the poetic laboratory itself (our own, necessarily, not Heine's or Pushkin's) and start the transformation process afresh with more gleaming and more cunningly startling words and similes? Shall we talk of the *ambient stupor of the surf,* in fastidious fear of *waves that go foaming and streaming?* What shall we betray, the irradiated simplicity of the German, or the zest and shock of the English word?

There is no set answer. But we must not wholly despair of achieving some of the careless, deceptively casual felicity of interrhyming and rhythmically interechoing tritenesses with similar materials in English—if we wish to call what we strive for a translation, and not an *imitatio,* a poem of the second order, a poem-inspired poem. Is not the true translator, after all, what the lamented Poggioli called in an essay the *added* artificer, *artifex additus artifici?* English resources of rhyme and rhythm, within the given range of lexical elements, may accommodate us—even unto half the kingdom—by a constellation of happy coincidence and restless ingenuity; and if we then make the unit of translation large enough, we may hope, through a kind of mosaic technique, to achieve a similarly harmonious pattern of linguistic building stones, associative relays, and rhythmic elements.

Such interlingual salvage operations, and their cost, can be illustrated, if not assessed, by a crude little experiment in which several translation processes are linked in a chain reaction. I once chose a random quatrain from Swinburne's "Chorus from Atalanta" and asked each of several sensitive and long-suffering friends to render it, successively, from English into French, from French into German, from German into Russian, and from Russian back into English. Here are three links in this cycle of cumulative compromises:

> For winter's rains and ruins are over,
> And all the season of snows and sins;
> The days dividing lover and lover,
> The light that loses, the night that wins.

> Car les pluies et les deuils de l'hiver ont cessé,
> Et le temps de la neige et le temps du péché;
> Les heures qui séparent l'amant de l'aimée,
> La lumière qui meurt, et la nuit couronnée.

> Denn Winterschauer, -trauer sind vergangen,
> Die Zeit, die Sünde mit dem Schnee gebracht;

Die Stunden, da entrückt zwei Liebste bangen,
Das Licht das stirbt, und die gekrönte Nacht.

For winter's gusts and griefs are over,
Snowtime weather and sin-time blight,
Lone ache of lover for distant lover,
The light that dies, and the throne of night.

The versions are like turns in a spiral, coiling out ever farther
from the sprightly though undistinguished original in spirit, tone,
and rhythm. We notice that the last coil, which is English again, has
sprung back, after all these vicissitudes, into a skippy four-footed
rhythm very like the original's; and it has salvaged the identical
end rhyme of one couple. Otherwise one observes a certain loss of
simplicity, accretion of material, some obscurity and loss of tension
in the last line. "The night that wins" lost its innocence by way of
"la nuit couronnée" and "gekrönte Nacht" and "u trona noči." Still—
the result is not as unrecognizable as was the rule in the similar
post-office game of our youth, where a short message was hurriedly
whispered from ear to ear in a circle of players, and the result was
a hilarious shambles. After all, we deliberately courted here the
cumulative effect of four subtle acts of "treason," and what emerged
was by no means a complete travesty of the original.

A more general interlingual and intercultural translation problem
than that of simplicity is that of allusiveness. Here a more or less
esoteric allusion, or a whole sequence of intramural associations,
more specific than those of linguistic hyperbole or estrangement, is
to be set quivering and tittering in the reader's mind like a mobile.
Here the translator has three choices, all distasteful: he may brave
it out with high-handed, literal brevity; or he may have to expand
a pregnant line or two into three or four lightly loaded ones; or he
may give up the precious form and goad the reader up a pile of
footnotes. The latter way, alas, was Nabokov's with his prose para-
phrase of *Onegin*.

On this kind of dilemma I know no better example than one that
the late Dudley Fitts furnished in a thoughtful essay a few years

ago. It concerns an anonymous Greek epigram about a girl called Daphne:

> Lektron henos pheugousa lektron polloisin etukhthe.

One may translate this, to a close equivalent of overt message and rhythm, as follows:

> She who fled from the bed of one
> A bed for many has become.

But this leaves the covert message, a multiple twinkling of simultaneous allusions, at the mercy of chance and faint hope. What to do? Shall one leave it at that and hope that the slow fuse will burn its meandering way by half-buried landmarks into those recesses of the reader's mind where his classical mythology languishes—and risk that when the spark arrives, there is nothing there to flash up in recognition? Or shall the allusive sentence be studded with essential little signposts, to lose all bite in the process? To quote Fitts:

> By the time we have reflected that the girl who owns the bed is named Daphne and that *daphne* is laurel in Greek, and that her bed is made of laurel, and that upon that bed, since she is a gallant lady, she entertains the men that visit her, and that for this reason she is inappropriately named for the original Daphne, a nymph, who, far from being a gallant lady, was so prim that she preferred to be turned into a laurel bush rather than to submit to the advances of a god, that god being inflamed Apollo himself. . . .

By the time the fuse has burned this far, not secretly and in one flash of associative delight, but slowly and prosaically, and all of it has been pondered and savored and made explicit, nothing is left but a laborious learned exegesis, as dead as an explained joke. The reader will give the three widely spaced guffaws once attributed to Austrian field marshals when told jokes—one laugh when the joke is told, another when it is explained, and a third when it is understood.

The very opening lines of *Onegin* contain a similar headache of an allusion. The elegant young scamp, summoned to the bedside of

a dying, moneyed uncle, ponders the legacy and its irksome price—
a few weeks' attendance at the sickbed, feigned solicitude, dancing
in and out with poultices and sympathy; and he begins an inner
monologue like this: "My uncle of most honest principles . . ."
He invokes most clearly, to Russians of his and later ages, the
start of a famous Krylov fable: "A donkey of most honest prin-
ciples . . ." Where to go for an equivalent literary allusion in En-
glish? Provided you have caught the allusion in the first place?

By way of strategic retreat from the whole painful subject, let us
consider the following attempts at Pushkinian stanzas; first in plain
prose, then in my verse rendering:

Onegin, VII, 2

LITERAL TRANSLATION

How sad I feel at your appearing,
Spring, spring—season of love!
What languid stir
(Is) in my soul, in my blood!
With what a heavyhearted tenderness
I rejoice in the wafting of spring
As it breathes against my face
In the lap of rustic silence!
Or is enjoyment alien to me,
And all that gladdens, animates,
All that exults and glistens,
Brings boredom and languor
Upon the soul long dead,
And all seems dark to it?

VERSE RENDERING

How I am saddened by your coming,
O time of love, o time of *bud!*
What languid stir you send *benumbing*
Into my soul, into my blood!
What painful tender feeling seizes
The heart, as spring's *returning* breezes
Waft to my face *in silken rush*
Here in the lap of rural hush!

Have I become so alienated
From all things that exult and glow,
All things that joy and life bestow,
That now they find me dull and sated,
And all seems *dark as burnt-out coal*
To the long-since insentient soul?

Onegin, III, 14

LITERAL TRANSLATION

I shall recount the simple speeches
Of father and old uncle,
The children's appointed meetings
By the old lindens, by the brook:
The torments of luckless jealousy,
Separation, tears of reconciliation;
I shall set (them) at odds again, and at last,
I shall lead them under the wreath. . . .
I shall cite the speeches of passionate tenderness,
The words of languishing love,
Which in days gone by
At the feet of a beautiful lady-love
Have come to my tongue,
Of which I have now lost the habit.

VERSE RENDERING

I shall recount the simple speeches
Of dad and uncle *in my book,*
The children's trysts by ancient *beeches,*
And on the borders of the brook;
The ravages of jealous torment,
Partings, reunion tears, *long dormant,*
I shall stir up once more, and then
In marriage soothe them down again. . . .
The language of impassioned pining
Will I *renew,* and love's *reply,*
The like of which in days gone by
Came to me as I lay *reclining*
At a dear beauty's feet, *enthralled,*
And which I have not since recalled.

I have juxtaposed a literal prose translation, conceding for the moment that even such a thing is possible, and my published version in the so-called Onegin stanza of the original. The stanza, as must be evident, is dismayingly intricate in its ordered interplay of masculine and feminine rhymes, and its three differently patterned iambic tetrameter quatrains with a couplet at the end. The italics mark the departures the translator was forced into: mostly padding necessitated by the shorter English breath, some rearrangement of the mosaic stones, some omissions. Predictably, most occur at the end of the lines.

Other offenses against literal fidelity occurred in substituting for the rhythmic and structural grandeur achieved by the long Russian words a careful modicum of the more semantic and metaphoric ornateness expected in English—but all of it only under dire duress. If the translator makes similar accommodations in his work, has he tacitly conceded that his enterprise has failed, or was impractical from the start? Has he falsified the poem? Or has he rather shown it the surpassing loyalty of a daring and creative sympathy? Is he a *traduttore,* or a *traditore?* For any corpus of poetry, only a handful of scholar-poets are qualified to say.

Nabokov's recent two-volume commentary in English on *Eugene Onegin* attempts to call into question again, not *a* verse translation, but verse translation itself. This happens once or twice in every literary period. The work illustrates this attitude of militant resignation by continually substituting exhaustive and highly imaginative exegesis for translation—while, however, retaining the word "translation" in its title. It will be clear now that I cannot regard the essential legitimacy of poetic translation—as distinct from the means and the areas and limits of tolerable compromise—as highly controversial. I would endorse the more challenging majority view of the task, which is that the task exists, and must be tackled. The goal is to create a poem in the target language, which should simulate, as near as may be, the total effect produced by the original on the contemporary reader. Total effect to me means *import* as well as *impact,* i.e., both what the poem imparts to the mind and how it strikes the senses; cognitive as well as aesthetic (stylistic, formal, musical, "poetic") values, pretending for just a moment that these two congruent entities can somehow be analytically separated. Again, "import as well as impact" means import *through* and *congruent with* impact; it does not mean a message in garbled prose, with subsequent assurances by way of stylistic and other commentary that the corpse in its lifetime was poetry. Eugene Nida has phrased the same postulate rather baldly like this:

> Translation consists in producing in the receptor language the closest natural equivalent to the message of the source language, first in meaning, and secondly in style.

I find precarious in this only the suggestion of consecutiveness or priority in the terms *first* and *secondly*. But then, Nida spoke of prose.

This disposes, to my mind (at least for culturally kindred languages like German and English, and even Russian and English), of both counsels of insouciance and counsels of despair; that is, on the one hand, of remote imitations or adaptations in distant meters and, on the other hand, of the spavined pony of would-be "literal" prose.

The central problem of verse translation, then, in a sense the only one, is not whether there can and should be simultaneous fidelity to content and form, but rather how to decide, first, what constitutes double fidelity in a given case and how it can best be approximated. The proper formal frame of accuracy, i.e., the largest allowable unit of form within which maximum fidelity must be achieved, is a delicate matter of balancing the poetic pulse of the original against the stylistic sense of the reader in the target language, and against his syntactic comprehension span; but luckily a large enough unit *can* usually be chosen to afford desperately needed latitude for transposing and rearranging within it elements of message and lexical-stylistic effects. This latitude somewhat soothes the notorious enmity between form and content in the recasting process—what I am now tempted to call the Nabokov Relation of fated failure.

When I spoke of reproducing the total impact on the *contemporary* reader, I meant, in a sense, the reader contemporary to the author, not the author's present-day native public. I realize that here I am on more controversial ground. But I am convinced that the diction used in the target language, save for deliberate archaisms used by the author, should be essentially modern, as that of the original was modern at its first appearance. Here "modern" may embrace the still resonant linguistic strata of the past one hundred, perhaps one hundred and fifty years. The antiquarian pursuit of archaizing the language used, to approximate the surface quaintness or patina that the original may by now have acquired among its native readers, is tempting; but I feel it is not only a foredoomed quest—technically too formidable and treacherous—but essentially wrongheaded. It is not the translator's business to produce an imitation period piece, to fake up that "classic" of a translation, which at the time remained unborn because no Schlegel and Tieck or no Zhukovsky happened to pick up the original. No one should—and few could—try to make himself into a ghostly Heine because in his time Heine *might* have produced the ideal translation of his contemporary Pushkin's *Onegin*.

Let me go back for a moment to the "unit of fidelity." In prose, except for extreme cases that tend to depart from prose, the problem of the unit of fidelity is not acute. The unit is normally the sentence, and only extremes of syntactic yapping or hacking, as in some German expressionism, or of syntactic convolution as in Thomas Mann or Tolstoy, raise the question of where the demands of naturalness must call a halt to close stylistic-syntactic imitation. But in poetry, especially rhymed poetry, the rigors of prosody bring "naturalness" and fidelity into conflict much sooner and oftener— in fact, sometimes at every step. "Meaning" acquires a more rigorous, because more comprehensive sense; freshness of vision and linguistic novelty are of the essence of what is stated, meaning *is* form and form meaning, over quite small units of discourse. To *just that* particular poetic impact of a line or phrase, there seem to be no alternative "plain" forms that could produce it. By the same token, literal translation, so-called (i.e., atomistic and sequential substitution of lexical pieces, morphological devices, and syntactic structures), not only runs into the hard wall of rhythm and rhyme, but is intrinsically absurd and self-defeating. Poetic utterance is not produced from some underlying, neutral, merely cognitive statement by linguistic manipulation; and if it were, the manipulations could not be the same in language A as in language B, or else they would be the *same* language. Hence sequential literalness becomes worse than irrelevant. . . . All this would have been comically redundant to say again, had the notion of literalness as a technique not been resurrected by Nabokov in relation to a major work of world literature, and had it not been respectfully (or at least gingerly) handled by at least some critics.

The first and constantly recurring decision, then, which the translator of poetry faces, is that of choosing the unit of fidelity. In some short articulated forms like the sonnet or the quatrain, or in long narrative poems whose overall unity is as brilliantly quantified as Pushkin's *Onegin* into stanzas, each of which is a viable and substructured microcosm of mood and meaning, the obvious outer unit is the stanza; within it, the whole delicate balancing act of restructuring and tint-matching necessarily consummates itself. What original effects have not been caught up within the translated stanza have been lost and cannot be made up before or beyond it. Within the outer unit, almost invariably there are subordinate ones that should be preserved, but with a less degree of rigor; for the poetic *mora* of the whole statement has not lapsed till the end of the stanza or other unit of fidelity: the ear is still open, all is yet in suspense.

Thus a mosaic technique of reconstitution within the unit, somewhat independent of the original order of poetic effects and certainly of the kind and sequence of linguistic elements, is possible, and not only possible, but necessary; and not only necessary *faute de mieux,* but often as a condition of fidelity. What the original, say, renders verbally (by verb) near the end of the first line, may or should be rendered adverbially, nominally, adjectivally, or even syntactically, say in the middle of the second line or still later—if thus the mosaic-making rules of the target language, its aesthetics and poetics demand it for the overall stanzaic impact. If, after a few days, the translator finds he cannot quite remember the stanza in the original, I submit this is not always a bad sign, or a symptom of a fatuous vanity.

Now if a line, or a larger subunit within the stanza, cries out for separate status as an integral felicity, or an inimitable local effect that cannot be moved or compensated elsewhere, it should be tackled in its place. But if move it must, then as likely as not it is the poetics and linguistics of the target language that demand it, not necessarily the denseness or stupor of the translator. The scar of the excision, or the local opaqueness caused in the image, may yet be partially remedied elsewhere; or the loss must simply be borne. It may be found that in such cases the light merely strikes another facet of the stanza; and the spatial sense of the reader may yet perceive, with luck, a refraction of the same jewel turned to another angle.

WALTER ARNDT

ON READING PUSHKIN*

While reading in his verse it is as though
I were vouchsafed a sudden flash of wonders,
As if of some high harmony beyond us
Had been released an unsuspected flow.

Its sounds do not seem made in this world's fashion:
As if, pervaded with his deathless leaven,
All earthly stuff—emotions, anguish, passion—
Had been transmuted to the stuff of heaven.

A. N. Majkov

* 1887, on the fiftieth anniversary of his death.

METRIC TRANSLATIONS

Shorter Poems

LIBERTY   [1817]

AN ODE

Begone out of my sight and flee,
Oh, feeble princess of Cythera!
Thou, haughty muse of Liberty,
The bane of kings, come here, come nearer!
The flowered garland from me wrench,   5
Break in my hand the pampered lyre . . .
I sing of Freedom's conquering fire,
Scourge vice enthroned on royal bench.

Of that exalted son of Gaul
Point me the footsteps all admired—   10
In whom 'mid storied ills, recall,
You once audacious hymns inspired.
You, fickle Fortune's favored knaves,
The tyrants of the nations, tremble!
And you with manhood fresh assemble   15
And listen: Rise, of fallen slaves!

Alas, where'er my eye may light,
It falls on ankle chains and scourges,
Perverted law's pernicious blight
And tearful serfdom's fruitless surges.   20
Where has authority unjust
In hazes thick with superstition
Not settled—slavery's dread emission
And rank vainglory's fateful lust?

Unstained by human freedom choked
A sovereign's brow alone is carried
Where sacred liberty is married
With mighty law and firmly yoked;
Where its stout roof enshelters all,   25
And where, by watchful burghers wielded,
Law's sword impends, and none are shielded   30
From its inexorable fall.

Before whose righteous accolade
The minions of transgression cower,
Whose vengeful hand cannot be stayed   35
By slavering greed or dread of power.
Oh, kings, you owe your crown and writ
To Law, not nature's dispensation;
While you stand high above the nation,
The changeless Law stands higher yet.   40

And woe betide the common weal
Where it incontinently slumbers,
Where Law itself is rendered feal
Be it to kings or strength of numbers!
To this one martyr witness bears,   45
Heir to his forebears' famous errors,
Who in the storm of recent terrors
Laid down his royal head for theirs.

Unto his death King Louis went,
His speechless offspring watching after,   50
His head bereft of crown he bent
To fell Rebellion's bloodied rafter.
Mute is the Law, the people too,
And down the axe of outrage rattles . . .
And an unholy purple settles   55
Upon a Gaul enchained anew.

Yes, I abhor thee and thy throne,
Oh, miscreant in despot's clothing!
Thy doom, thy children's dying groan,
I witness them with mirthful loathing.   60

Upon thy brow one reads the sign
Of subject peoples' execration,
World's horror, blemish of creation,
Reproach on earth to the Divine.

When by Nevá the midnight star   65
Hangs sparkling on the somber waters,
And carefree sleepers near and far
Have drooped to slumber in their quarters,
The singer finds his gaze and thought
The tyrant's lonely statue roaming,   70
Its ominous torpor in the gloaming,
And the forlorn imperial court—

And Clio's awesome tones he hears
Behind those awesome casements tolling,
Caligula's last hour appears   75
Before his sight anew unrolling,
He sees, beribboned and bestarred,
By venom and by wine befuddled,
The clandestine assassins huddled
With brazen brow and wolfish heart.   80

And silenced is the faithless guard,
The drawbridge downed at midnight season,
In secrecy the gate unbarred
By hands of mercenary treason.
Oh, shame! Of horror newly found!   85
The janissars burst in, appalling
Like beasts, the impious blows are falling . . .
And slaughtered lies the miscreant crowned.

Henceforward, rulers, know this true:
That neither blandishments nor halters   90
Make trusty buttresses for you,
Nor dungeon walls, nor sacred altars.
Be ye the first to bow you down
Beneath Law's canopy eternal:
The people's bliss and freedom vernal   95
Will keep forever safe your crown.

TO CHAADAEV[1]   [1818]

Love, hope, our private fame we banished
As fond illusions soon dismissed,
And Youth's serene pursuits have vanished
Like dreamy wisps of morning mist;
Yet 'neath the fateful yoke that bows us   5
One burning wish will not abate:
With mutinous soul we still await
Our Fatherland to call and rouse us.
In transports of impatient anguish
For sacred Liberty we thrill,   10
No less than a young lover will
Yearn for the promised tryst and languish.
While yet with Freedom's spark we burn
And Honor's generous devotion,
On our dear country let us turn   15
Our fervent spirit's fine emotion!
Believe, my friend: Russia will rise,
A joyous, dazzling constellation,
Will dash the slumber from her eyes;
On Tyranny's stark wreck the nation   20
Will our names immortalize!

[1] Petr Yakovlevič Chaadaev or Chadaev (1793–1856), Western-oriented Russian philosopher who in his late twenties began to circulate, in French manuscript, his *Lettres philosophiques.* They contained a profound critique of Russian historical evolution on premises of a quasi-Catholic world view. The first of these *Letters,* published in Russian in 1836, caused the journal *Telescope* to be shut down, and Chaadaev to be declared insane and put under house arrest. Pushkin had known and admired him ever since Chaadaev was stationed at Tsarskoe Selo as a young officer.

TO THE AUTHOR OF
HISTORY OF THE RUSSIAN STATE[1]   [1818]

In his *Historia* are proved and pointed out
With grace, simplicity, and judgment fair and cool,

[1] N. M. Karamzin (1766–1826), the noted stylist and pioneer of new literary movements, whose famous *History* was conservative and strongly monarchist in tone.

The timeless need for autocratic rule
And the charms of the knout.

HISTORY OF A VERSIFIER   [1818]

He catches with accustomed ear a
    Tweet;
Bedabbles single-mindedly the
    Sheet;
Recites to settle everybody's   5
    Hash;
Then publishes, and into Lethe
    Splash!

HISTORY OF A VERSIFIER   [1818]
(*freer version*)

He cultivates his sympathetic
    Nerve;
He squanders paper with ascetic
    Verve;
Recites to haunt his neighbor's harried   5
    Sleep;
At last is published, whew! and buried
    Deep.

IN THE COUNTRY   [1819]

I bid thee welcome, oh, sequestered nook,
Refuge of quietude, of toil and inspiration,

Wherein my days meander like an unseen brook,
    Sunk in oblivious elation.
I'm thine—I have exchanged those shameful Circe's yokes,   5
Luxurious merriment, carousal, dissipation,
For the quiescent fields, the peace of murmurous oaks,
For heedless idleness, the friend of inspiration.

    I'm thine—I love this garden dim,
      By bloom and morning cool anointed,   10
This pastureland with aromatic hayricks pointed,
Where in the spinneys freshets purl and gleam.
The scene before my gaze abounds in lively graces:
On this side twofold lakes extend their azure spaces,
Where every now and then a fisher's sail will shine,   15
Behind them quilted fields and rows of hillocks swelling,
    And farther, here and there a dwelling,
On luscious water-meadows wandering herds of kine,
Mills with their wings spread, drying-sheds with smoke-plumes
      welling,
    Toil and contentment showing sign on sign . . .   20

Here, freed from bonds of idle fuss and clutter,
I teach myself to taste of bliss without a flaw,
With spirit truly unconstrained to worship law,
To pay no heed to the untutored rabble's mutter,
With fellow-feeling to respond to bashful pleas,   25
    And not to grudge their fated ease
To fool or evildoer in their ill-got grandeur.

    Oracles of the ages, here I question you!
      In solemn and secluded splendor
      Your solace rings more clear and true.   30
      Sloth's sullen slumber is forsaken,
      To toil my ardent senses leap,
      And your creative thoughts awaken
      To ripeness in the spirit's deep.

But then a daunting thought casts gloom on mankind's lover: 35
    'Mid flowering crops and slopes
At every step his soul is saddened to discover
The infamy of ignorance that blights all hopes.

Purblind to tears, deaf to entreaty,
By destiny ordained for man's distress,   40
A barbarous barondom, devoid of law or pity,
By usurpation and the knout of ruthlessness
Preys on the peasant's goods and time and hardship.
Bent to a ploughshare not his own, subdued by rods,
Here hollow-chested servitude in furrows plods   45
    For an inexorable lordship.
Here all drag on the ponderous yoke unto the tomb,
Their souls too crushed to nourish hope or aspiration,
    Here in their freshness maidens bloom
    But for some brute's capricious inclination.   50
The dear support that every aging father craves,
His adolescent sons, companions of his labors,
Go from the native cabin but to join their neighbors
And swell the rosters of exhausted manor slaves.
Ah, that my voice could quicken hearts to indignation!   55
Wherefore into my breast were idle embers cast
Not to be bursting into fierce heroic blast?
Shall I behold, friends, an unshackled population,
And serfdom overthrown by an imperial hand?
Upon enlightened liberty's new fatherland   60
    Will there break forth a lovely dawn at last?

SECLUSION   [1819]

Blest he who in secluded leisure,
Far from the numskull's brazen ways,
Between hard work and slothful pleasure,
Old thoughts, new hopes, divides his days;
Whose friends by kindly fate were chosen   5
So as to save him, lucky pup,
Both from the bore that sends you dozing,
And from the boor that wakes you up.

THE DAGGER   [1821]

By Lemnos'[1] god, avenging knife,
For deathless Nemesis wert fashioned,
The secret sentinel of Freedom's threatened life,
The final arbiter of rape and shame impassioned.

Where Zeus's thunder sleeps, the sword of law is drowsing,   5
Thou art executor of curse and hope,
In wait within the throne room's housing,
Beneath the gleam of festive cope.

Like Hades' ray, Jove's bolt, the villain sees
The silent steel flash in his eye and quiver,   10
That makes him look behind and shiver
Amidst his revelries.

For everywhere thy blade will carve a sudden path,
On land, upon the seas, in temple or in tavern,
Thrice-guarded strong room, hidden cavern,   15
Upon his couch, by his own hearth.

Forbidden Rubicon[2] has suffered Caesar's tread,
Majestic Rome succumbed, the law inclined its head;
But Brutus righted Freedom's damage:
You struck down Caesar—and he staggered, dead,   20
Against great Pompey's haughty image.

The hordes of grim rebellion raise their outcry hoarse,
Detested, black of visage, sanguine,
Arose the misbegotten hangman
On slaughtered Freedom's headless corse.   25

Henchman of death, to wearied Hades he
With thumb-signs victims indicated,
But a supreme tribunal fated
For him the Eumenids[3] and thee.

[1] Hephaistos, in charge of Metallurgy, Thermodynamics, and Mechanical Engineering.

[2] The border stream between Cisalpine Gaul and Italy. Caesar crossed it with his army, violating the terms of his senatorial mandate and precipitating the civil war that ended the Republic.

[3] The propitiatory term for the dreaded Erinyes (the Latin Furies), the ancient divinities of retribution.

Oh, righteous youth, the Fates' appointed choice,   30
    Oh, Sand,⁴ you perished on the scaffold;
    But from your martyred dust the voice
    Of holy virtue speaks unmuffled.

In your own Germany a shadow you became
    That grants to lawless force no haven—   35
    And on your solemn tomb ungraven
    There glows a dagger for a name.

⁴ The German nationalist student Karl Ludwig Sand (1795–1820), who in 1819 shot the reactionary German playwright and Russian official August Friedrich von Kotzebue (1761–1819), who was also an intermittent Bonapartist. Sand was executed in 1820, and thus became a martyr to anti-Napoleonic Europe.

EPIGRAM ON A. A. DAVYDOVA¹   [1882]

One had Agláya by attraction
Of raven curls and martial stance,
One for his money (no objection),
A third because he was from France,
Cleon by dint of being clever,   5
Damis for tender songs galore;
But, my Agláya, say, whatever
Did your own husband have you for?

¹ Aglája Davydova, née Duchesse de Grammont, the promiscuous wife of General Alexander Davydov (the southern Decembrist's brother), whose favors Pushkin also enjoyed briefly.

TO A FOREIGN GIRL   [1822]

This valedictory effusion
Pleads in a tongue you do not speak,
And yet for it by fond illusion
Your understanding I would seek.

My dearest, till a pall may smother   5
These senses while we are apart,
While I can feel, you and no other
Will be the idol of my heart.
On strangers now your gazes bending,
Go on believing just my heart,   10
As you believed it from the start,
Its passions never comprehending.

A LITTLE BIRD   [1823]

In alien lands devoutly clinging
To age-old rites of Russian earth,
I let a captive bird go winging
To greet the radiant spring's rebirth.

My heart grew lighter then: why mutter   5
Against God's providence, and rage,
When I was free to set aflutter
But one poor captive from his cage!

NIGHT   [1823]

My murmurous soliloquy of thee oppresses
The hush of midnight with its languorous caresses.
Beside the couch whereon I drowsing lie there glows
A fretful candle, and my verse wells up and flows
Till purling streams of love, full-charged with thee, run
      through me.   5
Then, shimmering through the dusk, thy lustrous eyes turn to me,
They smile at me and make a whisper as they shine:
My dearest, tender one . . . my love . . . I'm thine . . . I'm
      thine.

[1823]

"Forth went the sower to sow his seeds . . ."

  As freedom's sower in the wasteland
Before the morning star I went;
From hand immaculate and chastened
Into the grooves of prisonment
Flinging the vital seed I wandered—   5
But it was time and toiling squandered,
Benevolent designs misspent . . .

  Graze on, graze on, submissive nation!
You will not wake to honor's call.
Why offer herds their liberation?   10
For them are shears or slaughter-stall,
Their heritage each generation
The yoke with jingles, and the gall.

ON COUNT VORONTSOV   [1824]

One half Milord, one half in trade,
One half a sage, one half a dunce,
One half a crook, but here for once
There's every hope he'll make the grade.

TO THE SEA   [1824]

Farewell to you, unharnessed Ocean!
No longer will you roll at me
Your azure swells in endless motion
Or gleam in tranquil majesty.

A comrade's broken words on leaving,   5
His hail of parting at the door:

Your chant of luring, chant of grieving
Will murmur in my ears no more.

Oh, homeland of my spirit's choosing!
How often on your banks at large   10
I wandered mute and dimly musing,
Fraught with a sacred, troubling charge!

How I would love your deep resounding,
The primal chasm's muffled voice,
How in your vesper calm rejoice,   15
And in your sudden, reckless bounding!

The fisher's lowly canvas slips,
By your capricious favor sheltered,
Undaunted down your breakers' lips:
Yet by your titan romps have weltered   20
And foundered droves of masted ships.

Alas, Fate thwarted me from weighing
My anchor off the cloddish shore,
Exultantly your realm surveying,
And by your drifting ridges laying   25
My poet's course forevermore.

You waited, called . . . I was in irons,
And vainly did my soul rebel,
Becalmed in those uncouth environs
By passion's overpowering spell.   30

Yet why this sorrow? Toward what fastness
Would now my carefree sails be spread?
To one lone goal in all your vastness
My spirit might have gladly sped.

One lonely cliff, the tomb of glory . . .   35
There chilling slumber fell upon
The ghost of mankind's proudest story:
There breathed his last Napoleon.

There rest for suffering he bartered;
And, gale-borne in his wake, there streams   40

Another kingly spirit martyred,
Another regent of our dreams.[1]

He passed, and left to Freedom mourning,
His laurels to Eternity.
Arise, roar out in stormy warning: 45
He was your own true bard, oh, Sea!

His soul was by your spirit haunted,
In your own image was he framed:
Like you immense, profound, undaunted,
Like you nocturnal untamed.   50

Bereft the world . . . where by your power,
Oh, Sea, would you now carry me?
Life offers everywhere one dower:
On any glint of bliss there glower
Enlightenment or tyranny.   55

Farewell then, Sea! Henceforth in wonder
Your regal grace will I revere;
Long will your muffled twilit thunder
Reverberate within my ear.

To woods and silent wildernesses   60
Will I translate your potent spells,
Your cliffs, your coves, your shining tresses,
Your shadows and your murmurous swells.

[1] Lord Byron, who had perished at Missolonghi that year.

——————   [1824]

Rose-maiden, no, I do not quarrel
With these dear chains, they don't demean:
The nightingale embushed in laurel,
The sylvan singers' feathered queen,

Does she not bear the same sweet plight,   5
Near the proud rose's beauty dwelling,
And with her tender anthems thrilling
The dusk of a voluptuous night?

THE GRAPE   [1824]

No, not by fleeting roses saddened
That passing spring will fade and kill,
By clustered grapes will I be gladdened
That ripen on the sloping hill,
On my fair vale delight bestowing,   5
The golden autumn's richest pearl,
As supply-tapered, freshly-glowing
As fingers of a sweet young girl.

———————— [1824]

Liza is afraid to love.
Or could this be just her fashion?
What if Dian's not above
Keeping dark her taste for passion?
Downcast lids, might they at all   5
Hide sly glances, holding wily
Muster of us, searching shyly
Which of us might help her fall?

———————— [1825]

When first the roses wither,
Their breath ambrosia yields,
Their airy souls fly thither
To the Elysian fields.

And there, where waters vagrant   5
Oblivion bear and dreams,
Their shadows honey-fragrant
Bloom over Lethe's streams.

EX UNGUE LEONEM   [1825]

One day I flicked my whip-o'-verse a little
And let the thing go out without my name;
Some scribbler pounced on it with ink and spittle
And had them print his piece unsigned, for shame.
Oh, Lord! The hack or I had never reckoned   5
That our generic marks gave us away:
He knew me by my talons in a second,
I knew him in an instant by his bray.

ANDRÉ CHÉNIER[1]   [1825]

(*dedicated to N. N. Raevsky*)

Ainsi, triste et captif, ma lyre
toutefois s'éveillait . . .

While awestruck all of Europe bends
Its gaze upon the urn of Byron,
And he the choir of bards attends,
A shade in Dante's high environ,

I hear another shadow call,   5
Who once, of songs and sobbing cheated,
By Terror's bloodstained planks retreated
Beneath the grave's umbrageous pall.

[1] The French poet (1762–94), one of Pushkin's early political heroes and poetic models, who died on the guillotine. The dedication is to Nikolaj Raevsky, son of the military hero of 1812, with whom Pushkin was on intimate terms when he traveled in the south with the Raevsky family in 1820 and enjoyed flirtations with two of the daughters.

Sepulchral flowers I bring the poet
Of love and groves and comity.   10
A lyre resounds, though none yet know it.
I sing—heard but by him and thee.

TO . . .   [1825]

I recollect that wondrous meeting,
That instant I encountered you,
When like an apparition fleeting,
Like beauty's spirit, past you flew.

Long since, when hopeless grief distressed me,   5
When noise and turmoil vexed, it seemed
Your voice still tenderly caressed me,
Your dear face sought me as I dreamed.

Years passed; their stormy gusts confounded
And swept away old dreams apace.   10
I had forgotten how you sounded,
Forgot the heaven of your face.

In exiled gloom and isolation
My quiet days meandered on,
The thrill of awe and inspiration,   15
And life, and tears, and love, were gone.

My soul awoke from inanition,
And I encountered you anew,
And like a fleeting apparition,
Like beauty's spirit, past you flew.   20

My pulses bound in exultation,
And in my heart once more unfold
The sense of awe and inspiration,
The life, the tears, the love of old.

WINTER EVENING   [1825]

Storm has set the heavens scowling,
Whirling gusty blizzards wild,
Now they are like beasts a-growling,
Now a-wailing like a child;
Now along the brittle thatches   5
They will scud with rustling sound,
Now against the window latches
Like belated wanderers pound.

Our frail hut is glum and sullen,
Dim with twilight and with care.   10
Why, dear granny, have you fallen
Silent by the window there?
Has the gale's insistent prodding
Made your drowsing senses numb,
Are you lulled to gentle nodding   15
By the whirling spindle's hum?

Let us drink for grief, let's drown it,
Comrade of my wretched youth,
Where's the jar? Pour out and down it,
Wine will make us less uncouth.   20
Sing me of the tomtit hatching
Safe beyond the ocean blue,
Sing about the maiden fetching
Water at the morning dew.

Storm has set the heavens scowling,   25
Whirling gusty blizzards wild,
Now they sound like beasts a-growling,
Now a-wailing like a child.
Let us drink for grief, let's drown it,
Comrade of my wretched youth,   30
Where's the jar? Pour out and down it,
Wine will make us less uncouth.

▬▬▬▬ [1825]

What if life deceives and baits you,
Never bridle, never grieve!
Bide the dismal day, believe
That a day of joy awaits you.

By the future lives the heart;   5
And if dreary be the present,
All is fleeting, will depart,
And departed, will be pleasant.

BACCHIC SONG   [1825]

Who laid our gay revel to rest?
Resound, bacchanalian cadence!
A toast to the amorous maidens
And tender young lovelies who loved us the best!
Pour full every glass to the edges!   5
The bottoms shall sing
With rings that we fling
In rich wine as our reverent pledges!
Up beakers as one, and a flourish in season!
Salute to the Muses, salute to man's reason!   10
Thou holiest sun, be aglow!
As this candelabrum has faded
Before the bright dawn, even so
Shall flicker and die every sophistry jaded
At reason's unperishing spark.   15
Salute to the sunrise, and vanish the dark!

▬▬▬▬ [1825]

The season's final blossoms bring
More dear delight than buds of spring.

They stir in us a live communion
Of sorrowfully poignant dreams.
Thus oft the hour of parting seems   5
More vivid than a sweet reunion.

TEMPEST   [1825]

You saw perched on a cliff a maid,
Her raiment white above the breakers,
When the mad sea reared up and played
Its whips of spray on coastal acres
And now and then the lightnings flush,   5
And purple gleams upon her hover,
And fluttering up in swirling rush,
The wind rides in her airy cover?
Fair is the sea in gales arrayed,
The heavens drained of blue and flashing,   10
But fairer on her cliff the maid
Than storms and skies and breakers crashing.

TO FRIENDS   [1825]

My foes—just for the nonce I may seem frozen,
And my quick wrath extinguished like a light;
But you have not escaped my field of sight,
Someone, some day, will all at once be chosen:
He shan't evade my penetrating claws   5
When for my swift, relentless swoop I picked him.
Thus the fierce hawk guards hen and goose for victim
As in the clouds his lazy rounds he draws.

PROSE AND POETRY   [1825]

Why, writer, toil with plodding prose?
Give me whatever thought you chose:
To pointed sharpness I will edge it.
With wingèd meters will I fledge it,
Will fit it to the tautened thew,   5
And bending my obedient bow,
Will send it flashing far and true,
And woe betide our common foe!

━━━━━━━━   [1825]

You're the kind that always loses,
Bliss and you are all at odds:
You're too sweet when chance refuses
And too clever when it nods.

━━━━━━━━   [1825]

Oh, Muse of satire, breathing fire!
Oh, come and heed my urgent call!
I do not need the thundering lyre,
Hand me the scourge of Juvenal!
Not the pedestrian imitators,   5
Not the penurious translators,
Nor rhymesters echoless, poor lambs,
Shall fester from my epigrams!
Peace to the poet wan with hunger,
Peace to the journals' gossipmonger.   10
Peace unto every harmless fool!
But as for you, my scoundrels cool,
Come forward! I shall surely hook one,
Hook all you scum with piercing pen,
And if by chance I overlook one,   15

Please do remind me, gentlemen!
Ah, mugs with sallow slander horrid,
Ah, forehead after brazen forehead,
All due from my avenging hand
The ineradicable brand!   20

ON ALEXANDER I   [1825]

Reared as he was to drum and banner
Our Emperor was no mean commander:
At Austerlitz ran out of breath,
In Eighteen-Twelve was scared to death,
(Albeit a fair frontline professor).   5
The front, though, proved unpicturesque . . .
Now he's collegiate assessor
Behind some Foreign Office desk.

════════   [1826]

Beneath the azure heaven of her native land
    She gently languished, gently faded . . .
She waned away at last and her young shade has fanned
    Its wings o'er me, I am persuaded;
Between us, though, a secret gulf has come to be.   5
    In vain I sought a sense of sharing:
Words from uncaring lips announced her death to me,
    And I took note of it uncaring.
So this was she whom I had loved with heart on fire,
    With strain of passion unto sadness,   10
With such slow ache of languishing desire,
    With such long agony, such madness!
Where is my pain, where is my love? Alas, my soul
    Relives those sweet dead days no longer;
It pays that luckless, all too trustful shade no toll,   15
    Be it of tears, be it of anger.

TO VYAZEMSKY   [1826]

So Ocean, man-devourer strident,
Has fanned your genius with fire?
You serenade with golden lyre
Hoar Neptune's awe-inspiring trident.

Recant! Our age's savage bent   5
Has allied earth and Neptune wizened.
Man is in every element
Tyrant or traitor or imprisoned.

TO YAZYKOV   [1826]

Yazykov, tell us from what source
Wells up your word of wild elation,
Now sweet, now like a gamboling horse,
Abrim with feeling, reckless force,
And young impulsive exaltation!   5
No—not Castalia's limpid blue
Has fed the notes of your Camoena,[1]
A vastly different Hippocrene[2]
Did Pegasus strike forth for you:
Not cooling waters calmly pouring,   10
With turbid ale afroth and soaring;
It's potent stuff and highly strung,
Like that new potion nobly rounded,
From rum and wine conjointly sprung,
With water's vileness uncompounded,   15
Which at Trigorsk our thirst unbounded
Revealed to us when we were young.

[1] Camoenae or Camenae were soothsaying nymphs of the springs in ancient Italic folklore, equated since Livius Andronicus with the Greek Muses. The one most often cited, Egeria, came to stand in a general sense for "the Muse" who inspired the poet.

[2] Hippocrene is the source that, according to Greek legend, sprang up under the hoofbeat of Pegasus and was thought of as the fount of poetic imagination.

CONFESSION [1826]

I love you—though I rage at it,
Though it is shame and toil misguided,
And to my folly self-derided
Here at your feet I will admit!
It ill befits my years, my station,   5
Good sense has long been overdue!
And yet, by every indication,
Love's plague has stricken me anew:
You're out of sight—I fall to yawning;
You're here—I suffer and feel blue,   10
And barely keep myself from owning,
Dear elf, how much I care for you!
Why, when your guileless girlish chatter
Drifts from next door, your airy tread,
Your rustling dress, my senses scatter   15
And I completely lose my head.
You smile—I flush with exultation;
You turn away—I'm plunged in gloom;
Your pallid hand is compensation
For a whole day of fancied doom.   20
When to the frame with artless motion
You bend to cross-stitch, all devotion,
Your eyes and ringlets down-beguiled,
My heart goes out in mute emotion
Rejoicing in you like a child!   25
Dare I confess to you my sighing,
How jealously I chafe and balk
When you set forth, at times defying
Bad weather, on a lengthy walk?
And then your solitary crying,   30
Those twosome whispers out of sight,
Your carriage to Opochka plying,
And the piano late at night . . .
Aline! I ask but to be pitied,
I do not dare to plead for love;   35
Love, for the sins I have committed,
I am perhaps not worthy of.
But make believe! Your gaze, dear elf,
Is fit to conjure with, believe me!

Ah, it is easy to deceive me! . . .   40
I long to be deceived myself!

TO I. I. PUSHCHIN[1]   [1826]

My oldest friend, companion peerless!
I too blessed fate when far up north
In my retreat remote and cheerless,
Adrift in dismal snow, so fearless
Your little sleigh bell tinkled forth.   5

Now providential dispensation
Grant that my voice may bless, I pray,
Your soul with equal consolation,
And bear into your prison station
Of bright Lyceum days a ray!   10

[1] Ivan Ivanovich Pushchin had been P.'s close friend ever since they were class-
mates at Tsarskoe Selo (1811–17). Undeterred by P.'s latest official disgrace, Push-
chin used a convenient family connection at Pskov to visit P. in January, 1825, at
the nearby family estate of Mikhailovskoe, which P. inhabited under surveillance
from both state and church authorities from 1824 to 1826. This was especially risky
in view of Pushchin's own active role in the inner circle of the Decembrist con-
spiracy. The friends had a heartwarming reunion, both fearing, correctly, that
under the circumstances it might be their last. Pushchin was condemned to Siberia
after the Decembrist revolt, and on arriving at the remote prison camp, three years
after that visit, was handed the present poem.
  We owe to Pushchin an invaluable set of sensitive and penetrating memoirs
covering the fourteen years of their close association.

STANZAS[1]   [1826]

In hopes of fame and bliss to come
I gaze ahead with resolution;
The dawn of Peter's sun was glum
With turmoil and with execution.

[1] (On the accession of Nicholas I.)

But he used truth to conquer hearts,   5
Enlightenment to soften manners;
He honored Dolgoruki's[2] arts
Above wild janissaries' banners.

He with a sovereign's fearless hand
Lit page on page of learning's story;   10
He did not spurn our native land,
Aware of its predestined glory.

He was now sage, now hero-king,
Now wright, now mate, as might determine
His spirit all-encompassing—   15
Eternal craftsman born to ermine.

Hold, then, your kin in proud regard,
Your life in all to his comparing,
Unflagging be like him, and hard,
And like him, of resentment sparing.   20

[2] Count Vasily Lukich Dolgoruki (1672–1739) was among the first young Russians to be sent abroad by Peter I to be educated. He served for a time as his foremost ministerial counselor and was entrusted with several important embassies. His later career was both less fortunate and less savory.

TO THE EMPEROR NICHOLAS I   [1826?]

He was made emperor, and right then
Displayed his flair and drive:
Sent to Siberia a hundred-twenty men
And strung up five.

WINTER JOURNEY[1]   [1826]

Brightly from its watery swathing
Sallies forth the lunar horn,

[1] Both in metric form and lyrical atmosphere this poem oddly resembles Nikolaus Lenau's "Der Postillon," conceived in the same general period, although there can scarcely be any connection between the two.

Yonder mournful clearings bathing
In its mournful light forlorn.

Down the dismal snow-track swinging   5
Speeds the troika, and the drone
Of the sleigh bell's tuneless ringing
Numbs me with its monotone.

Something stirring, something drowsing
Haunts the coachman's singsong too,   10
Chanting now of wild carousing,
Now of lovers' plaintive rue.

No black hut, no hearth-light sparkling,
Snow and desolation reign,
Mileposts only flash their darkling   15
Stripes and hurry past and wane.

Waste and gloom . . . but back tomorrow,
By your chimney, love, at will
Shall I muse, forgot all sorrow,
Gaze, and never gaze my fill.   20

When the clock's unhurried finger
Rounds its beat and strikes adieu,
Bidding strangers not to linger,
Midnight will not part us two.

Cheerless, love, the sleigh bell's ringing,   25
Drear my path across the fen,
Stilled the coachman's drowsy singing,
Dim the watery moon again.

THREE SPRINGS   [1827]

In this world's wasteland, borderless and bitter,
Three springs have broken forth with secret force:

The spring of youth, abubble and aglitter
Wells up and runs its swift and murmurous course.
Castalia's spring of flow divine is letting   5
In this world's wasteland exiles drink their fill.
The last, cool spring, the spring of all-forgetting,
Will slake the burning heart more sweetly still.

ARION   [1827]

We sailed in numerous company.
A few of us drew fast the sheeting,
The rest with mighty oar were beating
The brine; while, calm on slumbrous sea,
Our skillful helmsman clasped the rudder   5
To guide the laden vessel's thrust,
And I, at ease in carefree trust,
I sang to them . . . A sudden gust
Swept down and set the deep ashudder,
And crew and helmsman, all were lost!—   10
I only, secret singer, tossed
Upon the coast by seas in torment,
I sing my anthems as before,
And by a boulder on the shore
Dry in the sun my sodden garment.   15

THE POET   [1827]

   When on the poet Lord Apollo
Does not for mystic homage call,
To worldly bustle, pastimes hollow,
He lives in petty-minded thrall;
Then the celestial lyre is muted,   5
Chill torpor does his heart befall,
Amid life's idle and unsuited
He seems the idlest wretch of all.

Yet once the god-engendered word
But touches on the vivid senses,   10
The poet's soul awakens, tenses
Its pinions like an eagle stirred.
He chafes in worldly dissipation,
From human colloquy he flees,
Before the idol of the nation   15
He is too proud to bend his knees.
Then will he rush, uncouth and somber,
Astir with sounds and wild unease,
Toward the shores of desolate seas,
To murmuring wildwoods' vast penumbra.   20

THE TALISMAN   [1827]

Where the sea forever dances
Over lonely cliff and dune,
Where sweet twilight's vapor glances
In a warmer-glowing moon,
Where with the seraglio's graces   5
Daylong toys the Mussulman,
An enchantress 'mid embraces
Handed me a talisman.

'Mid embraces I was bidden:
"Guard this talisman of mine: 10
In it secret power is hidden!
Love himself has made it thine.
Neither death nor ills nor aging,
My beloved, does it ban,
Nor in gales and tempest raging   15
Can avail my talisman.

"Never will it help thee gather
Treasures of the Orient coast,
Neither to thy harness tether
Captives of the Prophet's host;   20
Nor in sadness will it lead thee
To a friendly bosom, nor

From this alien southland speed thee
To the native northern shore.

"But whenever eyes designing   25
Cast on thee a sudden spell,
In the darkness lips entwining
Love thee not, but kiss too well:
Shield thee, love, from evil preying,
From new heart-wounds—that it can,   30
From forgetting, from betraying
Guards thee this my talisman."

TO DAWE, ESQ.[1]   [1828]

Why does your wondrous pencil strive
My Moorish profile to elicit?
Your art will help it to survive,
But Mephistopheles will hiss it.

Draw Miss Olenin's face. To serve   5
His blazing inspiration's duty,
The genius should spend his verve
On homage but to youth and beauty.

[1] George Dawe (1781–1829), English portrait painter and mezzotint engraver in
the manner of Sir Joshua Reynolds. Went to Russia and was named First Painter
to the Court of Russia by Alexander I, who had him paint about 400 portraits of
army men who served in the Napoleonic Wars. Several of Dawe's paintings hang
in the Hermitage Museum in Leningrad.

REMEMBRANCE[1]   [1828]

When for us mortal men the noisy day is stilled,
        And, the mute spaces of the town

[1] A continuation of this poem, to more than double its length in print, exists in
a manuscript version that shows a few single-word gaps. These, and an unex-
plained reference to "two dear shades, angels given me by fate in bygone days,"
may explain Pushkin's decision not to include the rest of the poem in editions
printed in his lifetime.

With half-transparent nightly shadow filled,
      Sleep, daily toil's reward, drifts down,
Then is it that for me the gloom and quiet breed   5
      Long hours of agonized prostration;
On my nocturnal languor more intently feed
      The asps of mortal desolation;
Then fancies seethe at will, and the despondent mind
      Groans with excess of grim reflection;   10
Relentless Memory will wordlessly unwind
      Her long, long scroll for my inspection;
With loathing I peruse the record of my years,
      I execrate, I quail and falter,
I utter bitter plaints, and hotly flow my tears,   15
      But those sad lines I cannot alter.

THOU AND YOU   [1828]

The pale "you are" by warm "thou art"
Through careless slip of tongue replacing,
She sent within the love-struck heart
All sorts of happy fancies racing.
I stand before her all beguiled;   5
I stare at her, and the old Adam
Blurts out: You are all kindness, Madam!
And thinks: God, how I love thee, child!

YOUNG MARE   [1828]

Whither, mettlesome young filly,
Pride of the Caucasian brand,
Wildly bolting? Willy-nilly
Bridle time is close at hand.
Squint affrighted at my shadow,   5
Kick your hooves up in the air,

Down the smooth and spacious meadow
Freely canter all you care:
Tarry; soon I shall direct you,
In my thigh-grip meekly bound,   10
And with shortened rein deflect you
To an even-tempered round.

FOREBODING   [1828]

Once again there hang beclouded
My horizons, dark with rain;
Envious Fate, in malice shrouded,
Lies in wait for me again.
Will I find the strength to treat it   5
With disdain and, head unbowed,
Go with fortitude to meet it
As I did when young and proud?

Calmly, though my sails are riven,
I await what lies in store;   10
Once again I may be driven
Safely to a placid shore.
But foreboding, I confess it,
Brings me parting's fearful knell;
To your hand I fly to press it,   15
Angel, for a last farewell.

Angel meek and undefiant,
Gently whisper me good-bye,
Mourn: your loving gaze compliant,
Cast it down or raise it high.   20
In your heart enshrined forever,
I shall not grow faint or old:
Shall be young in hope, and never
Aught but gay and proud and bold.

─────── [1828]

Raven doth to raven fly,
Raven doth to raven cry:
Raven, where is carrion tender?
What shall be the day's provender?

Raven answers raven thus: 5
Well I know of meat for us;
On the fallow, by the willow
Lies a knight, a clod his pillow.

Why he died, who dealt the blow,
That his hawk alone can know,   10
And the sable mare that bore him,
And his bride who rode before him.

But the hawk now sails the air,
And the foe bestrode the mare,
And the bride a wreath is wreathing   15
For a new love, warm and breathing.

─────── [1828]

Capital of pomp and squalor,
Stately jail of souls unfree,
Firmament of greenish pallor,
Frost and stone and misery—
Still you set my heart to throbbing,   5
For at times there, down a street,
Comes a golden ringlet bobbing,
Trips a pair of slender feet.

THE UPAS TREE   [1828]

On acres charred by blasts of hell,
In sere and brittle desolation,
Stands like a baleful sentinel
The Upas, lone in all creation.

Grim Nature of the thirsting plains   5
Begot it on a day of ire
And steeped its leaves' insensate veins
And filled its roots with venom dire.

The poison trickles through its bark
And, melting in the noonday blazes,   10
It hardens at the fall of dark
In resinous translucent glazes.

That tree of death no bird will try
Or tiger seek: the storm wind vicious
Alone will darkly brush it by   15
And speed away, its breath pernicious.

And should a rain cloud overhead
Bedouse the brooding foliage, straying,
The boughs a lethal moisture shed,
The glowing sands with venom spraying.   20

Yet to that tree was man by man
With but an eyelid's flicker beckoned,
Sped duly forth that day, and ran,
And brought the poison by the second:

Brought waxen death back, and a bough   25
With leaves already limp and faded,
And from his wan and pallid brow
The sweat in clammy streams cascaded.

He brought it, faltered, and lay prone
On reeds beneath the vaulted tenting   30
And, luckless slave, died at the throne
Of that dread magnate unrelenting.

And on this venom arrows fed,
Obedient to the prince's orders,
And death and desolation spread   35
On fellowmen beyond the borders.

━━━━━━━━━ [1828]

    The dreary day is spent, and dreary night has soon
In leaden-colored draperies the heavens shrouded,
And over firry groves has risen all beclouded
A wan and spectral moon;
All these in me a mood of dark unease engender . . .   5
Up yonder far the moon ascends in splendor,
There is the air with sunset warmth replete,
There would the ocean like a sumptuous sheet
Beneath a sapphire sky enfold us . . .
This is the time, I know, she walks the mountain brow   10
Toward the strand besieged by surging, plunging shoulders,
There, at the foot of hallowed boulders
Forlornly and alone she must be sitting now . . .
Alone . . . no one to weep before her, none to languish,
No one to kiss her knees in rapt, oblivious anguish . . .   15
Alone . . . and no one's lips she suffers to be pressed
Upon her shoulders, her moist lips, her snowy breast,
No one is worthy of the heaven in her arm . . .
You surely are alone . . . in tears . . . then I am calm.
But if . . .   20

━━━━━━━━━ [1828]

Blest he who at your fancy's pleasure
Your dreamy, languid ardor won,
Whose every glance you heed and treasure,
Before all eyes by love undone;

But pity him who, heart and bowels   5
With love's consuming flame ablaze,
Must hear in silence your avowals,
While jealous anguish clouds his gaze.

—————   [1829]

I loved you: and the feeling, why deceive you,
May not be quite extinct within me yet;
But do not let it any longer grieve you;
I would not ever have you grieve or fret.
I loved you not with words or hope, but merely   5
By turns with bashful and with jealous pain;
I loved you as devotedly, as dearly
As may God grant you to be loved again.

—————   [1829]

As down the noisy streets I wander
Or walk into a crowded shrine,
Or sit with madcap youth, I ponder
Bemusing reveries of mine.

I say: the years speed by unhalting,   5
And we, as many as are here,
Will pass beneath the eternal vaulting,
And someone's hour is drawing near.

Or gazing at an oak tree lonely,
I muse: this patriarchal sage,   10
It has not passed my forebears' only,
It will outlive my own dim age.

Or fondling some dear child is reason
For me to think: I make thee room,

Farewell to thee! It is the season   15
For me to fade, for thee to bloom.

Each day, each passing year of aging,
In deep abstraction now I spend,
At pains among them to be gauging
The year-day of the coming end.   20

And where, fate, is my death preparing?
At sea, a-roving, in the fray?
Or will this nearby vale be bearing
Within its earth my feel-less clay?[1]

Although my flesh will be past caring   25
About the site of its decay,
Yet I would gladly still be sharing
The dear haunts of my earthly day.

And close to my sepulchral portals
I want young life to be at play,   30
And Nature, unconcerned with mortals,
To shed its beauty's timeless ray.

[1] This query is echoed by, among many others, Heinrich Heine when he asks *ca.* 1825 in "Wo?":

Wo wird einst des Wandermüden/ Letzte Ruhestätte sein?/ Unter Palmen in dem Süden?/ Unter Linden an dem Rhein?// Werd' ich wo in einer Wüste/ Eingescharrt von fremder Hand?/ Oder ruh' ich an der Küste/ Eines Meeres in dem Sand?// Immerhin! Mich wird umgeben/ Gotteshimmel, dort wie hier,/ Und als Totenlampen schweben/ Nachts die Sterne über mir.

AT THE BUST OF A CONQUEROR[1]   [1829]

You're wrong to think his likeness garbled:
The eye of art has truly seen
Upon his lips that smile enmarbled,
Wrath on his forehead's frigid sheen.
No wonder that his bust reflected   5
This potentate's internal strife:

[1] Directed at Alexander I.

His feelings ever were bisected,
A harlequin in face and life.

THE MONASTERY ON MT. KAZBEK   [1829]

Above thy brother summits' rows,
Kazbek, thy royal tentment glows
Aloft with everlasting lusters.
Thy monastery, past cloudy musters,
An ark afloat in vaporous height,   5
Just shows above the mountain clusters.

Oh, far-away, oh, longed-for site!
Could I but leave behind this canyon
And, soaring far beyond those shrouds,
Withdraw, with God for my companion,   10
Into a cell above the clouds! . . .

THE SNOWSLIDE   [1829]

On frowning boulders dashed to spray,
The waters roar and foam away,
Aloft the murmuring wildwoods sway,
        And eagles scream,
And through the watery haze of gray   5
        The summits gleam.

A slide broke off this mountain face
And in its thundering downhill pace
Dammed up the gorge's narrow space
        With ponderous force,   10
And Terek's mighty water race
        Blocked in its course.

Abruptly then becalmed and caged,
Your clamor, Terek, was assuaged;
But stubborn onslaught grimly waged   15
      The rearward ranks,
Broke through the snow bar, while enraged
      You swamped your banks.

And long the ruptured barrier so
Lay on, a thawless hulk of snow,   20
And sullen Terek ran below,
      His watery dust
Bedewing in his lathered flow
      The icy crust.

Across it lay a pathway wide,   25
There palfreys pranced and oxen plied,
And traders of the steppe would guide
      Their camels there,
Where sky-born Aeol, none beside,
      Now cleaves the air.   30

————————— [1830]

What use my name to you, what good?[1]
It will die down like the sad jingle
Of waves awash on distant shingle,
Like night sounds in the toneless wood.

Upon your mind it will for long   5
Leave but a lifeless trace, unspoken
Like on a tomb the lacy token
Of an unfathomable tongue.

What use is it? Long since suppressed
By fresh and turbulent emotion,   10
It will not stir within your breast
Old thoughts of tender, pure devotion.

[1] Written in response to a request to write his name in the album of the Polish beauty, Countess Karolina Sobańska, already immortalized by the love of Mickiewicz.

But one still day, forlorn, bereft,
Pronounce it as your tears are welling;
Say: memory of me is left,   15
A heart on earth for me to dwell in!

———————   [1830]

At moments when your graceful form
In my embrace I long to capture,
And from my lips a tender swarm
Of love's endearments pour in rapture—
Without a word your supple shape   5
From my encircling arms unfolding,
You make your answer by escape
And smile at me, all trust withholding;
Too keenly mindful in your heart
Of past betrayal's doleful mention,   10
You bide in listless inattention
And hear me not and take no part . . .
I curse the cunning machinations
That were my sinful youth's delight,
Those hours awaiting assignations   15
In gardens, in the dead of night.
I curse the lover's whispered suing,
And tuneful verse's magic aids,
Caress of rashly trusting maids,
Their tears, and their belated ruing.   20

FOUNTAIN AT TSARSKOE SELO   [1830]

Out of her fingers the urn must have slipped and burst on a boulder.
    Sorrowing there she sits, holding the useless shell.
Lo! from the jagged urn the jet springs still, and the maiden
    Over an endless flow leans in unending dismay.

CONJURY[1]   [1830]

Oh, if it's true that in the night,
When quietude the living covers,
And liquidly the lunar light
Glides down and on the tombstones hovers,
Oh, if it's true that then appear   5
Their tenants on the ghostly common,—
Leyla I wait, her shade I summon:
To me, my love, come here, come here!

Appear to me, beloved shade,
As you appeared before we parted,   10
In pallid wintry chill arrayed,
By deathly agony distorted.
Come like a star of outmost sphere,
Like a faint sound, an emanation,
Come like a dreadful visitation,   15
I care not how: Come here, come here!

I call you—not because I crave
To chastise those before whose malice
My love took refuge in the grave,—
Or as my spy in Hades' palace,   20
Or yet because I know the fear
Of doubt . . . but sorrowing above you,
I want to say that still I love you,
And still am yours: Come here, come here!

[1] Barry Cornwall (pseudonym for the minor English dramatist and poet B. W. Procter, 1787–1874) published a poem with a similar title which, like other works of his, had some influence on Pushkin in this period.

─────────   [1830]

Bound for the distant coast that bore you,
You left behind this alien clime,
And long that hour I wept before you,
That unforgotten, mournful time.

With fingers chill and numbed of feeling   5
I clutched you, begged you not to leave,
Parting's fierce pangs with moans appealing
To nourish still and let me grieve.

But from our sorrowing embraces
You tore away your lips and hand,   10
And from an exile's prison-places
You called me to another land.
"Let us await another meeting
'Neath skies of everlasting blue,
In olive shades," you kept repeating,   15
"Love's kisses, friend, we shall renew."

But there, alas, where heaven's quarters
Are steeped in azure lucence deep,
Where olives shade the sheltered waters,
You fell into eternal sleep.   20
Now all your beauty, all you suffered,
Are lost in the sepulchral urn,
And those reunion kisses proffered—
But I shall claim them, comes my turn.

AT KUTUZOV'S GRAVE   [1831]

Before the hallowed burial-stead
I linger here with lowered head . . .
All sleep, save in the twilight solemn
The temple candelabra gild
Tall granites, column after column,   5
And rows of standards, pendent, stilled.

Beneath them lies that lord of clans,
That idol of the northern lands,
The mighty realm's revered defender
Who all its enemies subdued,   10

The last of that illustrious gender,
Imperial Catherine's eagle brood.

Live ardor in your grave-site glows!
From it a Russian story flows,
Relates that hour when by the nation   15
Your silver-templed age was bid
With voice of trustful invocation
To "come and save!" You rose—and did.

Now hark again the voice of trust,
Arise and save the Tsar and us,   20
One instant, ancient grim preserver,
Appear at the sepulchral cleft,
Appear, and breathe new dash and fervor
Into the regiments you left.

Appear, and with your sacred hand   25
Point out among our leaders' band
Your true inheritor, your chosen . . .
But mute the temple chambers loom,
In calm, eternal slumber frozen
Sleeps the indomitable tomb.   30

TO THE SLANDERERS OF RUSSIA[1]   [1831]

Bards of the Nations, say, what set you seething,
Threats of Anathema at Russia breathing?
What roused your wrath? That Poland stirs again?
Desist: this strife pits Slavs against each other
It has been weighed by Fate, like many another   5
In an old dispute, past your scope and ken.

   Long since these tribes of hostile brothers
   Have vied among themselves and warred,

[1] This poem is Pushkin's angry reply to the clamor of indignation and calls for intervention generated in Western Europe by the brutal suppression of the Polish uprising of 1831, of which his friend Mickiewicz became the spokesman and spiritual leader abroad.

And now the ones and now the others
Have had to bow before the sword.   10
Who shall outlive that grim commotion,
The boastful Pole, the stalwart Russ?
Shall Slavic brooklets merge in Russia's ocean,
    Shall it dry out? Leave it to us!

Desist: to you these bloodstained tables   15
Remain unread, the clannish fables
Of this our internecine feud
Are undeciphered, unreviewed;
The voice of Kremlin, Praga,² calls you
But stirs no echo; the mystique   20
Of desperate fortitude enthralls you,
And then your hatred of us . . . Speak:

Is it for this, perchance, you hate us
That Moscow's blazing shell defied decrees
Of a vainglorious dictator's,   25
While you were writhing on your knees?
Or that we smashed that idol towering
Above the realms, so Europe gained release
And, saved by Russian blood, is flowering
    Anew in freedom, honor, peace?   30

Come, challenge us with deeds, not ringing quarrels!
Is the old hero, resting on his laurels,
Unfit to mount the Ismail³ bayonet?
Has then the Russian Tsar's word lost its omen?
Are we unused to Western foemen,   35
With Russian triumphs sated yet?
Are we too few? From Perm to Tauris gleaming,
From Finnish crags to ardent Colchis teeming,
From Kremlin, rocked upon its stand,
To China's battlements unshaken,   40
Bright steel her bristles, shall not waken,
Shall not rise up the Russian land?
Send on, then, sacred mischief-makers,
Send your embittered sons and braves:
There's room for them in Russian acres   45
Amid not unfamiliar graves.

² The suburb of Warsaw where the insurgents made their last desperate stand.
³ The Turkish fortress in Bessarabia stormed by Suvorov in 1790.

ECHO[1]   [1831]

Where beasts in trackless forests wail
Where horns intone, where thunders flail,
Or maiden chants in yonder vale—
    To every cry
Through empty air you never fail   5
    To speed reply.

You listen to the thunder knells,
The voice of gales and ocean swells,
The shepherd's hail in hills and dells
    And you requite;   10
But unrequited stay . . . This spells
    The poet's plight.

[1] The motif of this lyric appears to have been drawn from Barry Cornwall, see footnote to "Conjury," p. 42.

IN A BEAUTY'S ALBUM   [1832]

All harmony, all wondrous fairness,
Aloof from passions and the world,
She rests, with tranquil unawareness
In her triumphant beauty furled.
When all about her eyes hold muster,   5
Nor friends, nor rivals can be found,
All our beauties' pallid round
Extinguished wholly by her luster.

And were you bound I know not where,
Be it to love's embraces bidden,   10
Or what choice vision you may bear
In heart's most private chamber hidden,—
Yet, meeting her, you will delay,
Struck by bemusement in mid-motion,
And pause in worshipful devotion   15
At beauty's sacred shrine to pray.

ALBUM VERSE   [1832]

True, my pen these private pages
Has not touched in many a day;
In my drawer, I must say,
Lorn of friendly lines for ages
Languishing your album lay.   5
On your nameday then addressing
Timely compliments to you,
Let me wish you every blessing,
Every soothing solace too,
Lots of thunder on Parnassus,   10
Lots of days of restful calm,
And a conscience free of harm
From a single album passus
Owed to friend or to *Madame*.

───────────   [1833]

But for my soul's obscurely asking
And pining for I know not what,
I would stay here forever, basking
In bliss at this forgetful spot:
Desire's vain tremors never missing,   5
I'd count the world a dreamy wisp,
Those slender feet forever kissing,
Forever hearing that sweet lisp.

───────────   [1833]

Don't let me lose my mind, oh, God;
I'd sooner beg with sack and rod
    Or starve in sweat and dust.

Not that I treasure my poor mind,
Or would bemoan it should I find   5
    That part from it I must:

If they but left me free to roam,
How I would fly to make my home
    In deepest forest gloom!
In blazing frenzy would I sing,   10
Be drugged by fancies smoldering
    In rank and wondrous fume.

And I would hear the breakers roar,
And my exultant gaze would soar
    In empty skies to drown: 15
Unbridled would I be and grand
Like the great gale that rakes the land
    And mows the forest down.

But woe befalls whose mind is vague:
They dread and shun you like the plague,   20
    And once the jail-gate jars,
They bolt the fool to chain and log
And come as to a poor mad dog
    To tease him through the bars.

And then upon the evenfall   25
I'd hear no nightingale's bright call,
    No oak tree's murmurous dreams—
I'd hear my prison-mates call out,
And night attendants rail and shout,
    And clashing chains, and screams.   30

——————— [1835]

Bitterly sobbing, the maid chid the youth with jealous reproaches;
    Facing her, propped on a shoulder, sleep took him all unawares.
Straightway the maiden was still, lulling his gossamer slumber,
    Letting her tears flow on, quietly smiling at him.

——————   [1835]

I was assured my heart had rested
Its urge to suffer long before;
What used to be, I had protested,
Shall be no more! shall be no more!
Deceitful dreams forever hidden,   5
Forsaken raptures, sorrows banned . . .
Yet here afresh they stir me, bidden
By Beauty's sovereign command.

——————   [Between 1827 and 1836]

She looks at you with such soft feeling,
Her artless chatter so appealing,
Her gaiety so full of snap,
Her eyes replete with melting sweetness,
Last night she snuggled with such neatness   5
Beneath the sheltering table-nap
Her pretty foot into my lap!

FROM PINDEMONTE[1]   [1836]

I have but little use for those loud "rights"—the phrase
That seems to addle people's minds these days.
I do not fault the gods, nor to a soul begrudge it
That I'm denied the bliss of wrangling over a Budget,
Or keeping king from fighting king in martial glee;   5
Nor do I worry greatly if the Press is free
To hoax the nitwits, or if censors-pokers
Spoil journalistic games for sundry jokers;
All this is merely "words, words, words," you see.
Quite other, better rights are dear to me;   10
I crave quite other, better liberation:

[1] Italian poet (1753–1828), to whom Pushkin ascribed this ode to privacy solely
in order to hoodwink the censorship.

To be dependent on a king, or on a nation—
Is it not all the same? Good riddance! But to dance
To no one else's fiddle, foster and advance
One's private self alone; before gold braid and power   15
With neither conscience, thought, nor spine to cower;
To move now here, now there with fancy's whim for law,
In Nature's godlike works to take delight and awe,
And start before the gifts of art and inspiration
With pangs of trembling, joyous adoration—   20
There's bliss for you! There are your rights . . .

Narrative Poems, Fairy Tales, and Ballads

TSAR NIKITA AND HIS FORTY DAUGHTERS [1822]

Introductory Note

Tsar Nikita and His Forty Daughters was written in 1822 in the colorful, raw frontier town of Kishinev in Bessarabia. Unlike the earlier *Gabri-Iliad,* a brilliantly sacrilegious spoof of the sacred story of the Annunciation, which was charmingly rendered into English by Max Eastman and published in a limited edition in 1929, this rollicking piece of ribaldry does not seem to have been previously translated into English.

TSAR NIKITA AND HIS FORTY DAUGHTERS

Tsar Nikita once reigned widely,
Richly, merrily, and idly,
Did no good or evil thing:
So his realm was flourishing.
He kept clear of toil and bother,   5
Ate and drank and praised our Father.
With some ladies he had squired
Forty daughters had he sired,
Forty maids with charming faces,
Four times ten celestial graces,   10
Sweet of temper, full of love.
Ah, what ankles, Heaven above!
Chestnut curls, the heart rejoices,
Eyes—a marvel, wondrous voices,
Minds—enough to lose your mind: 15
All from head to toe designed
To beguile one's heart and spirit;
There was but a sole demerit.
Oh? What fault was there to find?
None to speak of, never mind.   20
Or at most the merest tittle.
Still, a flaw (though very little).
How explain it, how disguise
So as not to scandalize

That cantankerous old drip,   25
Sanctimonious Censorship?
Help me, Muse—your poet begs!
Well—between the lassies' legs . . .
Stop! Already too explicit,
Too immodest, quite illicit . . .   30
Indirection here is best:
Aphrodite's lovely breast,
Lips, and feet set hearts afire,
But the focus of desire,
Dreamed-of goal of sense and touch,   35
What is that? Oh, nothing much.
Well then, it was this in fact
That the royal lassies lacked.

This unheard-of malformation
Caused dismay and consternation   40
In each loyal courtly heart,
And much sorrow on the part
Of their Sire and stricken mothers.
From the swaddling-women others
Soon found out what had occurred;   45
All the nation when it heard
Ah'ed and oh'ed at such an earful,
Gaped and gasped, amazed and fearful;
Some guffawed, but most were leerier:
(This could land you in Siberia!).   50

Sternly Tsar Nikita summoned
Courtiers, mummies, nannies, "Come and
Here the stricture I impose:
Any one of you who sows
In my daughters' minds suggestions   55
Or provokes unseemly questions,
Or so much as dreams to dare
Hint at that which is not there,
Deal in doubtful words and notions,
Or perform improper motions—   60
Let there be no shred of doubt:
Wives will have their tongues cut out,

Men a member more essential,
Intumescent in potential."

Stern but just, such was the Tsar,   65
And his eloquence went far
To induce a wise complaisance;
All resolved with deep obeisance
That the counsel of good health
Was to hold one's mouth and wealth.   70
Noble ladies went in terror
Lest their men be found in error,
While the men in secret thought:
Oh, I wish my wife were caught!
(Ah, disloyal hearts and base!)   75

Our Tsarevnas grew apace.
Sad their lot! Nikita's Grace
Called his Council, put his case:
Thus and so—not unavowedly
But in whispers, not too loudly,   80
Pas devant les domestiques . . .
Mute the nobles sat and wondered
How to deal with such a freak.
But a gray-haired Nestor pondered,
Rose, and bowing to and fro,   85
Dealt his pate a clanging blow,
And with venerable stutters
To the potentate he utters:
"May it not, Enlightened Sire,
Be accounted wanton slyness   90
Or offend your Gracious Highness:—
Sunken yet in carnal mire,
A procuress once I knew,
(Where's she now? What does she do?
Likely in the same vocation.)   95
She enjoyed the reputation
Of a most accomplished witch,
Curing any ache or itch,
Making feeble members sound.
Pray let my advice be heeded: 100

If that witch could just be found,
She'd install the thing that's needed."

"Instantly," exclaimed and frowned,
Thunder on his brow, Nikita,
"Send for her and let me meet her,   105
Let the sorceress be found!
If, however, she deceive Us,
Of Our shortage not relieve Us,
Lead Us up the garden path
With sly tricks—she'll know Our wrath!   110
Let me be not Tsar but duffer
If I do not make her suffer
Death by fire—of which is token
This my prayer! I have spoken."

    Confidentially, discreetly,   115
Envoys were despatched who fleetly
Sped by special courier post,
Searched the realm from coast to coast,
Scampered, scurried, faster, faster,
Tracking witches for their Master.   120
One year passes, nothing's heard,
And another, not a word.
Till at last a lad of mettle
On a lucky trail did settle,
Rode into a forest dread   125
Just as though by Satan led;
There he found the little cottage
Where the witch lived in her dotage,
Boldly passing gate and bar
As an envoy of the Tsar,   130
He saluted the magician
And revealed the Tsar's commission:
What the quest was all about,
What his daughters were without.
She, with instant understanding,   135
Thrust him back onto the landing,
Hustled him straight on and out:
"Shake a leg, don't look about,
Do not linger or I'll plague you,

Strike your limbs with chills and ague;   140
Wait three days and then come back
For your answer and your pack;
But no later than the crack
Of that dawn!" Then she remembers
To lock up, fans golden embers . . .   145
Three-score hours she brewed her spell,
Conjured up the Prince of Hell,
And so soon as she could ask it,
He produced a brassbound casket
Stocked with countless feminine   150
Wherewithals of men's sweet sin.
Curly beauties, choice examples,
Every size, design, and shade,
What a marvelous parade!
Sorting out her wealth of samples,   155
Soon the sorc'ress had arrayed
Forty of superior grade
All in damask napkin dressed,
And had locked them in the chest.
This she handed to the willing   160
Envoy with a silver shilling,
And he rides . . . till in the west
Sinking sun commends a rest.
Just a bite to stay one's hunger,
Spirit keeps the body younger,   165
Vodka keeps the spirit mellow;
This was a resourceful fellow,
And he carried in his sack
Victuals for the long way back.
So he took this pleasant course,   170
Loosed the harness of his horse,
And sat munching in the shadow,
While his charger cropped the meadow.
Happily he sat and mused
How the Tsar would be enthused   175
With what nestled in his basket,
Might appoint him, what a fluke,
Knight or Baron, Viscount, Duke . . .
What was hidden in the casket
That the witch was sending him?   180

Just that oaken lid to mask it
For the journey's interim . . .
Tightly grooved, though . . . all looks dim.
Terror of the Tsar's decree
Yields to curiosity,   185
The temptation's too delicious:
Ear laid close against the fissures,
Long he listens—but in vain;
Sniffs—familiar scent . . . Egad!
What profusion there, what wonder!   190
Just a glimpse could not be bad;
If one pried the lock asunder . . .
And before he knew, he had.
Whoosh! the birdies, swarming out,
Light on branches all about,   195
Tails aflirt. In vain our lad
Loudly calls them back to casket,
Throws them biscuit from his basket,
Scatters morsels—all no good.
(Clearly such was not their diet);   200
Why return if you could riot
Sweetly chanting in the wood,
To be cooped in gloom and quiet?

Meanwhile in the distance stumbles,
All bent double by her load,   205
Some old woman down the road.
Our poor envoy up and bumbles
Quite distracted in her wake:
"Granny, help, my head's at stake!
Look, there sit my birdies scattered,   210
Chattering as if nothing mattered,
How can I entice them back?"
That old woman craned her neck,
Spat, and with her crook did beckon:
"Though you asked for it, I reckon,   215
Do not fret or worry so:
All you need to do is show—
And they'll all come back, I warrant."
Our young fellow thanked the crone,
And the moment he had shown—   220

Down they fluttered in a torrent,
Swarming off their firs and birches,
And resumed their former perches
In the envoy's box; and he,
To forestall some new disaster,   225
Clapped them under lock and key,
And rode homeward to his Master,
Thanking God he had retrieved them.
When the princesses received them,
Each one promptly found its cage;   230
And the Tsar in royal glee
Graciously was pleased to stage
A gigantic jubilee.
Seven days they spent in fêting
And a month recuperating.   235
The entire House of Lords
He allotted rich rewards,
Nor forgot the witch herself:
On the Art Museum's ladders
Reaching for the highest shelf,   240
They brought down to send the elf
Skeletons, a brace of adders,
And in spirits in a jar
Half a candle, famed afar.
And of course the envoy bold   245
Had his prize. My tale is told.

Some will ask me, eyebrows climbing,
Why I wrought such fatuous rhyming,
What the reason for it was?
Let me answer them: Because.   250

THE GYPSIES [1824]

Introductory Note

The Gypsies (begun in 1823/24 in Odessa, finished in October, 1824, at Mikhailovskoe) is an anti-Rousseauean drama built on Rousseauean premises. It is a tragedy of ungovernable human drives —the "fateful passions" of the rueful closing lines of the epilogue. These urges possess man and destroy him regardless of his own volition, and the central dramatic issue of flaw or guilt becomes almost irrelevant. Aleko, the haunted hero who bears a variant of Pushkin's own name, is twice undone by the elemental passion of possessive jealousy; once (it is barely hinted in the nightmare scene) during his life in urban civilization, another time in the free, simple environment which he has himself sought in a vain attempt to escape personal guilt and "enlightened corruption"—civilization and sophistication seen as a curse in the manner of Rousseau. Of the triad of principal actors, only the artistically subdued central figure, the old gypsy, has conquered, at great cost, the helpless serfdom of the human condition and thus, achieving full harmony with frugal nature and a life reduced to the bare essentials, attained the peace and wisdom of resignation. This achievement, however, has no explicit parallel among the other followers of the nomad life, whether "naturals" or romantic fugitives from the city —for *ot sudeb zaščity net :* there is no refuge from the fates.

The Gypsies is the most mature and thoughtful of Pushkin's southern narrative poems. In it he has completely discarded the romantic vagueness of background and the arid habit of narcissistic self-projection, which he had come to condemn in the Byronic poem and its thinly disguised author-hero—both powerful influences upon him in the earlier years of his "southern exile."

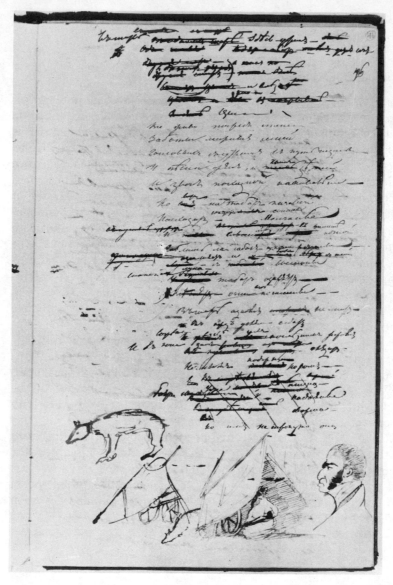

An early manuscript page of THE GYPSIES *with sketches of covered Bessarabian gypsy wagons and a girl (Zemfira?) nursing a baby.*

THE GYPSIES

Between Moldavian settlements
In clamorous throng the gypsies wander.
Tonight they spread their tattered tents
Encamped beside the river yonder.
Gay is their camp, like freedom gay,   5
Their sleep beneath the stars untroubled;
Amid the wheels of van and dray,
Their sides with hanging carpets doubled,
The campfire burns, and over it bent
They cook their meal; at pasture scattered,   10
The horses graze; behind the tent
A tame bear lies at ease, unfettered.
A lively bustle stirs the scene:
The peaceful cares of clansmen keen
To move at daybreak, women singing   15
And children's shouts around the wains,
Above the traveling anvil's ringing.
But now the night with slumbrous balm
Descends on the nomadic camping,
And nothing stirs the prairie calm   20
But barks and horses' neighs and stamping.
Extinct at last the winking lights,
All lies in stillness, moonbeams shimmer
Alone from heaven's distant heights
And set the silent camp aglimmer.   25
But in one tent an aged man
Still lingers by the charcoal pan,
His limbs at dying embers warming,
And his old eyes alertly scan
The steppe, where mists of night are forming.   30
His youthful daughter, scarcely grown,
Has gone to roam the prairie yonder.
In willful freedom bred to wander,
She will be back; but day has flown,
And soon the moon will have receded   35
From heaven's far-beclouded fold—
Zemfira's still abroad; unheeded
Her father's poor repast grows cold.

But here she is; with her together—
A stranger to the old man's gaze—   40
A lad comes striding through the heather.
"My father," thus the maiden says,
"I bring a guest, found in the distance
Beyond the barrow as I went;
I bade him slumber in our tent.   45
He wants to share our own existence,
And I shall be his gypsy love;
For where he dwelt, the law pursues him.
His name—Aleko. He will rove,
He vows, where I rove; and I choose him."   50

OLD MAN

My welcome to you; if you meant
To rest till morning in our tent,
Or if indeed you came preparing
A longer sojourn, I am glad
To share my shelter and my bread.   55
Be ours—and our own lot preferring,
Espouse our humble, wayward faring,
And share my wagon too; and so
At dawn we shall set forth together;
Choose any of the trades we know: 60
Forge iron, or to market go
With songs and dancing-bear atether.

ALEKO

I choose to stay.

ZEMFIRA

He will be mine;
And who is there to drive him from me?
But it grows late . . . the new moon's rim   65
Has sunk from sight; the plains are dim
With mist, and sleep will overcome me . . .

———

Day breaks. The elder ambles nearer
About the sleep-enveloped tent.

"The sun is up. Arise, Zemfira,   70
Wake up, my guest; it's time we went!
Come, children, end your blissful slumber . . ."
Out pours the tribe in noisy swarms,
The tents are struck, and wagons lumber
As the accustomed cart train forms.   75
All moves at once, by wonted norms
Across the barren lowlands swaying,
The donkeys carry children playing
In baskets slung behind the reins,
Husbands and brothers, wives and maidens,   80
All ages line the wagon trains,
Hails, clamor, tunes of gypsy cadence,
The dance-bear's growling and his chain's
Impatient jangle, colors sparkling
From tattered motley rags of dress   85
On gnarled or tender nakedness,
The dogs' unending howl and barking,
The bagpipe's skirling, axles' creak—
All squalid, savage, all unsettled,
But how vivacious, highly mettled,   90
How alien to our pastimes bleak,
How foreign to those vapid pleasures,
Stale as a slave song's tuneless measures!

—————

   The youth in gloom of spirit viewed
The even steppelands, now deserted,   95
His reason fearfully averted
From the deep sources of his mood.
Black-eyed Zemfira's love to treasure,
The wide world his to roam at leisure,
The lofty sun above him gay   100
In festive noontime glamour shining—
What sets the youthful heart to pining,
What private torment, what dismay?

      Little bird, God's wingèd neighbor,
      Knows not toil or heart's unrest,   105
      Nor in unremitting labor

Weaves a long enduring nest;
Seeks a twig-perch when it darkens
And till sunrise folds its wings;
Come the dawn, God's voice it hearkens,   110
Shakes its feathers down and sings.
Spring, the year's adornment, fading,
In its turn the summer's blaze,
Tardy autumn will be shading,
Shrouding all in rain and haze,   115
Fretful sloth to humans bringing—
Past blue seas denied to men,
Southward bound the bird is winging
Till the spring returns again.

He, like that careless feathered singer,   120
A transient exile, would not linger
In safety by a sturdy nest,
Clove to no custom, sought no rest.
For him no beaten road was needed,
No inn bespoke, no route to chart,   125
Aroused by each new morn, he ceded
His day to God, life's cares unheeded
Stirred not the torpor of his heart.
At times, like far-off constellations,
He glimpsed renown's alluring ray,   130
And rare delights and dissipations
All unexpected came his way.
Though crashing thunderbolts not seldom
Above his lonely head would strike,
The same oblivious slumber held him   135
In storm and quietude alike.
His life ignored blind Fate and yielded
To her malignant guile no toll;
But God! what sway the passions wielded
Within his unresisting soul!   140
How in his ravaged breast their torment
They used to wreak and rage their fill!
How briefly, how much longer dormant,
Will they flare up once more? They will!

———

ZEMFIRA

Tell me, my friend: you are not grieving   145
For what you will not know again?

ALEKO

Know what again?

ZEMFIRA

          I mean your leaving
The cities, your own countrymen.

ALEKO

What should I grieve for? If you knew it,
Could comprehend—why would I rue it,   150
The bondage of the stifling towns!
There man in throngs, hemmed in by fences,
Tastes not the morning cool, nor senses
The vernal perfume of the downs;
There love is furtive, thought in bridles,   155
There liberty is bought and sold,
They bow in worship before idols
And beg for shackles and for gold.
What did I leave? Betrayers' babble,
Rank prejudice's smug decree,   160
The hounding of the mindless rabble
Or else resplendent infamy.

ZEMFIRA

But there they have apartments spacious,
With rugs of many-colored plaid,
And games and festivals vivacious—   165
The girls there go so richly clad!

ALEKO

What of the city's noisy mirth?
Where love is not, there is no pleasure.
The girls . . . Of how much greater worth
Are you than they, for all your dearth   170
Of costly garments, pearls, and treasure!

Don't ever change, my lovely fair!
And I . . . have but a single mission,
Your pastimes and your love to share,
An exile by my own volition.   175

OLD MAN

You like us and the life we lead,
Though nurtured by a wealthy nation.
Not always, though, is liberation
Dear to a man of tender breed.
Here an old tale is still related: 180
A dweller of the South[1] once came
Amongst us, by the Emperor fated
To live in exile here, the same
As you (the legend stated,
But I forget his curious name).   185
Though old in body, far from strong,
His guileless soul was younger, firmer—
He had the wondrous gift of song,
His voice like to the waters' murmur.
And long, beloved of everyone,   190
Here on the banks of Danube dwelling,
He lived, and gave offense to none
But charmed them with his storytelling.
As shy and feeble as a child,
He knew not how to make his living,   195
And fed on creatures of the wild,
On fish and fowl of strangers' giving.
When storm winds raged and winter came,
The rapid flow in frost entrapping,
They used to guard with furry wrapping   200
The saintly stranger's aged frame.
Yet years and habitude could never
Endear our humble, toilsome way,
But, pale and gaunt, he strayed forever
Amongst us and was wont to say   205
That an immortal's vengeful passion
Pursued him for some old transgression.
Deliverance his only thought,
Throughout his span, with piteous crying

[1] The legend alludes to Ovid, the Roman poet banished by Augustus in A.D. 8 to Tomi on the Black Sea, not far from Bessarabia, the setting of *The Gypsies* and Pushkin's own temporary place of exile.

The exile, restless and distraught,   210
Bestrode the banks of Danube, sighing
For his far city; lastly, dying,
He charged them earnestly to send
To the warm land of his allegiance
His sorrowing bones—this alien region's   215
Reluctant guests unto the end!

ALEKO

   Is such the fate, then, of your sons,
Majestic Rome of song and story!
Thou bard of the immortal ones,
Love's singer, tell me, what is glory?   220
Sepulchral echoes, honor's hail,
Renown from age to age redawning?
Or, told beneath a smoky awning,
An errant nomad's artless tale?

———

   Two years have passed. The gypsies wander   225
Upon their wonted peaceful quest,
As ever finding here and yonder
Both hospitality and rest.
Civilization's bonds disdaining,
Aleko wanders free as they;   230
Exempt from cares and uncomplaining,
He shares their ever-ranging day.
He is the same, so are his dear ones,
Their life is his; to all appearance
He scarce remembers former years.   235
He loves the dusk of their nocturnal
Bivouacs, sweet indolence eternal,
Their tuneful speech upon his ears.
Fled from the lair where once he bedded,
The shaggy sharer of his tent   240
In hamlets on the steppe-trail threaded,
Near some Moldavian settlement,
Performed his ponderous dance and snorted
Before a cautious gathering
And gnawed the noxious iron sling;   245

While, on his traveler's staff supported,
The elder with a lazy swing
Would set the cymbaled hand-drum ringing,
Aleko sang, Zemfira bringing
Their freely given offering.   250
Night falls; all three prepare their diet
Of unreaped millet gleaned and crushed;
The old man sleeps—and all is quiet . . .
The tent within is dark and hushed.

———

The ancient's failing pulses quicken,   255
New life the vernal sunshine brings;
And by the cot his daughter sings
Of love. Aleko listens, stricken.

ZEMFIRA

Graying man, cruel man,
Spare me not fire or knife,   260
Stab you can, burn you can,
Firm I am, spurn your strife.

And your love I deny,
And your wrath I defy,
For another I love,   265
For his love I will die.

ALEKO

Be still. Your singing wearies me,
I do not like those uncouth airs.

ZEMFIRA

Too bad! but it is not for thee
That I am singing them. Who cares?   270

Stab you may, burn you may,
Not a word will I say,
Graying man, cruel man,
You shall not learn his name.

How much fresher than spring,   275
Hot as summer-day gold,
Is my lad young and bold,
Is his love that I sing.

What caresses we shared
In the still of the night!   280
How we laughed at the sight
Of the gray in your hair!

ALEKO

Enough, Zemfira! Hush, be quiet . . .

ZEMFIRA

So thou hast read my song's intent?

ALEKO

Zemfira!

ZEMFIRA

Scold, then! Why deny it?   285
It is for thee my song is meant.
Goes off, singing "Graying man . . ."

OLD MAN

Yes, I remember—that old ditty
Was first in my young manhood sung,
And often since in mart and city
It has delighted old and young.   290
When in the steppelands of Kaǧula
We wandered, of a winter night—
Dandling her daughter, my Mariula
Would sing it by the firelight.
The years gone by with every hour   295
Grow dark and darker now, I find
But that refrain some secret power
Has graven deep into my mind.

———

Night; all is still. The moon has brightened
The southern heaven's azure span;   300
Zemfira wakens the old man:
"Oh, father, listen! I am frightened.
Such troubled sleep Aleko sleeps!
He groans as if in pain, and weeps."

OLD MAN

Keep silent, daughter. Do not touch him.   305
I often heard the Russians tell:
At midnight a domestic elf
May haunt the sleeper's rest and clutch him
To choke his breath; at dawn the spell
Is loosed. Sit by me, calm yourself.   310

ZEMFIRA

Oh, Father! Now he sobs: Zemfira!

OLD MAN

His very dreams reach out for thee:
Than all the world he holds thee dearer.

ZEMFIRA

His love is wearisome to me.
For freedom pines my soul and mutters—   315
Already . . . Hush! I hear him moaning . . .
It is another name he utters.

OLD MAN

Whose name?

ZEMFIRA

Oh, listen! Hoarsely groaning,
Gnashing his teeth as one insane!
I must awaken him.

OLD MAN

In vain;   320
Break not a nightbound spirit's spell
Before its own time.

ZEMFIRA

It is broken.
He's rising, calling . . . he has woken.
I'll go to him—sleep on; farewell.

ALEKO

Where have you been?

ZEMFIRA

I have been sitting   325
With Father; there was plaguing thee
An evil sprite; thy soul unwitting
Knew agonies. It frightened me,
For in thy slumber thou wert gritting
Thy teeth and calling me.

ALEKO

I dreamed   330
Of you. Between us, so it seemed . . .
I fancied horrors past endurance!

ZEMFIRA

Trust not dream fancies—they depart.

ALEKO

Ah, I trust nothing—not the art
Of dreams, or that of sweet assurance,   335
I do not even trust your heart.

———

OLD MAN

Wherefore, unruly youth, confess,
Wherefore forever sighing, pining?
Here men are free, the heavens shining,
And women famed for comeliness.   340
Weep not—grief will undo you. Rather . . .

ALEKO

Zemfira does not love me, Father.

OLD MAN

She is a child, friend; be consoled.
Perversely, foolishly you languish.
Your love is drudgery and anguish,   345
A woman's is all play. Behold!
Across the vaulted darkness soaring,
The heedless moon serenely strays,
On all creation gently pouring
Her undiscriminating rays.   350
She calls upon a cloudbank yonder,
Bedews it with a silver haze—
Lo! to another she will wander,
Again for but a fleeting gaze.
How fix on one among the stellar   355
Redoubts and bid her: Cease to range!
How fix a maiden's heart and tell her:
This you shall love, and never change?
Console yourself, my friend.

ALEKO

How tender
Her love! How willingly she sank   360
To my embraces as we drank
The wilderness' tranquil splendor!
Forever playful, childish-gay,
How often has she sweetly chattered
Or with her magic kisses scattered   365
Dark fancies, banished gloom away,
And to the moment's joy restored me!
And now? Zemfira gone astray!
Zemfira grown unkind toward me! . . .

OLD MAN

Attend, my son, and you shall know   370
What once befell me long ago:
When yet the Danube did not echo

To Moskal[2] arms encroaching here
(An ancient grief, you see, Aleko,
I must recall), we lived in fear   375
Of the Great Turk; and from the aerie
Of lofty-towered Ak-Kerman
A Turkish pasha ruled the prairie
Of the Budzhak[3] still. I was young,
My fervent spirits sparkled brightly,   380
And of my curly tresses none
Was yet with silver threaded whitely.
Among our youthful beauties one
There shone . . . and long my eyes upon her
In worship gazed, as on the sun,   385
And in the end, at last, I won her . . .

Alas, my youthful years were gone
Like fallen stars as soon as kindled!
But you, fulfillment's season, dwindled
More swiftly still; for not above   390
One year I held Mariula's love.

Not far from the Kağulan waters
We met a tribe; they staked their ropes
And pitched beside our canvas quarters
Their tents upon the mountain slopes.   395
Two nights that band spent near us, breaking
Their trek, and on the third decamped;
With them, Mariula left, forsaking
Her baby daughter, while I dreamt
In peaceful sleep. At dawn's first shining   400
I woke—my love was gone! I flew
To search, I called—no trace. Repining,
Zemfira cried, and I wept too!
That dark hour taught me to abhor
All this earth's maidens; I forbore   405
Henceforth to let my eyes admire,
Nor my lone idleness desire
The solace of a tender guest.

ALEKO

You gave not chase, then, to arrest

[2] Derogatory Slavic, especially Polish, term for "Muscovite."
[3] The Budzhak (Turkish: *bucak*, "corner," probably from the angle between the Prut and the Danube) is the extensive *puszta*-like prairieland of southern Bessarabia.

The faithless ingrate and to chasten   410
Her vile abductors, did not hasten
To plunge a dagger in their breast?

OLD MAN

To what end? Who would vainly try
To hold young love, free as a bird?
On each in turn is bliss conferred   415
What was, returns not.

ALEKO

No—not I
Would thus have cravenly resigned
My rights in a usurper's favor;
Or at the meanest I would savor
A sweet revenge. Were I to find   420
My foe on the deep sea, I swear,
Unarmed, asleep—I would not spare
The knave my foot: straightway, unblanching,
Into the raging waves would launch him;
The sudden terror of his waking   425
With savage laughter I would cheer,
And long his thrashings would be breaking
Like gleeful music on my ear.

YOUNG GYPSY

One more . . . one more kiss . . .

ZEMFIRA

Time is fleeting,
My man mean-spirited and cross.   430

GYPSY

Just one . . . but longer! One last greeting.

ZEMFIRA

Farewell, or he might follow us.

GYPSY

When shall we have another meeting?

ZEMFIRA

Tonight, then, when the moon takes cover,
Upon that tomb, beyond the mound.   435

GYPSY

She plays me false—will not be found!

ZEMFIRA

Run! Here he is! . . . I'll come, my lover.

———

Aleko sleeps, but in his mind
A vague and troubling vision lingers,
Till with a cry he wakes—to find   440
All darkness. His mistrustful fingers
Reach out . . . and shrink as they uncover
Cold blankets—far off is his lover . . .
Half-rearing with a shuddering start,
He listens: silence; sick at heart,   445
His limbs now chill, now fever-damp,
He rises, leaves the tent, goes walking
Between the wagons, grimly stalking
The slumbering fields about the camp.
Deep gloom; the moon is mist-beclouded,   450
The faltering starlight barely hints
The faintest trail of dewy prints
Toward the mounds in distance shrouded.
He follows with impatient haste
The path these ill-starred footprints traced.   455

White in the hazy dusk before him
There gleamed afar a roadside tomb . . .
And there his dragging footsteps bore him,
Weighed down by prescience of doom,
With quivering lips and shaking knees;   460

Until—is it a dream he sees?—
Nearby is heard a whispering sound,
And at his feet twin shadows hover
Upon the desecrated mound.

FIRST VOICE

It's time . . .

SECOND VOICE

No, wait . . .

FIRST VOICE

It's time, dear lover.   465

SECOND VOICE

Don't go—let us await the day.

FIRST VOICE

It's late.

SECOND VOICE

Be bolder, love, be joyous.
One moment more!

FIRST VOICE

You will destroy us.

SECOND VOICE

One moment!

FIRST VOICE

While I am away,
My husband may wake up! . . .

ALEKO

He may.   470
No, stay, you two, where are you flitting?
The graveside here is fine, is fitting.

ZEMFIRA

Run, dearest, hurry . . .

ALEKO

Where away?
Oh, no, my bonny lad, you stay!
Lie there!
Thrusts his knife into him.

ZEMFIRA

Aleko!

GYPSY

I am dying!   475

ZEMFIRA

Aleko, you will be his death!
Look: you are all with blood bespattered!
What have you done?

ALEKO

As if it mattered.
Now go and drink your lover's breath.

ZEMFIRA

Ah, no—I am not frightened of   480
Your rage! I scorn it, I abhor it,
Your bloody deed, I curse you for it . . .

ALEKO

Then die you too!
Strikes her.

ZEMFIRA

I die in love . . .

———

Resplendent Venus, star of morrow,
Across the dawning orient shone.   485
Upon the tomb beyond the barrow,
Blood-dabbled, knife in hand, alone
Aleko sat. And thus they found him,
Hunched by those dead, his stare insane.
Abashed, the gypsies shrank around him;   490
Some sidled to inter the twain
Not far away. In mournful train
The women followed one another
To kiss their eyelids. On the slain
In numb bereavement her old father,   495
Bleak desolation in his heart,
Sat gazing mutely and apart.
They lifted and bore off the supple,
Now lifeless, forms and laid the couple
Into the chilly earthen womb.   500
Aleko from the farther tomb
Looked on . . . but when the two were covered
With that last offering of earth,
Still mute, he teetered forward, hovered,
And sprawled headlong upon the turf.   505

Then spoke the ancient by his side:
"Depart from us, oh man of pride!
We are but wild, a lawless nation,
We keep no rack or hempen knot,
Need neither blood nor lamentation—   510
But live with slayers we will not.
The heathen freedom you have known,
You claim it for yourself alone;
Your voice henceforth would awe and grieve us,
For we are meek and kind of heart,   515
And you are fierce and wicked—leave us,
And peace be with you as we part."

He spoke—and with a bustling start
The light encampment rose as bidden
To leave the night's dread vale behind.   520
And soon the prairie's depth had hidden
The nomad train. A single cart,
Its frame with wretched cover vested,
Stood in the fateful field arrested.
Thus late in autumn one may find,   525
On plains where morning mists are clinging,
With cries above their gathering-stead
A tardy crane-flight southward winging;
But one, pierced through by mortal lead,
Forlorn in empty fields is lagging,   530
Its wounded pinion sadly dragging.
Dusk fell; behind the wagon's awning
That night no flickering fire arose,
And no one till a new day's dawning
Lay down there for a night's repose.   535

EPILOGUE

Thus song-craft with its potent magic
From memory's beclouded haze
Will conjure visions, now of tragic,
Now of serenely shining days.

Where long, so long, the conflagrations   540
Of warlike ardor did not cool,
Where once the Russian showed his nation's
Imperious borders to Stambul,
Where our old eagle double-headed
For parted glories still is dreaded,   545
There in the steppelands I would see
On some abandoned rampart's traces
The gypsies' peaceful camping places,
Wild freedom's humble progeny.
And often through those untamed shires   550
Behind their lazy troops I fared,
Their simple nourishment I shared,
And fell asleep before their fires.

As on those leisured treks I came,
Their cheerful ringing tunes I cherished,   555
And long with fond recital nourished
Sweet Mariula's tender name.

   Yet you, too, Nature's sons undaunted,
Are strange to happiness, it seems!
Your ragged shelters, too, are haunted   560
By omens and oppressive dreams,
Deep in your wilderness, disaster
For wandering tents in ambush waits;
Grim passion everywhere is master,
And no one can elude the Fates.   565

THE BRIDEGROOM   [1825]

Introductory Note

The stanza of this ballad, with its haunting alternation of dreamy singsong, hearty rollick, and ominous gallop, is, of course, borrowed *in toto* from G. A. Bürger's (1747–94) famous "Lenore," perhaps the most impressive work of infant Romanticism. Lenore's ghostly ride bewitched both Goethe and Schiller and scored an international triumph second only to the noble vapors spread by Goethe's own *Werther*. A characteristic stanza of "Lenore" goes as follows:

> Schön Liebchen schürzte, sprang und schwang
> Sich auf das Ross behende;
> Wohl um den trauten Reiter schlang
> Sie ihre Lilienhände;
> Und hurre hurre, hopp hopp hopp!
> Ging's fort in sausendem Galopp,
> Dass Ross und Reiter schnoben,
> Und Kies und Funken stoben.

It is interesting to note also that Natasha's "nightmare" in "The Bridegroom" in atmosphere and some particulars closely prefigures Tatyana's dream in *Eugene Onegin* V, 11–21, which was written in the same period.

THE BRIDEGROOM

Three days Natasha'd been astray,
Who was a merchant's daughter,
When running home in wild dismay
At last the third night brought her.
Her mother and her father plied   5
The maid with questions, tried and tried;
She cannot hear for quaking,
All out of breath and shaking.

But fret and wonder as they did
And stubbornly insisted,   10
They could not fathom what she hid
And in the end desisted.
And soon Natasha grieved no more,
But flushed and merry as before
Went with her sisters walking   15
Beyond the gate and talking.

Once at the gate of shingled ash
The maidens sat together,
Natasha too, when in a flash
Past speeded, hell-for-leather,   20
A dashing troika with a youth;
And rug-clad cobs he drove, forsooth,
Drove standing up, bespattered
All in his path and scattered.

He, drawing closer, glanced upon   25
The maid; her glance replying,
He like the whirlwind galloped on,
The maid was nigh to dying.
And arrow-straight she homeward fled,
"It's he, I knew him well!" she said,   30
"Stop him, it's he, no other,
Oh, save me, friend and brother!"

Her kinfolk listened, grave and sad,
And shook their heads with ruing:
"Speak out, my lass," her father bade,   35
"And tell us how you knew him.
If something untoward occurred,
Speak openly, say just a word."
Natasha's back to crying,
No further word replying.   40

Next day a marriage-gossip came,
Came unexpected rather,
She spoke Natasha fair by name,
Fell talking to her father:

"You have the wares, we want to trade;   45
My buyer is a fine young blade,
Is lithely made and comely,
Not evil-famed or grumbly.

"Has wealth and wits, to never a man
In low obeisance bending,   50
But rather, like a nobleman
He lives with easy spending.
He's like to give his chosen girl
A fur of fox-skin and a pearl,
Gold hoops for golden tresses,   55
And stiff brocaded dresses.

"Last night he saw her on his ride
Out by the towngate linger;
Let's shake, take ikons and the bride
And to the altar bring her!"   60
There over tea and cake she sits
And hints and yarns and snares their wits,
While the poor bride's uneasy,
All fidgeting and queasy.

"So be it, then," her father said,   65
"Go forth, God speed you, dearie,
Take wreath, Natasha, and be wed,
Alone upstairs it's dreary.
Comes time for maids no more to flit,
For swallows, too, their chirps to quit,   70
It's time to nest, to nourish
Young bairns at home and cherish."

Natasha tried to have her say,
Her back to wall and rafter,
But all ashudder sobbed away,   75
Now racked with tears, now laughter.
The gossip in dismay runs up,
Makes her sip water from a cup,
And all the rest she dashes
And on her forehead splashes.   80

Natasha's kinfolk moaned and wept.
But she, back in her senses,
Announced: "I honor and accept
What your high will dispenses.
It's time that to the feast you bade   85
The groom, and many loaves were made,
Mead choice of brew and hearty,
The law bid to the party."

"Command, Natasha, angel child,
To please you, I am ready   90
To give my life!" A feast is piled,
Prodigious, rich, and heady.
Now worthy guests arrive apace,
They lead the bride to take her place;
As bridesmaids sing with weeping,   95
A sledge and team come leaping.

Here is the bridegroom—all sit down,
Cup touches cup with ringing,
The toasting bowl goes round and round
To drunken shouts and singing.   100

The Bridegroom

"I say, my merry friends, abide,
I say, why is my pretty bride
Not serving, eating, drinking,
All lost in mournful thinking?"

Said bride to groom: "I'll tell my plight   105
As best I may be able:
I find no rest by day or night,
I weep abed, at table.
A horrid nightmare wears me out."
Her father wonders: "What about?   110
Whatever kind it may be,
Tell us, my own dear baby!"

The maiden said: "I dream that I
Walk where the wood grows thickly,

It's late, and from a cloudy sky   115
The moonlight glimmers sickly.
I've lost my way; in pine and fir
No living creature is astir,
The trees alone are brushing
Their crowns with wispy rushing.   120

"But clear as day I now make out
Ahead a hut emerging;
I reach it, knock: no answer, shout:
No sound; I hail the Virgin,
I lift the latch, go in, advance,   125
Inside a candle burns; I glance—
All gleams with heaping measure
Of gold and silver treasure."

The Bridegroom

"What is so bad about your dream?
It means you'll be in clover."   130

The Bride

"I ask your leave, sir, it would seem
The dream is not yet over.
On gold and silver, rugs untrod,
Brocade and silks from Novgorod,
I stood in silence gazing   135
With wonder and amazing.

"Now hoofbeats clatter, voices roar,
Here someone comes a-riding;
I quickly up and slam the door,
Behind the chimney hiding.   140
Then voices swell in mingled din,
Twelve lusty lads come trooping in;
With them in modest duty
A fair and pure young beauty.

"Without a bow they throng the place,   145
The ikons never heeding,

Sit down to dine without a grace,
And, cap on head, start feeding.
The eldest brother at the head,
The youngest at his right hand fed,   150
At left in modest duty
There sat the pure young beauty.

"Hubbub and clink, guffaw and scream,
Exuberant carousal . . ."

THE BRIDEGROOM

"What is so bad about your dream?   155
It bodes a gay espousal."

THE BRIDE

"Your pardon, sir, it is not done.
The drunken din goes roaring on,
But as they cheer and riot,
The maid sits sad and quiet.   160

"Sat mute and neither ate nor sipped,
In bitter tears and fretting,
The eldest brother, whistling, gripped
His knife and fell to whetting;
The fiend glanced at the maiden fair,   165
And sprang and seized her by the hair:
I saw him kill and fling her
To chop off hand and finger."

"Sheer raving, fancy run amuck,
I would not let it grieve me!   170
Yet," said the groom, "it bodes good luck,
My tender maid, believe me!"
She gazed at him both hard and long:
"To whom, pray, did this ring belong?"
She asked, and, half-arising,   175
All stared with dread surmising.

The trinket, slipping, clinked and bounced,
The bridegroom blanched and trembled.
The guests stood awed. The law pronounced:
"Stop, bind him, all assembled!"   180
The fiend was tried, in fetters strung,
And shortly from the gallows hung.
Natasha rose to glory!
And therewith ends my story.

COUNT NULIN [1825]

Introductory Note

During Pushkin's prolonged isolation at the remote little family estate of Mikhailovskoe in the mid-twenties he completed *The Gypsies* and continued his labor of love on the steadily expanding *Eugene Onegin*. But new literary interests had awakened. He intensified his exploration of Shakespeare, which had begun to engross him in his southern exile, studied the era of dynastic upheavals preceding the Romanovs in Karamzin's *History of the Russian State,* and dramatized it in his pioneering romantic tragedy in blank verse, *Boris Godunov*. At the same time, constant contact with the life of the rustic squirearchy and peasantry increasingly drew his mind to humbler and earthier themes, and from the poetic forms that still came most naturally to him to the neglected claims of prose. *Count Nulin,* completed in two days in 1825 and published after his return from exile, reflects some of these new influences and tastes. It is in small part a remote parody of the well-worn classical tale of the rape of Lucretia by Tarquin, which Pushkin had lately encountered again in Shakespeare's poem; and if this makes his story a miniature mock-epic, it is "classical" at two removes. But the transposition into a totally different milieu and idiom is almost complete, the parodical intent so faint as to be nearly irrelevant, and the treatment one of evocative contemporary realism in detail and setting. To the reader, whether he is familiar with the hoary Roman legend or not, *Count Nulin* need be no more, and no less, than a briskly moving, elegantly turned anecdote in verse on the comic discomfiture of a Frenchified titled dandy stranded for a night in the Russian countryside; spiced at the very end with an astringent grain of worldly innuendo.

COUNT NULIN

It's time, it's time! The horn resounds,
The whips, done up in hunting habit,
Are mounted by first light, the hounds
Strain at the leash for fox and rabbit.
The squire on his veranda base   5
With arms akimbo scans the action,
His nice "important duty" face
Alight with honest satisfaction.
He sports a coat in Cossack taste,
A Turkish knife tucked in his waist,   10
A rum flask, in his bosom placed,
A horn, hung from a bronzen straplet.
His wife peers out in shawl and chaplet,
Her eyes, yet barely open, glare
At that equestrian affair,   15
The whips' and beaters' noisy tussle . . .
Now they lead up his horse out there;
Up stirrup, withers, all abustle
He hails her: Don't wait up for me!
And canters off in joyful hustle.   20

    In late September, you'll agree,
(I speak in lowly prose, you see,)
The countryside is drear: foul weather,
Snow, autumn winds, the roads a mess,
And howling wolves. But these, I gather,   25
Elate your huntsman! Comfortless,
Through godforsaken fields he prances,
Wet through and cursing, yet, confess,
Delighted to take random chances
Of night's rest and malign success.   30

    But what, the while the husband's wooing
Diana, is his lady doing?
There's all too much to do, worse luck:
Salt down mushrooms, feed goose and duck,
Both lunch and dinner to be seen to,   35
An eye to keep on loft and vault,

Always some place one has not been to
Where something might be found at fault.

Our heroine, heedless of disaster . . .
(Why, I forgot to give her name.   40
Natasha—thus her lord and master
Called her—but we can't do the same:
Natalia Pavlovna) . . . I'd rather
Natalia Pavlovna were more
Inclined to stir herself and bother   45
About this kind of wifely chore,
But she'd been reared, I need not mention,
Not mindful of ancestral law,
But in a noble spinsters' pension
Run by a Madame Falbalat.   50

She's sitting by the window, sore
At odds with Letter Ninety-four
Of that four-volume tranquilizer,
The Love of Armand and Eliza:
From Family Letters of the Pair,   55
A novel classical and hoary,
A lengthy, monstrous lengthy story,
High-mindedly exhortatory,
And quite without romantic flair.

Natalia Pavlovna to start with   60
Had thought it middling hard to part with,
But shortly found herself agog
At an embroilment then proceeding
Outside the place where she was reading
Between a he-goat and a dog.   65
A gang of urchins were guffawing,
And underneath her sill a flock
Of turkey-hens with mournful cawing
Stalked in the wake of a wet cock.
Three ducks were splashing in a puddle,   70
A woman picked her muddy path
To hang some wash across the lath;
The weather worsened; of a sudden

It seemed that snow was threatening . . .
Then you could hear a sleigh bell ring.   75

    He who has led a drear existence
Deep in the country, friends, will know
How sleigh bells tinkling in the distance
Can set the doubting heart aglow.
A friend on a belated visit,   80
Playmate of one's wild youth? . . . or is it . . .
Great God, could it be she? No . . . still . . .
Close, closer yet . . . your heartbeat chases
The jingling sound . . . but past it races,
Grows fainter . . . dies beyond the hill.   85

    Natalia Pavlovna has hurried
Onto the balcony, all flurried
By the glad sound: there! By the mill
Behind the brook a coach comes flying,
Crosses the bridge—you see? Oh, please,   90
This way! No, turning left . . . She sees
It go and nearly bursts out crying.

    Oh joy! A sudden slant and, jarred,
The coach capsizes. "Fil'ka, Vas'ka,
Go quickly, yonder's a kolyaska,   95
Run it at once into the yard,
And ask the owner in for dinner!
I hope he's whole! Find out, you ninny,
Don't stand there, run!" Away he raced.

    Natalia Pavlovna posthaste   100
Whips up a storm of ringlets, closes
The curtain, quickly redisposes
A chair, puts on a shawl and waits.
"How long, good Lord?" At last the gates
Admit a travel-worn, much battered,   105
In weary journeys mud-bespattered
And barely dragging *équipage*.
Behind it, a young esquire stumbles,
His French valet, undaunted, mumbles,

Sustaining him: *allons, courage!* 110
This tandem passes double-jointed
Through porch and hall; the lord they show
Into a room, in haste appointed,
The door flung wide as it will go;
While Picard bustles and arranges, 115
And his young master slowly changes,
Shall I just tell you who he was?
Count Nulin, back from foreign shores,
Where he had flung to winds of fashion
His income and his future ration, 120
Now to Petropolis bestirred
To strut there like some gorgeous bird,
Complete with sundry dress suits, waistcoats,
Hats, cloaks, young ladies fans and mascots,
Spyglasses, corsets, little baskets 125
Of studs, bright ties, chic pantaloons,
Some of Guizot's[1] appalling rot,
A sheaf of villainous cartoons,
A new romance by Walter Scott,
The Paris court's risqué *bons mots,* 130
With Béranger's[2] last tuneful varia,
Paer's[3] and Rossini's latest aria,
And this and that, and these and those.

　　All's ready. Lunchtime comes and goes;
The hostess finds her patience tested. 135
At last the door admits her prize.
Natalia makes as if to rise,
Deplores, politely interested,
His fall, and could he walk, in fact?
The Count declares himself intact. 140
They're served. The Count is seated, ponders,
Then brings his instrument to bear
And enters colloquy with her;
He rails at Holy Russia, wonders

---

[1] François Guizot (1787–1874), French conservative statesman and historian, elected to the Academy. "Little books," as the original has it, were not Guizot's forte; some of his studies and memoirs ran from eight to thirty-one volumes. The diminutive here denotes contempt.

[2] Pierre Jean de Béranger (1780–1857), most popular writer of *chansons* of the century.

[3] Ferdinando Paer (1771-1839), Italian composer (Venice, Vienna, Dresden, Paris) of over forty operas.

How one can live amidst her snows   145
And yearns for Paris—ah, God knows!
"The theatre?" "Oh, barer, colder,
C'est bien mauvais, ça fait pitié.
Talma[4] stone deaf, about to molder,
And Mamselle Mars . . .[5] zut! getting older . . .   150
None but Potier,[6] *le grand Potier,*
Still sheds, alone among his nation,
His pristine brilliance on the scene."

    "What writer now holds domination?"
"All d'Arlincourt[7] and Lamartine."   155
"Here, too, they have been imitated."
"You don't say! Really? Then I bet
Taste's growing more sophisticated!
God grant we'll be enlightened yet!"
"How high are waists now?" "More than lowish,   160
Almost to . . . this point, more or less,
Here is a pattern I possess . . .
If I may just inspect your dress . . .
Yes, flounces, ribbons . . . all quite modish."
"We get the *Telegraph* sent out."   165
"No wonder then! . . . Now you might favor
Some charming vaudeville, no doubt."
He sings. "But Count, you do not savor
Your lunch." "I'm done." "Well, then we might . . ."

    They've risen. She performs the duties   170
Of hostess with uncommon cheer.
The Count, forgetting all the beauties
Of Paris, marvels: what a dear!
Time flies unchecked. The Count is fighting
Some slight unease. The lady's eyes   175
Now seem expressively inviting,
And now opaquely unrequiting . . .

[4] François Joseph Talma (1763–1826), brilliant tragedian (French classical drama and Shakespeare); chosen by Napoleon to play before a *parterre de rois* at Erfurt in 1808.

[5] Stage name of Anne Françoise Hippolyte Boutet (1779–1847), celebrated Paris actress, active for forty-seven years, like Talma a favorite of Napoleon's.

[6] Charles Potier (1775–1838), veteran Paris actor of the time, father of the prominent vaudeville playwright of the forties by the same name.

[7] Charles Victor Prévot, Vicomte d'Arlincourt (1789–1856), French poet, dramatist, and historical novelist.

Here's midnight, to their great surprise;
Long have the footman's snores been blowing,
Long has the neighbor's cock been crowing;   180
The watchman beats his iron tub;
The candle ends are barely burning.

  Natalia Pavlovna gets up:
"*Adieu,* bed waits, time for adjourning.
Sweet dreams." The Count is loath to stand,   185
And, kissing tenderly her hand,
Perceives . . . what do you think? A quiver . . .
(A flirt will stop at nothing, though!)
For our young scamp, may God forgive her,
Has slyly pressed his hand, you know.   190

  Undressed, Natalia's being ushered
To bed by her Parasha's hands.
Friends, you must know that this Parasha
Shares in her lady's moods and plans:
She sews, she washes, crimps her tresses,   195
Begs for discarded hats and dresses,
With master now will freely clown,
Now just as freely dress him down,
And lie to her young mistress bravely.
Just now she is discoursing gravely   200
About the Count and his concerns—
God knows how in one day she learns
The mass of trifles now outpouring.
At last her mistress stemmed the flow,
And saying: "That's enough, you're boring!"   205
Asked for her cap and robe, and so
Was soon alone and gently snoring.

  The Count, too, is by his valet
Peeled down to shirt and negligee.
He lies down, asks for a Havana,   210
Picard brings in accustomed manner
Carafe and cup of silver plate,
Cigar box, candlestick of copper,
Tweezers, alarm clock with a stopper,
And a romance in uncut state.   215

The Count finds his attention flagging,
Though his eyes read; his soul is not
Content in bed with Walter Scott,
A secret restlessness is nagging
At his composure, and he thinks: 220
"Could I have fallen for that minx?
Might it be possible . . . how splendid!
That would be grand, though unintended . . .
The lady likes me, I don't doubt."
And Nulin puts his candle out.   225

Restless, as in a raging fever,
By Satan, busy as a beaver,
Beset with sinful waking dreams,
He glows. Imagination seems
To conjure up in all its phases   230
Last night's events. Her speaking gazes,
The rather rounded, ample shape,
The wholesome country-pink complexion,
That truly feminine inflection,
The flush of health no rouge can ape.   235
He sees that dainty foot protruding,
Recalls—of course! had she not shown . . . ?
Her hand, one could not help concluding,
Had half at random squeezed his own;
Who but a fool . . . yes, he should never   240
Have missed that moment's mood! However,
There was a chance still. He supposed
Her door would not as yet be closed . . .
With instant resolution, fumbling
Into his gown of silken hues,   245
Here comes for his Lucretia (stumbling
Across a falling chair), previews
Of love's sweet harvest his attraction,
The latest Tarquin, braced for action.

Thus you may see a crafty cat,   250
The dainty darling of the servant,
Steal down the stove bench, eyes observant,
To stalk a mouse. His ears laid flat,

His lids contracted, tail-end twitching,
He inches, freezes, talons itching   255
On each sly paw . . . until, scritch-scratch,
He pounces on the luckless wretch.

    The Count, in amorous elation,
Gropes forth by blind manipulation,
With flaming passion all aseethe,   260
At creaking boards in trepidation,
And scarcely taking time to breathe.
By long pitch-dark perambulation
He finds that door, and with light touch
Bears on the handle: not so much   265
As one faint squeak; discreetly nosing
Into the gap, he sees light seep
From a dim lamp, but half disclosing
The room; his hostess blithely dozing,
Aslumber, or pretending sleep.   270

    He enters, lingers, interposes
A step back . . . plump! is at her feet;
And she . . . but here I would petition
The gentlewomen of St. Pete[8]
To picture how this apparition   275
Had our Natalia petrified,
And if she should . . . Well, you decide!

    She, speechless at the visitation,
Stares at him wide-eyed, and the Count,
With floods of ardent protestation   280
Lets his emboldened fingers mount
Upon the coverlet: which action
Caused her a moment's stupefaction;
But she revived and, mortified
By outrage and indignant pride   285
(And panic too, perhaps, one wonders?),
She swung on Tarquin with a thundrous
Ear-box. Oh, yes, a slap—in fact,
A haymaker, to put it mildly!

---

[8] Corresponds to *Piter,* a later colloquialism for St. Petersburg, not used in the original.

Thus contumaciously attacked,   290
The Count changed color, glaring wildly;
Who knows but that his rattled wits
Might have provoked him further, given
That blistering rebuff—but driven
From dreamless sleep by barking Spitz,   295
Parasha crossed the hall; and damning
The roof that sheltered him that night
And that young vixen's artful shamming,
He turned to ignominious flight.

For the ensuing who, what, whether—   300
You may imagine as you choose
How they ran out that night together!
I will not offer any clues.

Arising taciturn next morning,
Count Nulin dresses slowly, yawning,   305
And manicures his rosy nails,
Though not too thoroughly or gently,
Ties his cravat but negligently,
Nor yet with moistened brushes sails
Down well-trimmed waves on glossy trails.   310
I wonder what he may be thinking;
But here he's called for coffee-drinking.
What now? Not having mastered yet
His sheepishness and sullen pet,
He goes.

Miss Mischief, tightly pursing   315
Her rosy mouth, beneath bent brow
Hides wicked gleams, but starts conversing,
As best her twitching lips allow,
Of this and that. Abashed and harassed,
But slowly growing less embarrassed   320
He answers in a lighter vein,
And after thirty minutes scarcely,
His little sallies flow less sparsely,
And he is half in love again.
Hush—in the hall there's some commotion,   325

Who's this? "Good Lord, I had no notion . . ."
"Natasha!" "Meet my husband! Here,
May I present: Count Nulin, dear."
"Delighted, sir . . . what awful weather!
Well: at the smith's as I passed through,   330
I saw your coach—as good as new!
Down by the orchard in the heather,
Natasha, we tracked down a hare,
The brown kind . . . Hey, some vodka! Try us,
Count, it's from far away somewhere;   335
You'll stay for lunch—don't you deny us!"
"No, really, . . . I've already missed . . ."
"Oh, nonsense, Count, I must insist,
My wife and I . . . no, do be seated,
We dote on guests!"
           But rudely cheated   340
Of every hope by these appeals,
The gloomy count digs in his heels.
Picard, already well refueled
Against the trip, turns up endueled
With baggage, while two men approach   345
To screw the chest down in the coach.
Now it drives up to the veranda,
Picard has stowed all odds and ends;[9]
The Count departs. Here, in all candor,
The tale might well conclude. Quite true;   350
But let me add a word or two.

    The carriage still on the horizon
Our lady lost no time advising
Her husband of the whole affair,
And soon, indeed, was advertising   355
My Count's great exploit everywhere.
But who was most of all in stitches
You couldn't guess—he had a ball!
"Her husband?" Pooh! Not he at all.
He very nearly bust his britches   360
With outrage, called the Count a whelp,
A jackanapes, he'd make him yelp,
Would sic his pack at the young jackass
To skin him for that shameful fracas.

[9] No rhyme to this line in the original.

No—Lidin laughed a great deal more,   365
The squire aged twenty-three next door.

   Now without fear of contradiction
We claim, in our own day and house,
A lady faithful to her spouse,
My friends, is no outlandish fiction.   370

TSAR SALTAN [1831]

Introductory Note

Tsar Saltan was written in the summer of 1831 during Pushkin's honeymoon at Tsarskoe Selo. It is both the largest and the finest example of Pushkin's experimentation with an essentially new genre, the folk tale closely following authentic plots but artistically transformed with varying degrees of metric elaboration.

The traditional *skazka* is a folk tale typically containing elements of fantastic adventure, burlesque, and supernatural intervention, and is often placed in a setting of courts and knights and wise men, peasants, sprites, and wizards. Pushkin's mind was saturated from childhood with samples of this ancient oral form. During his confinement at Mikhailovskoe near Pskov (1824–26) at the height of the European romantic revival of folk values and the legendary past, while in the close daily company of his old nurse, Arina Rodionovna, the poetic potential of the *skazka* struck him with renewed force, and he wrote down the plots of several tales from her dictation. The vehicle of the *skazka* was prose, marked by much formulaic material, recurrent epithets, and the kind of cozy repetitiousness demanded by the audience of oral literature; or non-tonic syllabic verse of variable line lengths and occasional use of rhyme. Pushkin employed the second vehicle in several of his own exercises in this genre in the early thirties; but in his most brilliant successes, *Tsar Saltan* and *The Golden Cockerel,* the fable is transposed into rhymed trochaic tetrameters of a gracefully stylized naïveté that is uniquely Pushkinian. The pregnant simplicity and subdued *espièglerie* of the diction partakes of the charms of both fairy tale and puppet play, and the combination of succinctness in detail and leisurely narrative pace contributes to an overall effect that is delightfully sophisticated and wholly original—a note last heard in that highly complex blend of classical European and native elements, Pushkin's early *opus mirabile, Ruslan and Ljudmila* (1820). The harmonious permutations of the triple-structured plot are like a Mozartian dance suite in verse; and the whole is suffused with the luminous freshness, the pomp and gaiety in miniature of which a glimpse can be caught, in yet another medium of art, on the best of the Palekh lacquer boxes.

Prince Mirsky, the foremost admirer of Pushkin's folk tales among his critics, characterized them as follows in his biography[1]:

> The charm of these tales lies in their beautiful consistency of style and fairy-tale logic, and in their absolute freedom from "meaning." They are pure creations out of a given material—things of beauty. Their peculiarity is that in making these things Pushkin did not make his personal and traditional tastes the criterion of their beauty, but subordinated their composition to the inherent laws discovered by him in the possibilities of the given folk tales. This is why, perhaps, after all, in spite of the argument being "borrowed," they are the most purely creative of Pushkin's works. The making of these stories was the making of a world obeying its own immanent laws and independent of this world of ours. The beautiful and logical consistency of these laws may be regarded as Pushkin's highest achievement and his greatest claim to poetical preeminence, and *King Saltan* and *The Golden Cockerel* as his most perfect creations. It is just because of the absence in it of all "human significance" that *King Saltan* is the most universally human of Pushkin's works. For it is pure form, and as accessible to all those who understand Russian as pure ornament is to all those who have eyes. The child (I speak from personal experience) is as admiringly absorbed in the process of narration and in the flow of rhyme as is the sophisticated critic in the marvelous flawlessness of the workmanship and consistency of the "style." *King Saltan* is the only one of the three tales which quite answers to the definition of pure formal perfection. *The Golden Cockerel* is also full of charm, but it has a sting of irony in it, which enhances its intellectual, but perhaps diminishes its universal, appeal . . .

In his classic *A History of Russian Literature*,[2] Mirsky goes even further:

> The longer one lives, the more one is inclined to regard *King Saltan* as the masterpiece of Russian poetry. It is purest art, free from all

[1] D. S. Mirsky, *Pushkin* (New York: Dutton Paperbacks, 1963).
[2] Ed. Whitefield (New York: Knopf, 1926, 1927, 1949, 1958).

the irrelevancies of emotion and symbol, "a thing of beauty" and "a joy for ever." . . . It requires no understanding; its reception is immediate, direct, unquestionable. It is not frivolous, nor witty, nor humorous. But it is light, exhilarating, bracing. It has high seriousness, for what can be more highly serious than the creation of a world of perfect beauty and freedom, open to all?

I fully realize that the claim for *King Saltan* to be accepted as *the* masterpiece of Pushkin has little chance of getting a majority of votes. Such a majority is virtually pledged to the last great narrative poem of Pushkin—*The Bronze Horseman*. . . . This poem certainly has very substantial claims to absolute preeminence. There is no conception of poetic greatness from the standpoint of which this preeminence could be challenged, except that (hypothetic) standpoint which would demand of all poetry that it be as free from human irrelevancies as is *King Saltan* . . .

THE TALE OF TSAR SALTAN, OF HIS SON, RENOWNED AND MIGHTY PRINCE GUIDON SALTANOVICH, AND OF THE FAIREST PRINCESS SWAN

Three young maidens sat one night
Spinning in the window-bight.
"If I were the Tsar's elected,"
One of these young maids reflected,
"I would spread a festive board   5
For all children of the Lord."
"If I were the Tsar's elected,"
Her young sister interjected,
"I'd weave linen cloth to spare
For all people everywhere."   10
"Had I been the Tsar's elected,"
Said the third, "I'd have expected
Soon to bear our father Tsar
A young hero famed afar."

Scarcely had she finished speaking,   15
When the door was softly creaking,

And the Tsar himself came in,
That whole country's sovereign.
He had heard behind the shuttered
Window every word they uttered,   20
And the third young sister's boast
Suited him by far the most.
"Fair my maid, your wish is answered,"
Said he, "you shall be my consort,
And by late September see   25
That you bear that prince for me.
As for you, good sisters, mind you,
Leave this chamber, I consign you
To my retinue, and there
Serve me and your sister fair: 30
Serve us, one at weaving, stitching,
And the other in the kitchen."

   Spoke and strode into the hall;
Off to court went one and all.
Soon abroad the Tsar was heading,   35
That same night ordained the wedding
And was at the banquet seen
Seated with his youthful queen.
Then selected worthies led them
To their ivory couch to bed them,   40
And with ceremony due
Laid them down there and withdrew.
But the palace cook is grieving,
And the weaver weeps a-weaving,
Smarting both with envy keen   45
Of their sister, now their queen;
While our freshly purpled beauty,
Eager to discharge her duty,
That first night conceived and bore.

   But the country was at war.   50
On his goodly charger starting,
Tsar Saltan bade her at parting
Take good care, and not alone
For her sake but for his own.
While he leads his lusty yeomen   55

Fiercely battling far-off foemen,
God bestows on her the joy
Of an ell-long baby boy.
Perched above her offspring regal
Proudly like a mother eagle,   60
She sends off an envoy far
With a note to cheer the Tsar.
But the palace cook and seamstress,
Babarikha too, the schemestress,
Their perfidious plot all hatched,   65
Have the courier trailed and snatched.
In his place they send another
With false witness to their brother,
Saying that the Tsar had won
Neither daughter, neither son,   70
Nor of mouse or frog a litter,
But some quite unheard-of critter.

But the Father Tsar, apprised
Of the message thus devised,
Started raising blood and thunder   75
Ready to string up the runner;
But, his fury once allayed,
He had this decree conveyed:
"Let the Tsar's return be waited
And the case adjudicated."   80

Off the envoy with this writ,
And at length returns with it.
But the palace cook and seamstress
Babarikha too, the schemestress,
Intercept the Tsar's command,   85
Lard the lad with liquor, and
In his empty pouch of leather
Slip another altogether;
So that day the fuddled slouch
Pulls this order from his pouch: 90
"Let the Tsar's decree be heeded:
With no more delay than needed,
Be the Queen and what she bore
Cast into the ocean's maw."

Powerless at this disaster   95
To the Empress and their Master,
All the nobles in dismay
Pressed into her room to say
What the Tsar's command was suing
For her son's and her undoing.   100
Orders duly read and seen,
They enclosed the prince and queen
In a keg at once brought forward,
Tarred it up and rolled it shoreward
And committed it to sea,   105
As by Tsar Saltan's decree.

    Dark-blue skies and starlets flashing,
Dark-blue sea and wavelets plashing,
Cloud across the heaven slides,
Keg across the ocean glides.   110
Like a widow all bedraggled
In it wept the queen and struggled,
While the babe grew more, you'd say,
By the hour than by the day.
Gone the day, the queen is crying,   115
Pleads the babe, the rollers hying:
"Wave, my wave, I beg of thee,
Ever ranging, ever free,
Foaming far in feckless motion,
Rolling rocks beneath the ocean,   120
Coursing up the coastal crest,
Heaving hulks upon thy breast—
Do not let us perish, save us,
Up onto the mainland wave us!"
And the wave at once obeyed,   125
Bore the barrel hence and laid,
Oh, so softly and intently,
It ashore and ebbed off gently.
Queen and babe had safely reached
Land, the keg was firmly beached.   130
From the keg, though, who will bring them?
God perhaps alone might spring them?
Up on tippy-toes the babe
Braced himself against a stave,

On the bottom bore a trifle   135
With his head, said: "Lest we stifle,
Why not break a window cleft?"
Burst the bottom out and left.

   Free are now both son and mother,
See a mound across the heather,   140
All about, the dark-blue sea,
On the mound a green oak tree.
Son thought: solid food would rather
Suit the two of us, I gather.
From the oak a branch he breaks,   145
And a sturdy bow he makes,
Off his cross the silk he wrings it,
To the oaken bow he strings it;
Broke a twiglet off a joint,
Fined it to an arrow point,   150
And went down the yonder lee-side
Seeking game along the seaside.

   Barely as the shore he nears,
Something like a moan he hears . . .
He perceives the sea unquiet,   155
Looks and sees some evil riot:
'Mid the waves a swan's astir
And a kite hangs over her;
Wildly that poor bird is thrashing,
All the sea churned up and splashing . . .   160
That one has its talons spread,
Bloody beak all sharp and red . . .
Twang! the arrow sang and whistled,
In the crop it struck and bristled—
Bow at ease he stood; the kite   165
Stained with blood the breakers bright;
Down it plunges, plumes asunder,
Groans unbirdlike going under;
Swimming shoreward sails the swan,
And the foul kite pecks upon,   170
And his near perdition speeding,
Wings him hard and drowns him bleeding.
Then unto the Tsarevich

In the Russian tongue she speaks:
"Prince, you are my potent savior,   175
My redeemer, no one braver!
Pine not lest you, lost my meat,
Have three days no food to eat,
Or no arrow on the morrow:
All this sorrow—is no sorrow.   180
Your high service I will earn,
And will serve you in my turn:
Not a swan-bird's rescue, know you,
But a maiden's life I owe you,
Not a kite you brought to earth,   185
Killed a warlock; of your worth
Never henceforth need remind me,
Ever by your side you'll find me.
Now then, let all sorrow cease,
Turn again and sleep in peace."   190

  As the swan-bird soared to nesting,
Queen and prince, intent on resting
From the weary day they spent,
Settled and to slumber went.
On the morn the prince, awaking   195
And nocturnal visions shaking,
Marveled to behold ahead
A prodigious city spread,
Walls with crenellated arches,
Snowy bastions topped with churches,   200
Dazzling domes to heaven soar,
Holy monasteries galore.
"See what's there!" he wakes his mother,
She cries one Oh, then another,
"I can tell, my snowy bird   205
Is already well bestirred."
For the city making straightway,
Hardly have they passed the gateway,
Bells a-tolling peal tattoo
Fairly deafening our two;   210
Townsfolk throng to meet them, choirs
Sing Te Deums from the spires;
Gorgeous trains of courtiers wait,

Each in golden coach of state;
Every voice exalts them loudly,   215
And the prince is crested proudly
With a ducal diadem
As the sovereign over them.
With the Queen's consent attested,
There and then he is invested,   220
In his capital installed,
Duke Guidón[1] henceforward called.

   Seawind saunters there and thither,
Drives a little vessel hither,
Bowling down the ocean trail,   225
Tautly bulging every sail.
All the sailormen a-sailing
Crowd amazed against her railing,
On the well-known isle they sight
Marvels in the noonday light: 230
A new city gold-enweltered,
Pier by sturdy barrier sheltered,
Cannon firing from the pier
To command a landing here.
As they fetch the mooring station,   235
Comes a ducal invitation,
They are furnished drink and food
And for course and parley sued:
"Guests, what goods may you be bearing,
Whither are you further faring?"   240
And the sailormen speak out:
"We have sailed the world about,
Fur of sable held our boxes,
Likewise coal-and-russet foxes;
Past the island of Buyan,   245
Feal to famous Tsar Saltan,
We are bound on eastward bearing,
For accomplished is our faring . . ."
Duke Guidon dismissed them then:
"Make in safety, gentlemen,   250
Down the ocean-sea your passage,
Carry Tsar Saltan a message,

---

[1] The prince's name transliterated would be *Gvidon,* but since it was originally borrowed from the Italian, it is here restored to Guidon which is as half-exotic as Gvidon is to Russian. The stress is, as shown above, on the second syllable, but the mark will be omitted henceforth.

Say I send my compliments."
Visitors despatched, the Prince
From the coast with spirit ailing   255
Follows far their distant sailing;
Lo! on drifting swells offshore
Swims the snowy swan once more.
"Hail, fair Prince! But why beclouded,
Like a rain-day still and shrouded?"   260
She addressed the royal lad,
"Has some sorrow turned you sad?"
Bleakly said the Duke, replying,
"Sadness-sorrow sends me sighing,
Eats my dauntless heart entire: 265
I so long to see my sire."
Swan to Prince: "So that's your worry!
Listen, would you care to hurry
Where that sloop is out at sea?
Then, my Prince, a gnat shalt be."   270
And she set her pinions flashing,
Whipped the water, sent it splashing
Over him from tip to toe.
And as he was standing so,
Faster than an eyelid's blinking   275
To a gnat she had him shrinking;
Off he flew with piping shrill,
Caught the sloop a-sailing still,
And discreetly downward gliding,
Found a crack and went in hiding.   280

   Seawind blows a merry clip,
Merrily sails on the ship;
Past Buyan her passage gaining,
Where the famed Saltan is reigning,
They already sight the shore   285
Of the land they're destined for.
As they anchor in the shallows
They are summoned to the palace;
So they take the castle route;
Our bold lad flies in pursuit.   290
Tsar Saltan, all gold-ensheeted,
In his hall of state is seated

On his throne and in his crown,
Pensive sorrow in his frown.
But the palace cook and seamstress,   295
Babarikha too, the schemestress,
Near the Tsar have found a place
And sit gazing at his face.
Tsar Saltan commands them treated,
At his very table seated: 300
"Ho," he asks them, "Esquire guests,
Long your voyage? Far your rest?
Are things sound abroad or parlous,
Can you tell us any marvels?"
"Everything is fairly sound there,   305
Here's a marvel we have found there:
Lay an island steep and bald,
All unpeopled and unwalled,
Plain and bare from crest to shingle,
On it grew an oak tree single;   310
Now upon this island dwell
A new town and citadel,
Rich in churches golden-headed,
Donjon chambers green-embedded,
Duke Guidon, their ruling prince,   315
Bade us bring you compliments."
Says Saltan: "If God will spare me,
To that island I will fare me,
Land upon that magic coast,
Duke Guidon will be my host."   320
But the palace cook and seamstress,
Babarikha too, the schemestress,
Do not wish to let him fare
To that isle of wonders there.
"I declare, astounding, brothers,"   325
Winking slyly at the others,
Sneers the palace cook, "dear me!
There's a city by the sea!
Here's a marvel, by Saint Cyril:
Wildwood spruce, beneath, a squirrel,   330
Squirrel sings a song and struts
Pawing, gnawing hazel nuts,
Not plain nuts he puts his paws on,

Golden shells the squirrel gnaws on,
Kernels of pure emerald:
Such are truly marvels called!"   335
Harks the Tsar with bated breathing,
But the gnat is seething, seething . . .
Swoops and sinks his stinger sly
Straight into his aunt's right eye.   340
Mighty ill the cookie took it,
Whey-faced sat and frozen crooked;
Servants, sister, and the shrew
Hunt the gnat with view-halloo:
"Oh, you thrice-accursed mosquito,   345
Just you wait!" He poohs their veto,
By the open window free
Homeward soars across the sea.

    And again in restless motion
Scans the Duke the dark-blue ocean;   350
Lo! on drifting swells offshore
Swims the snow-white swan once more.
"Hail, fair Prince! But why beclouded,
Like drear day becalmed and shrouded?"
She addressed the royal lad,   355
"Has some sorrow made you sad?"
Said Guidon the Duke, replying,
"Sadness-sorrow sends me sighing,
There's a fabled fairy thing,
I should like to find and bring: 360
Lives a squirrel in the wildwood,
Magic past all dreams of childhood,
He sings songs, they say, and struts
Pawing, gnawing hazel nuts,
Not plain nuts he puts his paws on,   365
Golden shells the squirrel gnaws on,
Shells of gold with emerald core;
Folk, of course, have fibbed before."
"No," the swan assured the youthful
Prince, "that squirrel tale is truthful,   370
I have known of it long since;
Do not pine, my dearest Prince,
I will gladly give you token

Of our fellowship unbroken."
Cheered, the Duke betook him then   375
Back to his abode again.
For his central courtyard heading,
Lo! he sees a spruce a-spreading,
Squirrel nibbling 'neath the tree
Nuts of gold for all to see,   380
Little emerald cores extracting,
And the golden husks collecting
Neatly each upon its pile,
Whistling them this song the while,
To the good folk in the courtyard: 385
"In the garden, in the orchard."
"Well, I thank you," Duke Guidon
Said in wonder, looking on,
"Swan like none, may God be giving
You such joy as I am living."   390
Straightway for his squirrel sage
Built a crystal squirrel cage,
Put a watch on it unsleeping,
Set a deacon strictly keeping
Count of gems, and gold beside,   395
Prince's profit, squirrel's pride.

    Seawind roaming there and thither
Blows a little vessel hither,
Bowling down the ocean swell,
All her canvas drawing well,   400
Past the craggy island fastness,
Past the wonder city's vastness:
Cannon firing from the pier
Bid the ship to anchor here.
As they fetch the mooring station,   405
Comes a ducal invitation;
They are served both drink and food,
And for course and converse sued:
"Guests, what goods may you be bearing,
Whither are you further faring?"   410
And the sailormen speak out:
"We have sailed the world about,
Trading steeds, both foal and filly,

Ponies from the Donland hilly,
Done our stint, it's homeward ho—
But we still have far to go:
Past Buyan the island sailing,
Tsar Saltan's dominions hailing . . ."
Duke Guidon addressed them then:
"Make in safety, gentlemen,
Down the ocean-sea your passage,
Carry Tsar Saltan a message,
Tell him Duke Guidon afar
Sends his duty to the Tsar."

Then the guests, farewells accorded,
Sought their ship and went aboard it.
For the shore makes Duke Guidon,
In the surf he spies the swan.
Pleads the Duke, his spirit yearning,
All with ache and anguish burning . . .
Swam the swan again ashore,
Splashed him soundly as before,
To a little housefly shrinking,
He flew off and, downward sinking,
Twixt the sea and sky on deck,
Tucked himself into a crack.

Seawind blows a merry clip,
Merrily sails on the ship;
Past Buyan her passage gaining,
Where the famed Saltan is reigning,
They already sight the shore
Of the land they're destined for.
As they anchor off the commons,
They receive a royal summons,
So they take the castle route;
Our bold lad flies in pursuit.
Tsar Saltan, all gold-ensheeted,
In his hall of state is seated
On his throne and in his crown,
Sorrow in his pensive frown.
But the crooked cook, the weaver,
And their gossip Babarikha,

415

420

425

430

435

440

445

450

Sit like angry toads not far
From the footstool of the Tsar.
By command the guests are greeted,   455
At the Tsar's own table seated;
"Ho," he asks them, "Merchant guests,
Long your voyage? Far from rest?
Are things sound abroad or parlous,
Can you tell us any marvels?"   460
So the sailormen speak out:
"We have sailed the world about,
Life is fair enough out yonder,
While abroad we saw this wonder:
There's an isle at sea out there,   465
On the isle a city fair,
Rich in churches golden-headed,
Donjon chambers green-embedded;
And a spruce tree shades the tower,
Underneath, a crystal bower;   470
In it lives a well-trained squirrel,
Nay, a wizard, by Saint Cyril!
Squirrel sings a song and struts
Pawing, gnawing hazel nuts,
Not plain nuts he puts his paws on,   475
Golden shells the squirrel gnaws on,
Emerald is every nut;
Servants guard the squirrel's hut,
Serve in sundry ways to suit it;
They make officers salute it,   480
Have a clerk for nothing but
Keeping tally of each nut;
Then the golden shells as nuggets
Go to mint and leave as ducats;
Maidens sift the emerald hoard   485
In a strong room to be stored.
On this isle they live in plenty,
All have mansions, never a shanty;
Duke Guidon, their reigning prince,
Bade us give you compliments."   490
Marvels Tsar Saltan: "So spare me,
To that island I will fare me,
Land upon that magic coast,

Duke Guidon shall be my host."
But the palace cook and seamstress,   495
Babarikha too, the schemestress,
Do not wish to let him fare
To that isle of wonders there.
Says the seamstress to His Highness,
Wreathed in sneering smirks and slyness;   500
"There's a squirrel—true or not—
Gnawing little stones—so what?
Nuggets out of nutshells making,
Little mounds of emerald raking,
This won't make us throw a fit,   505
Even if there's truth in it.
Here's what counts as marvel for me:
Where the ocean wild and stormy
Seethes up high with hiss and roar,
Foaming up an empty shore   510
And in rushing runs recoiling—
Rise from out the backwash boiling
Thirty-three young giants tall,
Bold of spirit one and all,
Comely heroes thrice eleven,   515
Mail aglow like blaze of heaven,
All alike as soldiers matched,
To Dad Chernomor attached.
Talk of wonders, this one surely
Makes all others come off poorly!"   520
Mum, the prudent guests prefer
Not to bandy words with her;
Harks the Tsar with bated breathing,
But Guidon is seething, seething . . .
Up and with a buzzing cry   525
Lights upon his aunt's left eye.
Ashen-faced, the seamstress took it,
"Ai," she screeched and turned all crooked.
"Catch it, catch it," cried the lot,
"Snatch the sting-fly, snatch and swat,   530
Stay right there, hold still a little . . ."
But Guidon the Fly won't fiddle,
By the open window he
Soars back home across the sea.

And the Duke in restless motion   535
Strides and scans the dark-blue ocean . . .
Lo! on drifting swells offshore
Swims the snowy swan once more.
"Hail, fair Prince! But why beclouded,
Silent like a rain-day shrouded?   540
Has some sorrow made you sad?"
She addressed the royal lad.
Said Guidon the Duke, replying,
"Sadness-sorrow sends me sighing,
Prodigies to overwhelm   545
I would bring into my realm."
"Pray, what portent brings such luster?"
"Somewhere there's a storm abluster,
Ocean breakers howl and roar
Foaming up a desert shore,   550
Back in rushing sun recoiling,
Leaving in their backwash boiling
Thirty-three young giants tall,
Bold and mettlesome withal,
Comely heroes thrice eleven,   555
Mail aglow like blaze of heaven,
All alike as soldiers matched,
To Dad Chernomor attached."
Then the swan responded saying:
"So it's this you find dismaying!   560
Do not pine, my dearest Prince,
I have known of this long since.
Yonder sea-knights are no others
But my kin, my native brothers.
Don't you fret, but homeward fare,   565
They will wait upon you there."
Grief forgot, the Duke departed,
Climbed upon his keep and started
Gazing seaward; all at once,
'Gan the sea to heave and dance,   570
And in rushing runs retrieving
Surf and sough, retreated, leaving
Thrice eleven on the site,
Knights in blazing armor bright;
They approach in paired procession   575

And, his snowy floss a-flashing,
Chernomor in solemn state
Guides them to the city gate.
From the keep the Duke descended,
Greeting to his guests extended,   580
Forward flocked the city folk,
To the Duke the leader spoke:
"Aye, the Swan Princess despatched us
And as sentinels detached us,
Warders for your fair redoubt,   585
Walking guard the walls about.
Without fail we shall henceforward
Daily stride together shoreward,
Risen from the ocean wave
By your soaring bastions brave;   590
Shortly therefore you will sight us,
Meanwhile, though, the waves invite us,
For the air of earth is dense."
And they all went homeward thence.

Seawind saunters there and thither   595
Drives a little vessel hither,
Bowling down the ocean swell,
All her canvas drawing well,
Past the craggy island fastness,
Past the wonder city's vastness;   600
Cannon firing from the pier
Bid the ship to anchor here.
As they fetch the mooring station,
Comes a ducal invitation.
They are furnished drink and food   605
And for course and parley sued:
"Guests, what goods may you be bearing,
Whither are you further faring?"
And the sailormen speak out:
"We have sailed the world about,   610
Trusty Damask steel we traded,
Gold and silver finely graded,
Done our stint, it's homeward ho—
But we still have far to go:
Past Buyan the island sailing,   615

Tsar Saltan's dominions hailing."
Duke Guidon addressed them then:
"Make in safety, gentlemen,
Down the ocean-sea your passage,
Carry Tsar Saltan a message,   620
Say the Duke Guidon afar
Sends his greetings to the Tsar."

    Then the guests, farewells accorded,
Sought their ship and went aboard it.
For the shore makes Duke Guidon,   625
In the surf he spies the swan.
And again he speaks his yearning,
Soul with ache and anguish burning . . .
Swam the swan ashore again,
Splashed him soundly there and then,   630
And at once he turned much smaller,
To a bumblebee, no taller;
Taking off with buzzing sound,
Out at sea the ship he found,
Straight upon her poop he glided,   635
Down a crack and there subsided.

    Seawind blows a merry clip,
Merrily sails on the ship;
Past Buyan their passage gaining,
Where the famed Saltan is reigning,   640
They already sight the shore
Of the land they're destined for.
As they anchor off the commons,
They receive a royal summons,
So they take the castle route;   645
Our bold lad flies in pursuit.
Tsar Saltan, all gold-ensheeted,
In his hall of state is seated
On his throne and in his crown,
Pensive sorrow in his frown.   650
But the palace cook and seamstress,
Babarikha too, the schemestress,
Sit near by him, and to see
Have four eyes among the three.

When the guests are duly greeted,   655
At the Tsar's own table seated,
"Ho," he asks them, "Esquire guests,
Long your voyage? Far your rest?
Are things sound abroad or parlous,
Can you tell us any marvels?"   660
And the sailormen speak out:
"We have sailed the world about,
Life is fair enough out yonder,
While abroad we saw this wonder:
There's an isle at sea out there,   665
On the isle a city fair,
Daily there befalls a wonder:
Ocean rollers seethe and thunder,
Rearing high with hiss and roar,
Foaming up a desert shore   670
And with rush and run resurging,
Leave from out their lee emerging
Thirty-three young giants hale,
Comely youths, their coats of mail
All with gold aglow and flashing,   675
Thrice eleven heroes dashing,
Like of choice recruits a crew;
Chernomor the Ancient too
Rises with them, marches forward,
And in pairs conducts them shoreward,   680
There to ward the isle redoubt,
Walking guard the walls about;
Watchful warders, none more ready,
None more dauntless or more steady.
Duke Guidon, residing there,   685
Bids Your Highness greetings fair."
Marvels Tsar Saltan: "So spare me,
To that island I will fare me,
Land upon that magic coast,
Duke Guidon shall be my host."   690
From the palace cook or seamstress
Not a murmur—but the schemestress
Snickers and will have her say:
"This is to amaze us, pray?
From the water watchmen amble,   695

Round and round an island shamble,
Truth or lie, I see in that
Nothing much to marvel at.
Here's what stuns the world astounded:
There is fame abroad, well-founded, 700
Of a princess far, far off
No one can adore enough,
Who the gleam of day outbrightens,
And the gloom of night enlightens;
In her hair the moon is borne, 705
On her brow the star of morn,
Forth she flows in splendor vested
Like a peacock fanned and crested,
And the words she utters seem
Murmurs from a purling stream. 710
Here you'd say without a blunder,
There's a wonder that's a wonder."
Mum, the prudent guests prefer
Not to bandy words with her,
Harks His Highness, barely breathing, 715
And the royal prince, though seething,
Hesitant to cast a blight
On his poor old granny's sight,
Bumbles buzzing with his muzzle,
Plummets plumb upon her nozzle, 720
Stings her right into the nose,
Where a monstrous bump arose.
And again they fuss and bustle:
"Help, for God's sake, hustle, hustle,
Guardsmen, catch the you-know-what, 725
Catch that sting-bee, snatch and swat!
Just you wait! Hold still a little,
Wait a while!" . . . All wasted spittle—
By the window wings the bee
Calmly home across the sea. 730

    And the Duke in restless motion
Strides and scans the dark-blue ocean . . .
Lo! on drifting swells offshore
Swims the snowy swan once more.
"Hail, fair Prince! But why beclouded, 735

Silent like a rain-day shrouded?
Has some sorrow made you sad?"
She addressed the royal lad.
Said Guidon the Duke replying,
"Sadness-sorrow sends me sighing,   740
Folk have wives; I look about:
I alone am left without."
"Whom then would you fain have courted,
May I ask?" "It is reported
That a princess lives far off   745
No one can adore enough,
Who of day the gleam outbrightens
And of night the gloom enlightens;
In her hair the moon is borne,
On her brow the star of morn,   750
Forth she steps in splendor vested
Like a peacock fanned and crested,
And her speeches sweet, it seems,
Murmur like the purl of streams.
Is this truth," he asks, "or error?"   755
And awaits her words in terror.
Still and thoughtful thereupon,
Says at length the snowy swan:
"Yes, there is just such a maiden,
Wiving, though, is not like trading,   760
Wives are not, like mitts of pelt,
Plucked and tucked behind your belt.
Here is some advice to ponder—
Think about this as you wander
Homeward, ponder long and hard,   765
Not to rue it afterward."
Swore Guidon, as God his witness,
Timeliness as well as fitness
Called for wedlock, he had brought
All the thought to bear he ought.   770
For this maid of fairy fashion
He stood ready, such his passion,
Starting forthwith to bestride
Thrice nine kingdoms far and wide.
Spoke the swan-bird, deeply sighing,   775
"Wherefore fare so far a-trying?

Know then, Prince, your fate is nigh,
For the princess fair—am I."
Then her pearly pinions spreading
And atop the breakers heading   780
For the shore in diving rush,
She alighted in the brush,
Shook and shed her plumage fluted,
To a princess stood transmuted,
Crescent in her tresses borne,   785
On her brow the star of morn;
Forth she steps in splendor vested
Like a peacock fanned and crested,
And the speech she utters seems
Murmurous like purling streams.   790
Duke Guidon, his bride enfolding
In his tender arms and holding,
Leads her as his rightful spouse
To his loving mother's house.
Brings her in and, humbly kneeling,   795
"Dearest Queen," entreats with feeling,
"I have found my consort true,
Your obedient child; we sue
Your consent in joint communion
And your blessings on our union: 800
Concord blissful, love serene
Wish us both." The Mother-Queen,
Shedding tears of fond complaisance
As they bow in deep obeisance
To her wondrous ikon, pleads: 805
"Children, God reward your deeds."
Then Guidon no longer tarried,
Duke and princess up and married,
Settled down and did their best
For their union to be blessed.   810

    Seawind saunters there and thither,
Drives a little vessel hither,
Bowling down the ocean swell,
All her canvas drawing well,
Past the craggy island fastness,   815
Past the wonder city's vastness;

Cannon firing from the pier
Bid the ship to anchor here.
As they fetch the mooring station,
Comes a ducal invitation.   820
They are furnished drink and food
And for speech and answer sued:
"Guests, what goods may you be bearing,
Whither now are further faring?"
And the sailormen speak out: 825
"We have sailed the world about,
Sundry wares beyond our telling
None too cheaply were we selling,
Of our voyage home back east
What is left is not the least,   830
Past Buyan the island sailing,
Tsar Saltan's dominions hailing."
Duke Guidon addressed them then:
"Make in safety, gentlemen,
Down the ocean-sea your passage,   835
Carry Tsar Saltan my message,
And remind your Tsar once more
Of a visit twice before
Promised us in proper season—
Pledge neglected for some reason.   840
Then add greetings for the nonce."
Guests despatched, Guidon for once
Did not follow them but tarried,
Being but so lately married.

    Seawind blows a merry clip,   845
Merrily sails on the ship;
Past Buyan their passage gaining,
Where the famed Saltan is reigning,
They already sight the crest
Of the shore they know the best.   850
As they anchored in the shallows,
They were summoned to the palace,
Where the Tsar Saltan they found
Seated on his throne and crowned;
And the palace cook and seamstress,   855
Babarikha too, the schemestress,

Sit not far away and see
On four eyes among the three.
When the guests are duly greeted,
At the Tsar's own table seated,   860
"Ho," he asks them, "Merchant guests,
Long your voyage? Far your rest?
Are things sound abroad or parlous,
Can you tell us any marvels?"
And the sailormen speak out: 865
"We have sailed the world about,
Life is fair enough out yonder,
While abroad we saw this wonder:
There's an isle at sea out there,
On the isle a city fair,   870
Rich in churches golden-towered,
Donjon chambers busk-embowered;
And a spruce tree shades the tower,
Underneath, a squirrel bower;
In it lives a well-trained squirrel,   875
What a wizard, by Saint Cyril!
Squirrel sings a song and struts
Pawing, gnawing hazel nuts,
Not plain nuts he puts his paws on,
Golden shells the squirrel gnaws on,   880
Every nut an emerald bright;
And they tend him day and night.
There is still another wonder:
Ocean rollers seethe and thunder,
Rearing high with hiss and roar,   885
Foaming up a desert shore,
And with rush and run resurging,
Leave from out their lee emerging
Thirty-three young giants hale,
Comely youths, their coat of mail   890
All with gold aglow and flashing,
Thrice eleven heroes dashing,
Like of choice recruits a crew—
Chernomor the Ancient too.
Than this guard is none more ready,   895
None more dauntless or more steady.
And the Prince's little wife

You could look at all your life:
She of day the gleam outbrightens,
And of night the gloom enlightens,   900
Crescent in her tresses borne,
On her brow the star of morn.
Duke Guidon, who rules that country,
Warmly praised by all and sundry,
Charged us with good cheer to you,   905
But with plaint of grievance, too:
Of a visit in due season,
Undelivered for some reason."

This was all Saltan could stand,
Bade the fleet cast off from land.   910
Yet the palace cook and seamstress,
Babarikha too, the schemestress,
Do not wish to let him fare
To that wonder island there.
But for once he did not heed them,   915
With a royal roar he treed them:
"Say, what am I, Tsar or child?"
He demanded, driven wild.
"Off I go!" With stomp and snortle
He stalked out and slammed the portal.   920

At his window Duke Guidon
Mutely gazed the sea upon:
Never roaring, never seething
Lies the ocean, barely breathing,
On the skyline azure-blue   925
White top-gallants heave in view:
Ocean's mirror reaches bruising,
Comes the royal squadron cruising.
Duke Guidon then gave a leap,
Loudly shouted from his keep: 930
"Ho, my Mother, dearest Mother,
You, young Duchess, for another,
Look you over yonder, fast,
Here our Father comes at last!"
Guidon, through his spyglass peering   935
At the squadron swiftly nearing,

Spies the Tsar upon the stem
Gazing through his glass at them.
And the palace cook and seamstress,
Babarikha too, the schemestress,   940
Near him in amazement stand,
Staring at this unknown land.
Cannon boom from every barrel,
Carillons from belfries carol;
Lone, the Prince upon the pier   945
Greets the Tsar and at his rear
Both the palace cook and seamstress,
Babarikha too, the schemestress,
Leads them to the city wall,
Speaking not a word withal.   950

Now they pass the castle center,
Gorgets glisten as they enter,
And before the Sovereign's eyes
Thirty-three young giants rise,
Thrice eleven heroes dashing,   955
Comely knights in armor flashing,
Like of choice recruits a crew,
Chernomor the Ancient too.
And the Tsar steps in the spacious
Courtyard: lo, a squirrel gracious   960
'Neath a spruce tree sings and struts,
Gnawing golden hazel nuts,
Emerald kernels bright extracting
And into a pouch collecting,
All bestrewn the spacious yard   965
With the precious golden shard.
Hastening on, they meet, astounded,
Fair Her Grace and stand dumbfounded:
In her hair the moon is borne,
On her brow the star of morn;   970
On she walks in splendor vested,
Like a peacock fanned and crested,
Leading forth her Queen-in-law.
Tsar Saltan, he stares in awe . . .
Heart in throat, he marvels, ponders: 975
"By what magic? Signs and wonders!

How?" His pulses leaped and throbbed,
Then he burst in tears and sobbed,
In his open arms he caught her,
And his son, and his new daughter,   980
And they all sat down in strength
To a merry feast at length.
But the palace cook and seamstress,
Babarikha too, the schemestress,
Ran to hide in niche and nook;   985
Found at last and brought to book,
They confessed, all pale and pining,
Beat their breasts and started whining;
And the Tsar in his great glee
Let them all get off scot-free.   990
Late at night some subjects loyal
Helped to bed His Highness Royal.
I was there, had beer and mead,
Dip a whisker's all I did.

THE BRONZE HORSEMAN: A Tale of Petersburg   [1833]

Introductory Note

The Bronze Horseman, although overpraised by some, is perhaps the most significant of Pushkin's narrative poems, and certainly the most original among those that are not what the Soviet scholiasts blushingly call "indecorous." It was completed in 1833 and published posthumously, with some omissions due to censorship, in 1837, the year of Pushkin's death. The Prologue with the celebrated accolade to St. Petersburg and homage to Peter I is intriguingly at odds with the import of the poem as a whole. The setting, and part of the symbolic energizer of the poem on its historic-philosophical plane, is of course the great flood of the Nevá River in 1824—and it also carries the human plot on to its tragic conclusion.

The Bronze Horseman was previously translated into English some thirty years ago by Oliver Elton, who sought to preserve the metric form of the original, and later by Edmund Wilson, who did not. By far the best critical work on the poem was done by the distinguished Polish scholar, Wacław Lednicki. Lednicki was the first to perceive and document fully the poem's central significance in the ambivalent relationship between its author and his admired friend and political antagonist, the great Polish poet Adam Mickiewicz, and thus, indirectly, in the century-old rivalry between Poland and Russia; between the emerging Western commitment to pluralistic liberalism and humanism and Russia's instinctive revulsion against it, of which we witnessed the latest tragic example in Czechoslovakia. The poem may be legitimately read, in one of its aspects, as part of a complex long-distance dialogue in verse across an unbridgeable political gulf between two estranged friends, the hero-poets (in Carlyle's sense) of their estranged nations. Specifically, it is in this sense an attempted rebuttal of Mickiewicz's far more passionate and poetically opulent indictment of St. Petersburg in the "Digression" of his verse drama of 1832, *Forefathers' Eve, Part III*. In a magnificent blast of hot fury and cold contempt, Mickiewicz, in this cycle of poems, assails and morally annihilates St.

Petersburg, which he sees as a prime symbol of the tasteless megalomania and brutish malignity of imperial Russia. Mickiewicz's "Digression" and Pushkin's *Bronze Horseman* are so intimately linked that from the viewpoint of comparative literature and Slavic political history one would wish that they were always printed as companion pieces. Marjorie Beatrice Peacock has created a distinguished English translation of the former, which I believe is most accessible in the appendix to Lednicki's monograph, *Pushkin's Bronze Horseman: The Story of a Masterpiece* (Berkeley: University of California Press, 1955). Even this is now a rare book.

The tenor of Pushkin's private pronouncements about St. Petersburg in the thirties differs startlingly from the panegyric tone adopted in *The Bronze Horseman*. The records of his correspondence and conversation in the period from 1833 to 1837 are poignant testimony to his settled disgust with the "repulsive" city; a feeling not wholly attributable to the maddening frustrations of his professional and personal situation there, though admittedly it is more its society and court than the city itself that he abominates. Here are some typical examples from his letters, mostly to his wife; many more were collected forty years ago by Andrej Belyj and published with his study of Pushkin's diction in *The Bronze Horseman*[1]:

Petersburg is dreadfully depressing . . .

I spit and do my best to get out of Petersburg . . .

God, how I should like to light out for the fresh air . . .

You don't think by any chance that swinish Petersburg is not repulsive to me? That I enjoy living there among libels and denunciations? . . .

I am angry with Petersburg and rejoice in every sickening thing about it . . .

Brjulov is just leaving me for Petersburg, bracing his heart; he is afraid of the climate and the lack of freedom. I try to console him . . . (while) my own heart sinks to my boots . . .

[1] Andrej Belyj, *Ritm kak dialektika i Mednyj Vsadnik: Issledovanie.* Izdatel'stvo "Federacija" (Moskva, 1929), cf. p. 266 ff.

The Bronze Horseman, then, derives much of its troubling impact and its lasting freshness from a profound ambiguity. This is the sustained tension between the claims of *raison d'état*—lately in America more deceptively labeled the "national interest"—which in the poem are most overtly endorsed in the sonorous cadences of the Prologue; and the equally strong and more appealing claims of the humble (a key word of Pushkin's later poetry) individual in whose ostensible interest, but at whose crucial expense, the imposing edifice of the state is created and maintained. The external elements of authoritatively enforced law, discipline, and progress merge in the poetic mind into an aesthetic effect: the kind of ordered beauty, imposed on an ill-favored nature, which is still persuasive to the foreigner under the changeful sky over the water-mirrored pastel neoclassic of Leningrad.

Yet in numerous subtle ways Pushkin also identifies himself with his lowly, tormented, déclassé hero, Eugene. The green-cream-and-magenta charms of palaces and spires harbor nameless terrors and paralyzing frustration; the patterned grace of wrought-iron railings and granite banks confines not only classicist statuary and leafy parks but also private liberty and private need for fulfillment; and in this, Peter's city was and is ominously unlike Brühl's Dresden, William III's Amsterdam, or Canaletto's Venice, all of which seem to share collaterally in its urban pedigree. Peter the Great, Atarus, is both hero and anti-hero of *The Bronze Horseman.* With a combination of paternalistic ruthlessness, often faddish xenophilia, and deeply flawed success that is highly reminiscent of his pupil, Atatürk, in the 1920's, Peter had unfrocked, unbeavered, and unpriested his bewildered Russians. He had "made the trains run on time" like the bloated little Caesar of Fascist Italy whom so many befuddled foreign intellectuals fawned on before Ethiopia. But he and his imperial descendants, Alexander I of this poem, Nicholas I who was Pushkin's jailer and censor ("a lot of the staff sergeant in him, and a little of Peter the Great"), and their unanointed disciples of the last half-century have unalterably ranged against them the forces of intractable nature and elusive human privacy. This is what Mickiewicz's superb poems in the "Digression" are about; and this is what, despite Pushkin's conscious intentions, *The Bronze Horseman* came to be about also, under the compulsion of the Polish poet's fraternal genius.[2]

[2] A few excerpts from Mickiewicz's "St. Petersburg," in the Peacock translation, will serve to illustrate the extraordinary parallelism between the two works at certain key junctures:

> The ladies gleam like splendid butterflies/ With bright-hued cloaks and hats of brave design;/ Each glitters in Parisian elegance,/ Her small foot twinkling in a fur-lined shoe,/ Her face crab-red and snowy white of hue.—// . . . Pale-lipped with hate,/ He laughed, raised his clenched fist, and struck the stone,/ As though he summoned down a vengeful fate . . . //   His charger's reins Tsar Peter has released;/ He has been flying down the road, perchance,/ And here the precipice checks his advance./ With hoofs aloft now stands the maddened beast,/ Champing its bit unchecked, with slackened rein:/ You guess that it will fall and be destroyed./ Thus it has galloped long, with tossing mane,/ Like a cascade, leaping into the void,/ That, fettered by the frost, hangs dizzily./ But soon will shine the sun of liberty,/ And from the West a wind will warm this land.—/ Will the cascade of tyranny then stand?//

THE BRONZE HORSEMAN: A Tale of Petersburg   [1833]

The occurrence described in this narrative is based on truth. The details of the flood are drawn from journals of the time. The curious may consult the account composed by V. N. Berkh.

PROLOGUE

Upon a shore of desolate waves
Stood *he,* with lofty musings grave,
And gazed afar. Before him spreading
Rolled the broad river, empty save
For one lone skiff stream-downward heading.   5
Strewn on the marshy, moss-grown bank,
Rare huts, the Finn's poor shelter, shrank,
Black smudges from the fog protruding;
Beyond, dark forest ramparts drank
The shrouded sun's rays and stood brooding   10
And murmuring all about.

He thought;
"Here, Swede, beware—soon by our labor
Here a new city shall be wrought,
Defiance to the haughty neighbor.
Here we at Nature's own behest   15
Shall break a window to the West,
Stand planted on the ocean level;
Here flags of foreign nations all
By waters new to them will call,
And unencumbered we shall revel."   20

A century passed, and there shone forth
From swamps and gloomy forest prison,
Crown gem and marvel of the North,
The proud young city newly risen.
Where Finnish fisherman before,   25
Harsh Nature's wretched waif, was plying,
Forlorn upon that shallow shore,
His trade, with brittle net-gear trying
Uncharted tides—now bustling banks
Stand serried in well-ordered ranks   30
Of palaces and towers; converging
From the four corners of the earth,
Sails press to seek the opulent berth,
To anchorage in squadrons merging;
Nevá is cased in granite clean,   35
Atop its waters bridges hover,
Between its channels, gardens cover
The river isles with darkling green.
Outshone, old Moscow had to render
The younger sister pride of place,   40
As by a new queen's fresh-blown splendor
In purple fades Her Dowager Grace.

I love thee, Peter's own creation,
I love thy stern and comely face,
Nevá's majestic perfluctation,   45
Her bankments' granite carapace,
The patterns laced by iron railing,
And of thy meditative night
The lucent dusk, the moonless paling;

When in my room I read and write   50
Lampless, and street on street stand dreaming,
Vast luminous gulfs, and, slimly gleaming,
The Admiralty's needle bright;
And rather than let darkness smother
The lustrous heavens' golden light,   55
One twilight glow speeds on the other
To grant but half an hour to night.

    I love thy winter's fierce embraces
That leave the air all chilled and hushed,
The sleighs by broad Nevá, girls' faces   60
More brightly than the roses flushed,
The ballroom's sparkle, noise, and chatter,
And at the bachelor rendezvous
The foaming beakers' hiss and spatter,
The flaming punch's flickering blue.   65
I love the verve of drilling duty
Upon the playing fields of Mars,[1]
Where troops of riflemen and horse
Turn massed precision into beauty,
Where laureled flags in tatters stream   70
Above formations finely junctured,
And brazen helmets sway and gleam,
In storied battles scarred and punctured.
I love, war-queen, thy fortress pieces
In smoke and thunder booming forth   75
When the imperial spouse increases
The sovereign lineage of the North,
Or when their muzzles roar in token
Of one more Russian victory,
Or scenting spring, Nevá with glee,   80
Her ice-blue armor newly broken,
In sparkling floes runs out to sea.

    Thrive, Peter's city, flaunt thy beauty,
Stand like unshaken Russia fast,
Till floods and storms from chafing duty   85
May turn to peace with thee at last;
The very tides of Finland's deep
Their long-pent rancor then may bury,

[1] The parade grounds of St. Petersburg are called Mars Field.

And cease with feckless spite to harry
Tsar Peter's everlasting sleep.   90

    There was a time—our memories keep
Its horrors ever fresh and near us . . .
Of this a tale now suffer me
To tell before you, gentle hearers.
A grievous story it will be.   95

PART ONE

    Through Peter's darkened city rolled
November's breath of autumn cold.
Nevá, her clamorous waters splashing
Against the crest of either dike,
Tossed in her shapely ramparts, like   100
A patient on his sickbed thrashing.
Already dark it was and late;
A rainstorm pressed its angry spate
At windowpanes, with moaning driven
By dismal winds. Just then was seen   105
Back from a friend's house young Eugene—
(A pleasant name that we have given
The hero of our tale; what's more,
My pen was friends with it before.)
His surname may go unrecorded;   110
Though once, who knows but it was lauded
In native lore, its luster keen
Blazed by the pen of Karamzin,[2]
By now the world and rumor held
No trace of it. Our hero dwelled   115
In poor Kolomna,[3] humbly serving
Some office, found the great unnerving,
And cared for neither buried kin
Nor legend-woven origin.

    And so tonight Eugene had wandered   120
Back home, slipped off his cloak, undressed,
Composed himself, but found no rest,
As ill at ease he lay and pondered.

[2] Allusion to Karamzin's monumental *History of the Russian State.*
[3] Then an outlying faubourg of St. Petersburg.

What were his thoughts? That he was poor,
And by his labor must secure   125
A portion of esteem and treasure;
That God might well have eased his pains
With wits and cash; that men of leisure,
Endowed with luck if not with brains,
Could idly leave him at a distance,   130
And lead so carefree an existence!
He thought that in the post he held
He had attained but two years' rating;
That still the storm was not abating,
And that the banked-up river swelled   135
Still more—and since by now they surely
Had struck the bridges down securely,
He and Parasha must, he knew,
Be parted for a day or two.
And poet-like, Eugene, exhaling   140
A sigh, fell musing on his lot:

    "Get married? I? And, yet, why not?
Of course, it won't be easy sailing,
But what of that? I'm young and strong,
Content to labor hard and long,   145
I'll build us soon, if not tomorrow,
A simple nest for sweet repose
And keep Parasha free of sorrow,
And in a year or two, who knows,
I may obtain a snug position,   150
And it shall be Parasha's mission
To tend and rear our children . . . yes,
So we will live, and so forever
Will be as one, till death us sever,
And grandsons lay us both to rest . . ."   155
Thus ran his reverie. Yet sadly
He wished that night the wind would still
Its mournful wail, the rain less madly
Be rattling at the windowsill.
At last his eyelids, heavy-laden   160
Droop into slumber . . . soon away
The night's tempestuous gloom is fading
And washes into pallid day . . .

Disastrous day! Nevá all night
Has seaward strained, in hopeless muster   165
Of strength against the gale's wild bluster,
But now at last must yield the fight.

From morning, throngs of people line
The banks and marvel at the fountains
Of spray, the foam-tipped rolling mountains   170
Thrust up by the envenomed brine;
For now Nevá, her flow arrested
By the relentless sea-wind's force,
Reared up in fury, backward-crested,
And drowned the islands in her course.   175
The storm more fiercely yet upsoaring,
Nevá, engorged, with swell and roaring
As from a cauldron's swirl released,
Abruptly like a frenzied beast
Leaped on the city. At her onrush   180
All scattered, every place was swept
An instant void, swift waters crept
Into the deeply hollowed basements,
Canals rose gushing to the casements,
There streamed Petropolis, foam-laced,   185
Like Triton foundered to the waist.

Beset! Besieged! The vile surf charges
Through window frames like thieves, loose barges
Dash in the panes, stern forward wrenched.
Street-hawkers' trays, their covers drenched,   190
Smashed cabins, roofing, rafters reeling,
The stock-in-trade of thrifty dealing,
The wretched gain of misery pale,
Whole bridges loosened by the gale,
Coffins unearthed, in horrid welter   195
Float down the streets.
                In stricken gloom
All see God's wrath and bide their doom.
Alas! All founders, food and shelter!
Where now to turn?

That fateful year
Our famed late sovereign still was sitting   200
On Russia's throne—he sadly here
Upon his balcony did appear
And owned: "For tsars there is no pitting
Their power against the Lord's." His mien
All grief, he sat and contemplated   205
The fell disaster's desolate scene.
Into the squares to lakes dilated,
Debouched, like riverbeds inflated,
What had been streets. The palace stood
Like a lone cliff the waters riding.   210
The Tsar spoke out: and where they could,
By roadways near and distant gliding,
Upon their stormy path propelled,
The Emperor's generals went speeding
To save the people, who, unheeding   215
With fear, were drowning where they dwelled.

That night, where on Tsar Peter's square
A corner-house[4] new risen there
Had lately on its high porch shown—
One paw raised, as in live defiance—   220
A marble pair of guardian lions:
Astride upon the beast of stone
There sat, his arms crossed tight, alone,
Unmoving, deathly pale of feature,
Eugene. He was afraid, poor creature,   225
Not for himself. He did not hear
The evil breakers crest and rear,
His soles with greedy lashes seeking,
Nor feel the rain splash in his face,
Nor yet the gale with boisterous shrieking   230
Tear off his hat. Impaled in space,
His eyes held fast a distant border
And there in frozen anguish gazed.
There, mountainous, in wild disorder
From depths of chaos skyward raised,   235
Huge waves were towering and gloating,
There howled the storm and played with floating
Wreckage . . . God, God! Just there should be,

[4] The new edifice of the Ministry of War.

Set hard upon the inland sea,
Close, ah, too close to that mad billow,   240
A fence unpainted, and a willow,
And a frail hut: there dwelt those two,
Her mother and she, his bride bespoken,
Long dreamed-of . . . or was all he knew
A dream, naught but an empty token   245
All life, a wraith and no more worth,
But Heaven's mockery at Earth?

And he, as by a spell enfolded,
By irons to the marble bolted,
Could not descend; all within sight   250
Was an unending watery blight.
And o'er Nevá all spray-ensheeted,
Its back to where Eugene still clung,
There towered immobile, undefeated,
Upon its bronzen charger seated,   255
The Idol with its arm outflung.

PART TWO

With rack and ruin satiated,
Nevá, her wanton frenzy spent,
At last drew back her element—
By her own tumult still elated—   260
And nonchalantly abdicated
Her plunder. Thus a highwayman
Comes bursting with his vicious clan
Into some village, wrecking, slashing,
Destroying, robbing—shrieks and gnashing   265
Of teeth, alarms, oaths, outrage, roar—
Then, heavily with booty weighted,
Fearing pursuers, enervated,
The band of robbers homeward pour
And strew the wayside with their plunder.   270

The waters fell, and as thereunder
Dry footing showed, Eugene, heartsore,
Benumbed with sorrow, fear, and wonder,

Made headlong for the riverside,
Close on the barely ebbing tide.   275
For still Nevá, high triumph breathing,
Sent angry billows upward seething
As from live coals beneath her course,
And still the whitecaps heaved and slanted,
And heavily the river panted   280
As will a battle-winded horse.
Eugene looks round: a boat on station!
He greets it like a revelation,
Calls to the wherryman—and he,
With daring unconcern, is willing   285
To take him for a quarter-shilling
Across that formidable sea.

   And long he struggled hard to counter
The turmoil with his practiced strength;
Time after time their craft, aflounder   290
Between banked waves, seemed sure to founder
With its rash crew—until at length
They reached the shore.

              Eugene, fear-stricken,
Runs down the long-familiar lane,
By long-dear places, looks—in vain: 295
Unknowable, a sight to sicken
The heart, all stares in disarray,
This flung aside, that swept away,
Here half-uprooted cabins listed,
There others lay all crushed and twisted,   300
Still others stood misplaced—all round,
Strewn as upon a battleground,
Were scattered corpses. Barely living,
Eugene flies onward arrow-straight,
Worn-out with terror and misgiving,   305
Onward to where he knows his fate
Awaits him with a secret message,
As it might be a sealed despatch.
Here is the suburb now, the passage
Down to the bay, and here the thatch . . .   310
But what is this?

He stopped, confounded.
Retraced his steps and once more rounded
That corner . . . stared . . . half raised a hand:
Here is the place where it should stand,
Here is the willow. There, remember,   315
The gate stood—razed, no doubt. And where,
Where is the house? Distraught and somber,
He paces back and forward there,
Talks to himself aloud, soon after
Bursts out abruptly into laughter   320
And slaps his forehead.

        Night sank down
Upon the horror-shaken town;
But few found sleep, in every dwelling
They sat up telling and retelling
About the day just past.

        Dawn's ray   325
From pallid banks of weary gray
Gleamed down upon the silent city
And found of yesterday's alarm
No trace. The purple cloak[5] of pity
Already covered recent harm   330
And all returned to former calm.
Down streets re-won for old endeavor
Men walk as callously as ever,
The morning's civil service troops,
Emerged from their nocturnal coops,   335
Are off to work. Cool tradesmen labor
To open cellar, vault, and store,
Robbed by Nevá the night before,
The sooner to surcharge their neighbor
For their grave loss. They carted off   340
Boats from the courtyards.

        (Count Khvostov,
A poet whom Parnassus nurses,
Lamented in immortal verses
The blight Nevá had left behind.)

[5] This is assumed to refer either to imperial charity or to the calm dawn, or ambiguously to both.

My pitiful Eugene, though—evil   345
His lot; alas, his clouded mind
Could not withstand the brute upheaval
Just wrought on it. The clash and strain
Of flood and storm forever thundered
Upon his ear; his thoughts a train   350
Of horrors, wordlessly he wandered;
Some secret vision seemed to chill
His mind. A week—a month—and still
Astray from home he roved and pondered.
As for the homestead he forsook,   355
The landlord let his vacant nook
To some poor poet. Eugene never
Returned to claim it back, nor took
His left possessions. Growing ever
More alien to the world, he strayed   360
All day on foot till nightfall led him
Down to the wharves to sleep. He made
His meals of morsels people fed him
Through windows. His poor clothing frayed
And moldered off him. Wicked urchins   365
Threw pebbles at his back. The searching
Coachwhips not seldom struck him when,
As often now, he would be lurching
Uncertain of his course; but then
He did not feel it for the pain   370
Of some loud anguish in his brain.
Thus he wore on his luckless span,
A moot thing, neither beast nor man,
Who knew if this world's child, or whether
A caller from the next.

                    He slept   375
One night by the Nevá. The weather
Was autumn-bent. An ill wind swept
The river. Sullen swells had crept
Up banks and steps with plash and rumble,
As a petitioner might grumble   380
Unheard outside the judge's gate.
Eugene woke up. The light was failing,
The rain dripped, and the wind was wailing

And traded through the darkness late
Sad echoes with the watchman's hailing . . .   385

    Eugene sprang up, appeared to waken
To those remembered terrors; shaken,
He hurried off at random, then
Came to a sudden stop; again
Uncertainly his glances shifted   390
All round, wild panic marked his face.
Above him the great mansion lifted
Its columns. On the terrace-space,
One paw raised as in live defiance,
Stood sentinel those guardian lions,   395
And high above those rails, as if
Of altitude and darkness blended,
There rode in bronze, one arm extended,
The Idol on its granite cliff.

    Eugene's heart shrank. His mind unclouding   400
In dread, he knew the place again
Where the great flood had sported then,
Where those rapacious waves were crowding
And round about him raged and spun—
That square, the lions, and him—the one   405
Who, bronzen countenance upslanted
Into the dusk aloft, sat still,
The one by whose portentous will
The city by the sea was planted . . .
How awesome in the gloom he rides!   410
What thought upon his brow resides!
His charger with what fiery mettle,
His form with what dark strength endowed!
Where will you gallop, charger proud,
Where next your plunging hoofbeats settle?   415
Oh, Destiny's great potentate!
Was it not thus, a towering idol
Hard by the chasm, with iron bridle
You reared up Russia to her fate?

    The piteous madman fell to prowling   420
About the statue's granite berth,

And furtively with savage scowling
He eyed the lord of half the earth.
His breath congealed in him, he pressed
His brow against the chilly railing,   425
A blur of darkness overveiling
His eyes; a flame shot through his breast
And made his blood seethe. Grimly louring,
He faced the haughty image towering
On high, and fingers clawed, teeth clenched,   430
As if by some black spirit wrenched,
He hissed, spite shaking him: "Up there,
Great wonder-worker you, beware! . . ."
And then abruptly wheeled to race
Away full tilt. The dread Tsar's face,   435
With instantaneous fury burning,
It seemed to him, was slowly turning . . .
Across these empty spaces bound,
Behind his back he heard resound,
Like thunderclouds in rumbling anger,   440
The deep reverberating clangor
Of pounding hoofs that shook the ground.
And in the moonlight's pallid glamour
Rides high upon his charging brute,
One hand stretched out, 'mid echoing clamor   445
The Bronze Horseman in pursuit.
And all through that long night, no matter
What road the frantic wretch might take,
There still would pound with ponderous clatter
The Bronze Horseman in his wake.   450

    And ever since, when in his erring
He chanced upon that square again,
They saw a sick confusion blurring
His features. One hand swiftly then
Flew to his breast, as if containing   455
The anguished heart's affrighted straining;
His worn-out cap he then would raise,
Cast to the ground a troubled gaze
And slink aside.

A little island
Lies off the coast. There now and then   460
A stray belated fisherman
Will beach his net at dusk and, silent,
Cook his poor supper by the shore,
Or, on his Sunday recreation
A boating clerk might rest his oar   465
By that bleak isle. There no green thing
Will grow; and there the inundation
Had washed up in its frolicking
A frail old cottage. It lay stranded
Above the tide like weathered brush,   470
Until last spring a barge was landed
To haul it off. It was all crushed
And bare. Against the threshold carried,
Here lay asprawl my luckless knave,
And here in charity they buried   475
The chill corpse in a pauper's grave.

Selected Stanzas from *Eugene Onegin*
A NOVEL IN VERSE

EUGENE ONEGIN [1823–1831]

Introductory Note

Pushkin's mature art is concrete and of this world, humanly dimensioned, capable even of homey simplicity, though never petty or stuffy. It remains craftsmanlike and lucid even in the noblest flights of his early and, occasionally, late mode of Schilleresque pathos— the vein of "The Dagger" and "Liberty," and of the prologue to *The Bronze Horseman*. It does not shroud itself in the trailing draperies of diffuse cerebration or melt in the aquarelle sentimentalism that marks much of contemporary romanticism and inheres, to name a prominent example, in the very conceptual structure of Goethe's *Faust*. Although Pushkin pays Goethe the tribute of a distant and in large part, one suspects, dutiful and hearsay admiration, he would assuredly have snorted unprintably at such gaucheries of Goethean invention as Homunculus in his flood-lit sputnik, that curious amphibious Montgolfier of hot air, or that even more flatulent and even less durably buoyant classicist yeast cake, the hopskip-and-jump-to-glory skirt-chaser, Euphorion-Byron. The somewhat murky and infelicitous threnode to Byron in *Faust II* (lines 9907 to 9938) contrasts very instructively with Pushkin's terse and inspired lines to the same Continental idol in "To the Sea," conceived roughly simultaneously.

Not that Pushkin is always simple in form or earthbound in conception. Some of his structures, large and small, notably *Tsar Saltan* and *Eugene Onegin,* partake of the involute intricacy of a Chinese chess set; but they remain free of any cargo of bizarre symbolisms or clutter of baroque detail. Their complexity of structure and viewpoint is reminiscent rather—in a more purposeful and less mannered way—of the conceits that amused certain artists of the seventeenth and eighteenth centuries; those painted vistas, say, of the interior perspectives of a picture gallery. You enter the frame of the painting, as Alice entered her looking glass, and gain a limited, multiply abstracted, but infinitely suggestive view of a world of little worlds: foreshortened corridors alive with miniature por-

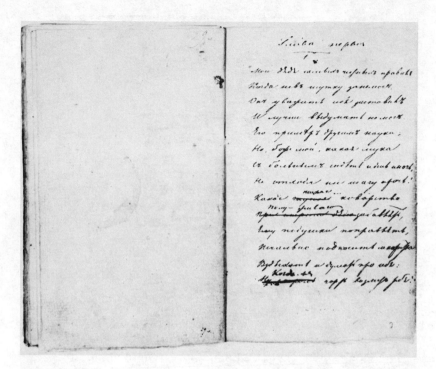

One of Pushkin's notebooks, opened to the first stanza of EUGENE
ONEGIN.

traits and landscapes and interiors in every manner and style, usually authentic and recognizable works, with mirrors placed here and there to double and quadruple, remove and ironize the sights, and doors half-open to glimpses of receding halls and cabinets and more corridors. There is a modest example of the kind in the Hermitage, and some finer ones in West European galleries. The finest of them all is *Eugene Onegin*.

For expert and far-ranging commentary on Pushkin's central work, *Eugene Onegin,* see volumes II and III of Vladimir Nabokov's *Aleksandr Pushkin, Eugene Onegin,* Bollingen Series, LXXII (New York: Pantheon Books, 1964). A succinct introduction to the work and a full

A page from Pushkin's notebooks showing rough drafts of stanzas II, 29, 30 of EUGENE ONEGIN. *Among the sketches is a self-portrait.*

translation in the metric form of the original are found in the latest
edition of my own *Alexander Pushkin : Eugene Onegin ;* A New Trans-
lation in the Onegin Stanza (New York : Dutton Paperbacks, 1963).

Selected Stanzas from EUGENE ONEGIN

I, 1

"Now that he is in grave condition,
My uncle, decorous old dunce,
Has won respectful recognition
And done a clever thing for once.
His act should be a guide to others;   5
But what a bore, I ask you, brothers,
To tend a patient night and day
And venture not a step away!
Is there hypocrisy more glaring
Than to amuse one all but dead,   10
Adjust the pillow for his head,
Dose him with melancholy bearing,
And think behind a public sigh:
Deuce take you, step on it and die!"

I, 2

Thus a young good-for-nothing muses,
As in the dust his post-wheels spin,
By a decree of sovereign Zeus's
The extant heir to all his kin.
Friends of Ruslan and of Ljudmila!¹   5
Allow me, with no cautious feeler
Or foreword, to present at once
The hero of my new romance:
Onegin, a dear friend of mine,
Born where Nevá flows, and where you,   10

¹ See Introduction, page xxx.

I daresay, gentle reader, too
Were born, or once were wont to shine;
There I myself once used to be:
The North, though, disagrees with me.[2]

II, 1

The manor where Onegin fretted
Was so enchanting a retreat,
No simple soul would have regretted
Exile so pastoral and sweet:
The manor house leaned, well secluded,   5
Against a hill, no wind intruded,
Close by a stream flowed; and away
There stretched a shimmering array
Of meads and cornfields gold-brocaded,
And hamlets winked; across the grass   10
A wandering herd would slowly pass;
Umbrageous arbors densely shaded
A park, far-rambling and unkempt,
Where sheltered dryads mused and dreamt.

II, 2

The mansion had been built for leisure,
As stately houses ought to be,
Hewn to the calm and rugged measure
Of our astute antiquity.
Room after room with lofty ceiling,   5
A tapestried salon, revealing
Ancestral[3] portraits hung in file
And stoves of many-colored tile.
All this has now been superseded,
Exactly why, I never learned;   10
But where Onegin was concerned,
In any case it was unneeded,
Because he yawned with equal gloom
In any style of drawing room.

[2] Allusion to Pushkin's recent banishment from St. Petersburg for writing subversive poetry.

[3] The manuscripts have either "tsars" or "ancestors" here; presumably it was suspected that the censor might take umbrage at the notion that displaying portraits of tsars was old-fashioned.

III, 22

With beauties have I been acquainted
As pure as winter and as kind,
Untouched, untempted, and untainted
Inviolate even to the mind;
I have admired their self-possession,   5
Their innate virtue and discretion,
And run for cover, I avow,
As if beholding at their brow
The dread inscription over Hades:
"Abandon hope who enter here."   10
To kindle feeling strikes with fear,
And to repel, delights these ladies.
On the Nevá's banks, I dare say
You have met vestals such as they.

III, 23

And others shine there, proudly wielding
Adherents to their service bent,
Themselves complacently unyielding
To passion's plea and blandishment.
And what was I amazed to witness?   5
When with a show of rigid fitness
They've driven bashful love away,
They lure it back into the fray
By a judicious use of kindness:
The words at any rate appear   10
At times less formal and severe—
And with impressionable blindness
The love-game's innocent recruit
Returns to the inane pursuit.

III, 25

A flirt allures with calculation,
Tatyana's love is his to keep,
Without reserve or hesitation,
As dear as children's and as deep.

She has not learned to whisper: tarry—   5
With choicer bait to trap the quarry
The more securely in the net,
Designing here with hope to whet
Vainglory, there to leave suspended
The doubting heart, then stoke desire   10
To higher blaze with jealous fire,
Lest, ardor in fulfillment ended,
The cunning slave should entertain
A restless urge to slip his chain.

IV, 38, 39

Reposeful slumber, reading, rambling,
The purl of brooks, the sylvan shades,
Betweentimes fresh young kisses sampling
From creamy-skinned and black-eyed maids,
An eager mount, to rein obedient,   5
Light dinner taken when expedient,
A glass or two of gleaming wine,
Seclusion, hush: thus in divine
Simplicity his life proceeded;
Unfeelingly, without a care,   10
He sipped its sweetness, unaware
Of summer's shining gait; unheeded
Alike his urban friends and treats
And tedious holiday conceits.

IV, 40

And yet our northern summer season
Like southern winter comes, and lo,
Is gone, and though for some odd reason
We won't admit it, it is so.
Autumn was in the air already,   5
The sun's gay sparkle grew unsteady,
The timeless day became more brief;
The forest, long in darkling leaf,
Unclothed itself with mournful rustle;

The fields were wrapped in misty fleece,   10
A raucous caravan of geese
Winged southward; after summer's bustle
A duller season was at hand:
November hovered overland.

IV, 41

Through frigid haze the dawn resurges,
Abroad the harvest sounds abate;
And soon the hungry wolf emerges
Upon the highway with his mate.
His scent scares into snorting flurries   5
The trudging horse; the traveler hurries
His way uphill in wary haste.
No longer are the cattle chased
Out of the byre at dawn, the thinning
Horn notes of cowherds cease the tune   10
That rounds them up again at noon.
Indoors the maiden sings at spinning
Before the crackling pine-flare light
Companion of the winter night.

IV, 42

At last a crackling frost enfolded
Fields silvered o'er with early snows:
(All right—who am I to withhold it,
The rhyme you knew was coming—*rose!*)
The ice-clad river's polished luster   5
No stylish ballroom floor could muster;
A joyous swarm of urchins grates
The frozen sheet with ringing skates.
A cumbrous goose on ruddy paddies
Comes waddling down the bank to swim,   10
Steps gingerly across the rim,
Slithers and falls; in swirling eddies
Descends the virgin snow and pranks
And showers stars upon the banks.

IV, 43

What in those winterbound recesses
To do? Take walks? One must agree,
The somber countryside depresses
With its austere monotony.
Across the frozen steppes to gallop?   5
Your horse, its iron's blunted scallop
Caught on a vicious icy clot,
Will have a fall, as like as not.
Stay in your cell and read: the highlights
Are Pradt and Walter Scott. No good?   10
Not interested? Well, you could
Check ledgers, sulk, drink—the long twilights
Will somehow pass, tomorrow's too,
And so the whole gay winter through!

—————————

V, 1

Fall lingered on as if it never
Would leave the countryside that year,
While Nature seemed to wait forever
For winter. Snow did not appear
Till the third January morning.   5
Up early, Tanya without warning
Finds roofs and fences overnight
Turned to exhilarating white,
Her window laced with subtle etching,
The trees with wintry silver starred,   10
Pert magpies sporting in the yard,
The softly covered hilltops stretching
'Neath winter's scintillating shawl. . . .
And clear is all, and white is all.

V, 2

Winter . . . the peasant, feeling festive,
Breaks in a track with sled and horse;

Sensing the snow, his nag is restive
And shambles at a trot of sorts;
Here passes, powdery furrows tracing,   5
A spirited kibitka[4] racing,
The coachman, on his box ahead,
In sheepskin coat and sash of red.
There runs a houseboy, having chosen
To seat his "Rover" on a sled,   10
Himself hitched up in charger's stead;
The rascal feels one finger, frozen
Already, with a wince and grin,
While Mother shakes her fist within.

V, 11

A wondrous dream Tatyana's dreaming.
It seems to her that she is out
On foot in wintry lowland gleaming
With snow; drear fog shrouds all about;
Ahead among the snowdrifts dipping,   5
Its angry waters swirling, ripping,
In somber grayness roared and strained
A stream, by winter not enchained.
Two slender boughs, ice-welded halfway
Afford a parlous, swaying bridge   10
Between the near and yonder ridge:
Across the roaring gulf her path lay,
And here, to nameless dread a prey,
Tatyana halted on her way.

V, 12

The stream, like rankling separation,
Moves her to chide it, as it were;
There's no one at the further station
To stretch a helping hand to her;
But there—a snowdrift heaves and surges,   5
And from beneath it who emerges?
A bear, disheveled all and swarth;
Tanya cries out, he stretches forth

4 Light cart or sleigh with a hood.

A mighty paw with razor talons
And growls; she with a shrinking hand   10
Supports herself upon it, and
In tremulously halting balance
Is borne across the torrent there;
And then—the bear comes after her!

V, 13

She dares no backward glance, unable
To spur her hurried steps enough,
And still the groom in shaggy sable
Refuses to be shaken off;
Still onward crashed the fiend and shuffled.   5
Woods loom ahead; tall firs unruffled
In their beclouded beauty frown,
Their sloping branches all weighed down
With pads of snow. Through the denuded
Treetops of linden, birch, and ash   10
The rays of heaven's lanterns flash.
No path leads here; all blurred and hooded
The brush and hillsides rise and fall,
Enveloped deep in snowy pall.

VI, 44

With new temptations I am lusting,
With yet untasted sorrow sad;
The first I find myself mistrusting,
And hanker for the grief I had.
Oh, dreams, my dreams, where is your sweetness?   5
Oh, youth's (the rhyme fair beckons) fleetness!
Can it be really true at last,
Its lovely bloom is past, is past,
In truth, in sober earnest ended?
All elegiac pose aside,   10
The springtime of my days has hied
(As hitherto I just pretended)?
Is it irrevocably noon?
Shall I be really thirty soon?

VI, 45

The afternoon of life is starting,
I see I must confront this truth.
So be it: friendly be our parting,
Oh nimble season of my youth!
For your delights my thanks I render,   5
For bitter grief, for torment tender,
For feasts and turmoil, storm and shine,
For all the bounty that was mine,
I render thanks to you. Your gladness,
Alike in tumult and in calm,   10
I relished, without stint or qualm;
Enough! I leave you, not in sadness,
Embarking for another shore,
To rest from what I knew before.

VI, 46

One backward glance; farewell, dear settings
Where my lone days were used to roll,
Instinct with ease and passion's frettings
And musings of the pensive soul.
But you, my verdant inspiration,   5
Keep ever green imagination,
Come winging oftener to this part;
Come quickening the slumbrous heart,
Let not the poet's soul grow frigid,
Or coarsen to a cruder cast   10
And turn to lifeless stone at last,
With worldly stupor numb and rigid,
In that vile quicksand where we lie
And wallow, brothers, you and I!

VII, 1

The snows from the surrounding mountains,
By spring's insistent rays beset,
By now cascade in turbid fountains
On meads already glistening wet,

And Nature from her slumber breaking   5
Greets with a smile the year's awaking.
The sky renews its azure sheen,
And with a downy haze of green
The still transparent forest rallies,
While from her waxen cell the bee   10
Goes gathering the meadow-fee.
Gay hues invade the drying valleys,
Herds rustle, and the twilight hush
Has thrilled to nightingale and thrush.

VII, 2

How I am saddened by your coming,
Oh time of love, oh time of bud!
What languid throb you send benumbing
Into my soul, into my blood!
How laggardly enchantment seizes   5
The heart, as spring's returning breezes
Waft to my face in silken rush
Here in the green secluded hush!
Have I become so alienated
From all things that exult and glow,   10
All things that joy and life bestow,
That now they find me dull and sated,
And all seems pale as burnt-out coal
To the long-since insentient soul?

VII, 6

By rolling mountains half-surrounded,
Come, let us wander where one sees
A brook meander, meadow-bounded,
Across a grove of linden trees.
Nightlong, the nightingale, spring's lover,   5
Sings there, and heather roses hover
Above the coursing water's drone;
And here a tomb and graven stone—
Two venerable firs impart it
Their shadow—tell the passing guest: 10

"Vladimir Lensky here found rest,
Who met death young and eager-hearted;
Such was the year, *so long* his lease.
Fair youth and poet, sleep in peace."

VII, 7

There, for a time, when night had ended,
On a low branch one might discern
A wreath, by unknown hand suspended,
Asway above the tranquil urn;
And for a time, two maidens yonder   5
At leisured eventide would wander
And by the rising moon be found
In mingled tears upon the mound.
But now . . . the mournful shrine is never
Sought out; the trail that passed beneath,   10
Untrod; the fir branch bears no wreath.
Alone the shepherd sings as ever,
Grizzled and frail, his simple air
And plaits his artless sandal there.

VIII, 1

When in the parks of the Lyceum
A carefree flower life I led,
And eagerly read *Apuleium,*
But *Ciceronem* left unread,
In springtime, when the stillness brought us   5
But swan calls over gleaming waters,
In valleys charged with mystery
The Muse began to visit me.
Into my monkish study breaking
Like sudden dawn, she would ignite   10
Gay fireworks of fancy-flight
And sing of childish merrymaking,
Our glorious dawn's heroic themes,
The heart's first palpitating dreams.

VIII, 2

And lo, the public smiled, and served us
The fairy food of early fame;
Derzhavin in old age observed us
And, gravebound, with his blessings came . . .

. . . .
. . . .
. . . .
. . . .
. . . .
. . . .
. . . .
. . . .
. . . .
. . . .
. . . .

VIII, 3

And I, for single law declaring
The passions' arbitrary cues,
My joys with chance companions sharing—
I brought my enterprising Muse
To roaring feasts and altercations,   5
Patrolmen's midnight imprecations,
And she among that boisterous horde
Exultantly her bounty poured,
Like a bacchante joined their revels,
And singing songs across her glass,   10
Was wooed with many a wanton pass
By those long-vanished gay young devils;
While I was proud to show and share
My giddy young companion there.

VIII, 4

But angry fortune glared upon me
And drove me far . . . She left me not,

My tender maid, and often won me
Sweet respite with a wondrous plot
That charmed the burden off my shoulders.   5
How often, 'mid Caucasian boulders
On moonlit gallops it was she
Who, like Lenore, rode with me!
How often by the Tauris' waters
She led the way through misty caves   10
Of night, to hear the murmuring waves,
The endless lisp of Nereus' daughters,
The breakers' deep, eternal choir
In praise of all creation's sire!

VIII, 5

The capital's ado and glitter
Forsworn as soon as left behind,
She roamed the humble tents of bitter
Moldavia, and found them kind.
In that bleak wilderness she rambled   5
With wandering tribes, and soon resembled
Her hosts, forgot for their scant tongue
That of the gods whence she had sprung,
And learned the airs of that steppe pleasance.
Then—sudden shift of scene all round—   10
In my own garden she was found,
Clothed in a country damsel's presence,
In wistful musing steeped her glance,
And in her hand a book from France.

THE ORIGINALS

WITH LINEAR TRANSLATIONS

Стихотворения

ВОЛЬНОСТЬ   [1817]

ОДА

Беги, сокройся от очей,
Цитеры слабая царица!
Где ты, где ты, гроза царей,
Свободы гордая певица?
Приди, сорви с меня венок,   5
Разбей изнеженную лиру...
Хочу воспеть Свободу миру,
На тронах поразить порок.

Открой мне благородный след
Того возвышенного галла,   10
Кому сама средь славных бед
Ты гимны смелые внушала.
Питомцы ветреной Судьбы,
Тираны мира! трепещите!
А вы, мужайтесь и внемлите,   15
Восстаньте, падшие рабы!

Увы! куда ни брошу взор —
Везде бичи, везде железы,
Законов гибельный позор,
Неволи немощные слезы;   20
Везде неправедная Власть
В сгущенной мгле предрассуждений
Воссела — Рабства грозный Гений
И славы роковая страсть.

Shorter Poems

LIBERTY   [1817]

ODE

Flee, vanish from [my] eyes,
Cythera's feeble princess!
Where [art] thou, where [art] thou, bane of kings,
Freedom's proud singer?
Come, tear from me the wreath,   5
Smash the effeminate lyre . . .
I want to sing [of] Freedom for the world,
Strike [at] vice upon thrones.

Unveil to me the noble trail
Of that exalted Gaul   10
In whom thyself 'mid famed calamities
Thou didst inspire audacious hymns.
Fosterlings of flighty Destiny,
Tyrants of the world! Tremble!
And ye, take heart like men and hearken,   15
Rise up, fallen slaves!

Alas! Wherever I cast [my] gaze—
Everywhere scourges, everywhere irons,
The laws' pernicious sham,
Serfdom's powerless tears;   20
Everywhere lawless Authority
In thickened fog of prejudices
Has settled—Slavery's dread Genius
And Glory's fateful passion.

[165

Лишь там над царскою главой   25
Народов не легло страданье,
Где крепко с Вольностью святой
Законов мощных сочетанье;
Где всем простерт их твердый щит,
Где сжатый верными руками   30
Граждан над равными главами
Их меч без выбора скользит

И преступленье свысока
Сражает праведным размахом;
Где не подкупна их рука   35
Ни алчной скупостью, ни страхом.
Владыки! вам венец и трон
Дает Закон — а не природа;
Стоите выше вы народа,
Но вечный выше вас Закон.   40

И горе, горе племенам,
Где дремлет он неосторожно,
Где иль народу, иль царям
Законом властвовать возможно!
Тебя в свидетели зову,   45
О мученик ошибок славных,
За предков в шуме бурь недавних
Сложивший царскую главу.

Восходит к смерти Людовик
В виду безмолвного потомства,   50
Главой развенчанной приник
К кровавой плахе Вероломства.
Молчит Закон — народ молчит,
Падет преступная секира...
И се — злодейская порфира   55
На галлах скованных лежит.

Самовластительный Злодей!
Тебя, твой трон я ненавижу,
Твою погибель, смерть детей
С жестокой радостию вижу.   60

There only on the royal head   25
[The guilt of] the nations' suffering has not come to lie
Where strong with sacred Liberty
Is mighty laws' conjunction
Where to all is proffered their firm shield,
Where, grasped by the faithful hands   30
Of the citizens, over equal heads
Their sword glides without choice

And strikes transgression from on high
With righteous impact;
Where incorruptible is their hand   35
By either avid greed or dread.
Potentates! to you crown and throne
The Law gives—and not nature;
Ye stand higher than the nation,
But higher than ye eternal Law.   40

And woe, woe to the tribe
Where it incautiously slumbers,
Where either for nations or for kings
It is possible to overrule the laws!
Thee I call to witness,   45
Oh, martyr of notorious errors,
Who for [his] forebears in the roar of recent storms
Laid down his royal head.

Up to his death steps Louis
In the sight of speechless posterity,   50
[His] uncrowned head he bowed
To the bloody scaffold of Mutiny.
Silent the Law—silent the nation,
There falls the criminal axe . . .
And lo—a villainous purple   55
Lies on the shackled Gauls.

Autocratic Miscreant!
Thee, thy throne I abhor,
Thy downfall, [thy] children's death
With cruel joy I see.   60

Читают на твоем челе
Печать проклятия народы,
Ты ужас мира, стыд природы,
Упрек ты богу на земле.

Когда на мрачную Неву   65
Звезда полуночи сверкает
И беззаботную главу
Спокойный сон отягощает,
Глядит задумчивый певец
На грозно спящий средь тумана   70
Пустынный памятник тирана,
Забвенью брошенный дворец —

И слышит Клии страшный глас,
За сими страшными стенами,
Калигулы последний час   75
Он видит живо пред очами,
Он видит — в лентах и звездах,
Вином и злобой упоенны,
Идут убийцы потаенны,
На лицах дерзость, в сердце страх.   80

Молчит неверный часовой,
Опущен молча мост подъемный,
Врата отверсты в тьме ночной
Рукой предательства наемной...
О стыд! о ужас наших дней!   85
Как звери, вторглись янычары!..
Падут бесславные удары...
Погиб увенчанный злодей.

И днесь учитесь, о цари:
Ни наказанья, ни награды,   90
Ни кров темниц, ни алтари
Не верные для вас ограды.
Склонитесь первые главой
Под сень надежную Закона,
И станут вечной стражей трона   95
Народов вольность и покой.

The nations read upon thy brow
The stamp of execration,
Thou [art] the horror of the world, the shame of nature,
Thou a reproach to God on earth.

When on the somber Nevá   65
The star of midnight sparkles,
And the carefree head
Quiet sleep weighs down,
The pensive singer gazes
Upon the menacingly sleeping 'mid the haze   70
Desolate monument of the tyrant,
The palace deserted to oblivion—

And hears the awesome voice of Clio
Behind those awesome walls,
Caligula's last hour   75
He sees vividly before [his] eyes,
He sees—in ribbons and stars,
By wine and spite intoxicated,
Go the clandestine murderers,
On [their] faces, insolence, in the heart, terror.   80

Silent is the faithless sentinel,
Let down in silence the drawbridge,
The gate unlocked in the nocturnal gloom
By treason's hired hand . . .
Oh, shame; oh, horror of our days!   85
Like beasts, the janissaries have thrust in! . . .
There fall the ignominious blows . . .
The crowned miscreant has perished.

And henceforth learn, oh, kings:
Neither punishment nor rewards,   90
Neither the cover of dungeons nor altars
Are faithful barricades for you.
Be the first to bow your head[s]
Beneath the trusty shelter of the Law,
And there will stand eternal guard of the throne   95
The nations' freedom and content.

К ЧААДАЕВУ   [1818]

Любви, надежды, тихой славы
Недолго нежил нас обман,
Исчезли юные забавы,
Как сон, как утренний туман;
Но в нас горит еще желанье,   5
Под гнетом власти роковой
Нетерпеливою   душой
Отчизны внемлем призыванье.
Мы ждем с томленьем упованья
Минуты вольности святой,   10
Как ждет любовник молодой
Минуты верного свиданья.
Пока свободою горим,
Пока сердца для чести живы,
Мой друг, отчизне посвятим   15
Души прекрасные порывы!
Товарищ, верь: взойдет она,
Звезда пленительного счастья,
Россия вспрянет ото сна,
И на обломках самовластья   20
Напишут наши   имена!

АВТОРУ
«ИСТОРИИ ГОСУДАРСТВА РОССИЙСКОГО»   [1818]

В его «Истории» изящность, простота
Доказывают нам, без всякого пристрастья,

TO CHAADAEV[1]   [1818]

Of love, of hope, of quiet glory
Not long I nursed the self-deceit,
Vanished are adolescent dallies
Like a dream, like the morning mist;
But still desire burns within us;   5
Beneath the press of fateful power
With impatient soul
We hark the native country's summons.
We bide with yearning expectation
The moment of sacred liberty,   10
As the young lover bides
The moment of the promised meeting.
The while with liberty we burn,
The while our hearts are quick for honor,
My friend, to our land we dedicate   15
The soul's exquisite raptures!
Comrade, believe: it will arise,
The star of captivating bliss,
Russia will rouse herself from sleep,
And on the ruins of despotism   20
Our names will be inscribed!

[1] Petr Yakovlevič Chaadaev or Chadaev (1793–1856), Western-oriented Russian philosopher who in his late twenties began to circulate, in French manuscript, his *Lettres philosophiques*. They contained a profound critique of Russian historical evolution on premises of a quasi-Catholic world view. The first of these *Letters*, published in Russian in 1836, caused the journal *Telescope* to be shut down, and Chaadaev to be declared insane and put under house arrest. Pushkin had known and admired him ever since Chaadaev was stationed at Tsarskoe Selo as a young officer.

TO THE AUTHOR OF
HISTORY OF THE RUSSIAN STATE[1]   [1818]

In his *History* elegance, simplicity
Prove to us without fear or favor

[1] N. M. Karamzin (1766–1826), the noted stylist and pioneer of new literary movements, whose famous *History* was conservative and strongly monarchist in tone.

Необходимость самовластья
И прелести кнута.

ИСТОРИЯ СТИХОТВОРЦА [1818]

Внимает он привычным ухом
    Свист;
Марает он единым духом
    Лист;
Потом всему терзает свету   5
    Слух;
Потом печатает — и в Лету
    Бух!

ДЕРЕВНЯ [1819]

Приветствую тебя, пустынный уголок,
Приют спокойствия, трудов и вдохновенья,
Где льется дней моих невидимый поток
    На лоне счастья и забвенья.
Я твой — я променял порочный двор цирцей,   5
Роскошные пиры, забавы, заблужденья
На мирный шум дубров, на тишину полей,
На праздность вольную, подругу размышленья.

    Я твой — люблю сей темный сад
    С его прохладой и цветами,   10
Сей луг, уставленный душистыми скирдами,
Где светлые ручьи в кустарниках шумят.
Везде передо мной подвижные картины:
Здесь вижу двух озер лазурные равнины,
Где парус рыбаря белеет иногда,   15
За ними ряд холмов и нивы полосаты,

The inevitability of autocracy
And the charms of the knout.

HISTORY OF A VERSIFIER   [1818]

He perceives with accustomed ear a
    "Whoosh";
Bedabbles singlemindedly the
    Page;
Then victimizes everybody's   5
    Ear;
Then publishes—and into Lethe
    Splash!

IN THE COUNTRY   [1819]

I greet thee, isolated nook,
Refuge of quietude, of toils and inspiration,
Where flows the invisible current of my days
    In the lap of happiness and oblivion.
I am thine—I have exchanged the sinful court of Circes,   5
Luxurious feasts, amusements, dissipations,
For the peaceful rustle of oak groves, for the quiet of fields,
For free idleness, the friend of reflection.

    I am thine—I love this dark garden
        With its cool and flowers,   10
This meadow, studded with fragrant hay-ricks,
Where bright streams murmur in the bushes.
Everywhere before me [are] animated pictures:
Here I see two lakes' azure expanses,
Where the sail of a fisherman whitely shines at times,   15
Behind them a row of hills and striped cornfields,

Вдали рассыпанные хаты,
На влажных берегах бродящие стада,
Овины дымные и мельницы крилаты;
   Везде следы довольства и труда...   20

Я здесь, от суетных оков освобожденный,
Учуся в истине блаженство находить,
Свободною душой закон боготворить,
Роптанью не внимать толпы непросвещенной,
Участьем отвечать застенчивой мольбе   25
   И не завидовать судьбе
Злодея иль глупца — в величии неправом.

Оракулы веков, здесь вопрошаю вас!
   В уединенье величавом
   Слышнее ваш отрадный глас.   30
   Он гонит лени сон угрюмый,
   К трудам рождает жар во мне,
   И ваши творческие думы
   В душевной зреют глубине.

Но мысль ужасная здесь душу омрачает: 35
   Среди цветущих нив и гор
Друг человечества печально замечает
Везде невежества убийственный позор.
   Не видя слез, не внемля стона,
На пагубу людей избранное судьбой,   40
Здесь *барство* дикое, без чувства, без закона,
Присвоило себе насильственной лозой
И труд, и собственность, и время земледельца.
Склонясь на чуждый плуг, покорствуя бичам,
Здесь рабство тощее влачится по браздам   45
   Неумолимого владельца.
Здесь тягостный ярем до гроба все влекут,
Надежд и склонностей в душе питать не смея,
   Здесь девы юные цветут
   Для прихоти бесчувственной злодея.   50
Опора милая стареющих отцов,
Младые сыновья, товарищи трудов,
Из хижины родной идут собой умножить
Дворовые толпы измученных рабов.

In the distance scattered huts,
Wandering cattle on the humid banks,
Smoky drying-sheds and winged windmills;
    Everywhere traces of contentment and toil . . .   20

Here I, freed from the bonds of daily vanities,
Am learning to find bliss indeed,
With free soul to worship law,
Not hearken to the unenlightened crowd's mutter,
With sympathy to answer shy entreaty   25
    And not to envy the lot
Of malefactor or of fool—in [their] unlawful grandeur.

Oracle of the ages, here I question thee!
    In [this] majestic isolation
    More audible is thy consoling voice.   30
    It chases off the sullen sleep of indolence,
    To labors stirs hot zeal in me,
    And thy creative thoughts
    Ripen in the soul's depth.

But a terrifying thought here darkens the soul: 35
    Amid blossoming crops and mountains
The friend of humanity sadly observes
Everywhere the murderous shame of ignorance.
    Not seeing tears, not hearing groan[s],
By destiny selected for men's undoing,   40
Here a savage class of squires, without feeling, without law,
Has arrogated to itself with the rod of violence
The labor, property, and time of the tiller of the soil.
Bent over alien plough, humbled to whips,
Here an exhausted slavedom plods along the furrows   45
    Of the implacable proprietor.
Here all drag on the ponderous yoke to the grave,
Not daring to nurse in their soul[s] hopes or inclinations,
    Here youthful maidens blossom
    For the caprice of an unfeeling evildoer.   50
The dear support of aging fathers,
Young sons, companions of [their] toils,
From the native cabin go to swell the numbers
Of the throng of worn-out manor serfs.

О, если б голос мой умел сердца тревожить!   55
Почто в груди моей горит бесплодный жар,
И не дан мне судьбой витийства грозный дар?
Увижу ль, о друзья! народ неугнетенный
И рабство, падшее по манию царя,
И над отечеством свободы просвещенной   60
Взойдет ли наконец прекрасная заря?

УЕДИНЕНИЕ   [1819]

Блажен, кто в отдаленной сени,
Вдали взыскательных невежд,
Дни делит меж трудов и лени,
Воспоминаний и надежд;
Кому судьба друзей послала,   5
Кто скрыт, по милости творца,
От усыпителя глупца,
От пробудителя нахала.

КИНЖАЛ   [1821]

    Лемносский бог тебя сковал
    Для рук бессмертной Немезиды,
Свободы тайный страж, карающий кинжал,
Последний судия позора и обиды.

Где Зевса гром молчит, где дремлет меч закона,   5
    Свершитель ты проклятий и надежд,
      Ты кроешься под сенью трона,
      Под блеском праздничных одежд.

    Как адский луч, как молния богов,
Немое лезвие злодею в очи блещет,   10

Oh, if my voice knew how to trouble hearts!   55
Wherefore burns in my breast a fruitless glow,
And heroism's formidable gift was not vouchsafed to me by fate?
Shall I see, oh friends, a nation unoppressed
And serfdom fallen by the emperor's sign of hand,
And on a fatherland of enlightened liberty   60
Will there arise at last a lovely dawn?

SECLUSION   [1819]

Blessed he who in remote shelter,
Far from demanding dunces,
Divides [his] days between labor and lazing,
Recollections and hopes;
To whom Fate has sent friends,   5
Who is hidden, by the Creator's mercy,
From the booby who puts [one] to sleep,
From the boor who wakes [one] up.

THE DAGGER   [1821]

The god of Lemnos[1] forged thee
For the hands of deathless Nemesis,
Freedom's secret guard, the avenging dagger,
The final arbiter of shame and offense.

Where Zeus's thunder is silent, where the sword of law slumbers,   5
Thou [art] executor of curses and of hopes
Thou hidest in the shelter of the throne,
Beneath the glitter of festive clothes.

Like Hades' ray, like lightning of the gods,
The mute blade gleams in the evildoer's eyes,   10

[1] Hephaistos, in charge of Metallurgy, Thermodynamics, and Mechanical Engineering.

И, озираясь, он трепещет
Среди своих пиров.

Везде его найдет удар нежданный твой:
На суше, на морях, во храме, под шатрами,
За потаенными замками,   15
На ложе сна, в семье родной.

Шумит под Кесарем заветный Рубикон,
Державный Рим упал, главой поник закон;
Но Брут восстал вольнолюбивый:
Ты Кесаря сразил — и, мертв, объемлет он   20
Помпея мрамор горделивый.

Исчадье мятежей подъемлет злобный крик:
Презренный, мрачный и кровавый,
Над трупом вольности безглавой
Палач уродливый возник.   25

Апостол гибели, усталому Аиду
Перстом он жертвы назначал,
Но вышний суд ему послал
Тебя и деву Эвмениду.

О юный праведник, избранник роковой,   30
О Занд, твой век угас на плахе;
Но добродетели святой
Остался глас в казненном прахе.

В твоей Германии ты вечной тенью стал,
Грозя бедой преступной силе —   35
И на торжественной могиле
Горит без надписи кинжал.

And looking around, he trembles
  Amidst his feasts.

Everywhere thy unexpected blow will find him:
On dry land, on the seas, in the temple, under tents,
  Behind concealed locks,   15
  On the couch of sleep, in his own family.

There splashes under Caesar the forbidden Rubicon,[2]
Imperious Rome has fallen, the law inclined its head;
  But Brutus freedom-loving rose:
Thou struckst down Caesar—and, dead, he embraces   20
  Pompey's proud marble.

The horde of mutinies lifts up [its] wrathful cry:
  Detested, gloomy, and bloody,
  Over the corpse of headless freedom
  The monstrous hangman has arisen.   25

Apostle of perdition, to the wearied Hades
  With [his] thumb he indicated victims,
  But the supreme tribunal sent him
  Thee and the Eumenid maiden.[3]

Oh, righteous youth, the choice of destiny,   30
  Oh, Sand,[4] thy age was extinguished on the scaffold;
  But of holy virtue
  The voice remained in the martyred dust.

In your Germany you became an eternal shade,
  Threatening woe to lawless force—   35
  And on the triumphal grave
  Burns without inscription a dagger.

[2] The border stream between Cisalpine Gaul and Italy. Caesar crossed it with his army, violating the terms of his senatorial mandate and precipitating the civil war that ended the Republic.

[3] The propitiatory term for the dreaded Erinyes (the Latin Furies), the ancient divinities of retribution.

[4] The German nationalist student Karl Ludwig Sand (1795–1820), who in 1819 shot the reactionary German playwright and Russian official August Friedrich von Kotzebue (1761–1819), who was also an intermittent Bonapartist. Sand was executed in 1820, and thus became a martyr to anti-Napoleonic Europe.

НА А. А. ДАВЫДОВУ   [1822]

Иной имел мою Аглаю
За свой мундир и черный ус,
Другой за деньги — понимаю,
Другой за то, что был француз,
Клеон — умом ее страща,   5
Дамис — за то, что нежно пел.
Скажи теперь, мой друг Аглая,
За что твой муж тебя имел?

ИНОСТРАНКЕ   [1822]

На языке тебе невнятном
Стихи прощальные пишу,
Но в заблуждении приятном
Вниманья твоего прошу:
Мой друг, доколе не увяну,   5
В разлуке чувство погубя,
Боготворить не перестану
Тебя, мой друг, одну тебя.
На чуждые черты взирая,
Верь только сердцу моему,   10
Как прежде верила ему,
Его страстей не понимая.

ПТИЧКА   [1823]

В чужбине свято наблюдаю
Родной обычай старины:
На волю птичку выпускаю
При светлом празднике весны.

ON A. A. DAVYDOVA[1]   [1822]

One man had my Agláya
For the sake of his uniform and black moustache,
Another for money—[that] I [can] understand,
Another for being French,
Cleon—thrilling her by his mind,   5
Damis—for his tender singing.
Tell [me] now, my dear Agláya,
What did your husband have you for?

[1] Aglája Davydova, née Duchesse de Grammont, the promiscuous wife of General Alexander Davydov (the southern Decembrist's brother), whose favors Pushkin also enjoyed briefly.

TO A FOREIGN GIRL   [1822]

In a language unintelligible to you
I write verses of leave-taking,
Yet in pleasant delusion
I beg your attention:
My dear, until I fade away,   5
Having lost [all] feeling in [our] separation,
I shall not cease adoring
You, my dear, you alone.
Gazing at alien features,
Believe only my heart,   10
As formerly you believed it,
Its passions not understanding.

A LITTLE BIRD   [1823]

In alien land I religiously observe
The native custom of old:
I give a little bird its freedom
On the lucent holiday of spring.

Я стал доступен утешенью;   5
За что на бога мне роптать,
Когда хоть одному творенью
Я мог свободу даровать!

НОЧЬ   [1823]

Мой голос для тебя и ласковый и томный
Тревожит позднее молчанье ночи темной.
Близ ложа моего печальная свеча
Горит; мои стихи, сливаясь и журча,
Текут, ручьи любви; текут полны тобою.   5
Во тьме твои глаза блистают предо мною,
Мне улыбаются — и звуки слышу я:
Мой друг, мой нежный друг... люблю... твоя... твоя!..

═══════════   [1823]

Изыде сеятель сеяти семена своя.

Свободы сеятель пустынный,
Я вышел рано, до звезды;
Рукою чистой и безвинной
В порабощенные бразды
Бросал живительное семя —   5
Но потерял я только время,
Благие мысли и труды...

Паситесь, мирные народы!
Вас не разбудит чести клич.
К чему стадам дары свободы?   10
Их должно резать или стричь.
Наследство их из рода в роды
Ярмо с гремушками да бич.

Consolation (I became accessible to) was vouchsafed me;   5
Why should I mutter against God,
When even to one creature
I was able to give freedom!

NIGHT   [1823]

My voice, caressing and languid for you,
Troubles the tardy silence of the dark night.
Near my couch a mournful candle
Burns; my verses, pouring forth and murmuring,
Flow, brooks of love, flow, full of you.   5
In the gloom your eyes glisten before me,
Smile for me, and sounds I hear:
My dear, my tender dear . . . I love . . . am yours . . . yours!

━━━━━━━━   [1823]

"Forth went the sower to sow his seeds . . ."

    Freedom's sower in wilderness,
I went out early, before the star;
With hand pure and guiltless
Into enslaved furrows
I flung life-giving seed—   5
But I merely lost time,
Benignant thoughts and labors . . .

    Pasture, peaceful nations!
You will not wake to honor's hail.
For what to herds the gifts of freedom?   10
They need to be slaughtered or shorn.
Their heritage from generation to generation
[Is] the yoke with jingles and the whip.

184]

НА ВОРОНЦОВА   [1824]

Полу-милорд, полу-купец,
Полу-мудрец, полу-невежда,
Полу-подлец, но есть надежда,
Что будет полным наконец.

К МОРЮ   [1824]

Прощай, свободная стихия!
В последний раз передо мной
Ты катишь волны голубые
И блещешь гордою красой.

Как друга ропот заунывный,
Как зов его в прощальный час,
Твой грустный шум, твой шум призывный
Услышал я в последний раз.

Моей души предел желанный!
Как часто по брегам твоим
Бродил я тихий и туманный,
Заветным умыслом томим!

Как я любил твои отзывы,
Глухие звуки, бездны глас
И тишину в вечерний час,
И своенравные порывы!

Смиренный парус рыбарей,
Твоею прихотью хранимый,
Скользит отважно средь зыбей:
Но ты взыграл, неодолимый,
И стая тонет кораблей.

Не удалось навек оставить
Мне скучный, неподвижный брег,
Тебя восторгами поздравить

TO VORONTSOV   [1824]

One-half milord, one-half shopkeeper
One-half sage, one-half ignoramus,
One-half villain, but there is hope
That he will be a whole one in the end.

TO THE SEA   [1824]

Farewell, free element!
For the last time before me
You roll [your] blue waves
And gleam in [your] proud beauty.

Like a friend's sorrowful mutter,   5
Like his call at the hour of leave-taking,
Your doleful sound, your sound of summons
I have heard for the last time.

My soul's longed-for realm!
How often along your shores   10
Have I roved, silent and bedazed,
Troubled by a cherished design!

How I loved your call-notes,
[Your] muffled sounds, the chasm's voice,
And [your] silence at the evening hour,   15
And [your] willful surges!

The humble sail of fishermen,
By your caprice preserved,
Glides bravely amid the breakers:
But let a playful mood seize you, indomitable one,   20
And a flock of ships founders.

I did not contrive to leave forever
The dull, immobile shore,
To greet you with surges of rapture

И по хребтам твоим направить   25
Мой поэтический побег!

Ты ждал, ты звал... я был окован;
Вотще рвалась душа моя:
Могучей страстью очарован,
У берегов остался я...   30

О чем жалеть? Куда бы ныне
Я путь беспечный устремил?
Один предмет в твоей пустыне
Мою бы душу поразил.

Одна скала, гробница славы...   35
Там погружались в хладный сон
Воспоминанья величавы:
Там угасал Наполеон.

Там он почил среди мучений.
И вслед за ним, как бури шум,   40
Другой от нас умчался гений,
Другой властитель наших дум.

Исчез, оплаканный свободой,
Оставя миру свой венец.
Шуми, взволнуйся непогодой: 45
Он был, о море, твой певец.

Твой образ был на нем означен,
Он духом создан был твоим:
Как ты, могущ, глубок и мрачен,
Как ты, ничем неукротим.   50

Мир опустел... Теперь куда же
Меня б ты вынес, океан?
Судьба людей повсюду та же:
Где капля блага, там на страже
Уж просвещенье, иль тиран.   55

Прощай же, море! Не забуду
Твоей торжественной красы

And by your crests to guide   25
My poet's flight!

You waited, you called . . . I was in fetters;
Vainly struggled my soul:
By a mighty passion spellbound,
At the shores I remained . . .   30

What is there to regret? Whither now
Would I direct [my] carefree way?
A single object in your wilderness
Might have struck my (soul) fancy.

One cliff, the gravestone of glory . . .   35
There were steeped in chill sleep
Memories majestic:
There Napoleon's flame died.

There he found rest amid agonies.
And in his wake like noise of tempest   40
Another genius sped from us,
Another potentate of our thoughts.[1]

He vanished, bemoaned by Freedom,
Leaving his wreath to the world:
Roar out, well up with stormy weather: 45
He was, oh Sea, your singer.

Your image had left its mark on him
He was created of your spirit:
Like you, mighty, deep, and darkling,
Like you, undaunted by anything.   50

The world has emptied . . . whither now
Would you bear me off, Ocean?
Earth's lot is everywhere the same:
Where there is a drop of bliss, there [stands] on guard
Already Enlightenment or a tyrant.   55

Farewell then, Sea! I shall not forget
Your festive beauty,

[1] Lord Byron, who had perished at Missolonghi that year.

И долго, долго слышать буду
Твой гул в вечерние часы.

В леса, в пустыни молчаливы   60
Перенесу, тобою полн,
Твои скалы, твои заливы,
И блеск, и тень, и говор волн.

───────   [1824]

О дева-роза, я в оковах;
Но не стыжусь твоих оков:
Так соловей в кустах лавровых,
Пернатый царь лесных певцов,
Близ розы гордой и прекрасной   5
В неволе сладостной живет
И нежно песни ей поет
Во мраке ночи сладострастной.

ВИНОГРАД   [1824]

Не стану я жалеть о розах,
Увядших с легкою весной;
Мне мил и виноград на лозах,
В кистях созревший под горой,
Краса моей долины злачной,   5
Отрада осени златой,
Продолговатый и прозрачный,
Как персты девы молодой.

And long, long shall I hear
Your deep roar in the evening hours.

To forests, wildernesses silent   60
Shall I transport, full of you,
Your cliffs, your bays,
And the glitter and shade and murmur of [your] waves.

—————————   [1824]

Oh rose maiden, I am in fetters;
But I am not ashamed of your fetters:
Thus the nightingale in the laurel bushes,
Feathered king of sylvan singers,
Near the proud and beauteous rose   5
Lives in delightful bondage
And tenderly sings songs for her
In the gloaming of the voluptuous night.

THE GRAPE   [1824]

I shall not regret the roses
Which have faded with the light spring;
The grape, too, on the vines is dear to me,
In clusters ripened on the hillside,
The glory of my fertile vale,   5
Solace of golden autumn,
Oblong and translucent
Like the fingers of a young maiden.

━━━━━━━━━ [1824]

Лизе страшно полюбить.
Полно, нет ли тут обмана?
Берегитесь — может быть,
Эта новая Диана
Притаила нежну страсть —   5
И стыдливыми глазами
Ищет робко между вами,
Кто бы ей помог упасть.

━━━━━━━━━ [1825]

Лишь розы увядают,
Амврозией дыша,
В Элизий улетает
Их легкая душа.

И там, где волны сонны   5
Забвение несут,
Их тени благовонны
Над Летою цветут.

EX UNGUE LEONEM   [1825]

Недавно я стихами как-то свистнул
И выдал их без подписи моей;
Журнальный шут о них статейку тиснул,
Без подписи ж пустив ее, злодей.
Но что ж? Ни мне, ни площадному шуту   5
Не удалось прикрыть своих проказ:
Он по когтям узнал меня в минуту,
Я по ушам узнал его как раз.

═══════   [1824]

Liza is afraid to love.
Come, is there not here deception?
Be on guard—(for) it may be,
This new Dian
Has concealed [her] tender passion—   5
And with eyes demure
Shyly makes a search among us
Who might help her fall.

═══════   [1825]

So soon as roses wilt,
Breathing ambrosia,
To Elysium wing(s) away
Their light soul[s].

And there, where sleepy waves   5
Bear oblivion,
Their fragrant shades
Bloom over Lethe.

EX UNGUE LEONEM   [1825]

Not long ago I gave a little flick in verses
And issued them without my signature;
Some clown of a journalist printed a little piece about them,
Releasing it without signature, the cad.
But fancy! Neither I nor [that] gutter clown   5
Succeeded in concealing our tricks:
He knew me in a minute by my talons,
I knew him by his ears right enough.

АНДРЕЙ ШЕНЬЕ   [1825]

Посвящено Н. Н. Раевскому

Ainsi, triste et captif, ma lyre toutefois
s'éveillait...

Меж тем, как изумленный мир
На урну Байрона взирает,
И хору европейских лир
Близ Данте тень его внимает,

Зовет меня другая тень,   5
Давно без песен, без рыданий
С кровавой плахи в дни страданий
Сошедшая в могильну сень.

Певцу любви, дубрав и мира
Несу надгробные цветы.   10
Звучит незнаемая лира.
Пою. Мне внемлет он и ты.

К ***   [1825]

Я помню чудное мгновенье:
Передо мной явилась ты,
Как мимолетное виденье,
Как гений чистой красоты.

В томленьях грусти безнадежной,   5
В тревогах шумной суеты,
Звучал мне долго голос нежный,
И снились милые черты.

ANDRÉ CHÉNIER[1]   [1825]

(*dedicated to N. N. Raevsky*)

Ainsi, triste et captif, ma lyre
toutefois s'éveillait . . .

While the dumbfounded world
Gazes at Byron's urn,
And to the choir of European lyres
His shade is hearkening close to Dante,

To me calls out another shade,   5
Long without songs, without sobbing
From the bloody scaffold in the days of suffering
Descended to the shelter of the grave.

To the singer of love, of groves and peace
I carry flowers for his tomb.   10
A lyre unknown resounds.
I sing. I am heard by him and thee.

[1] The French poet (1762–94), one of Pushkin's early political heroes and poetic models, who died on the guillotine. The dedication is to Nikolaj Raevsky, son of the military hero of 1812, with whom Pushkin was on intimate terms when he traveled in the south with the Raevsky family in 1820 and enjoyed flirtations with two of the daughters.

TO . . .   [1825]

I recollect a wondrous moment:
Before me *you* appeared,
Like a fleeting apparition,
Like the genius of pure beauty.

In the oppression of hopeless grief   5
In the concerns of noisy bustling,
Long I could hear [your] tender voice,
And dreamed of [your] dear features.

Шли годы. Бурь порыв мятежный
Рассеял прежние мечты, 10
И я забыл твой голос нежный,
Твои небесные черты.

В глуши, во мраке заточенья
Тянулись тихо дни мои
Без божества, без вдохновенья, 15
Без слез, без жизни, без любви.

Душе настало пробужденье:
И вот опять явилась ты,
Как мимолетное виденье,
Как гений чистой красоты. 20

И сердце бьется в упоенье,
И для него воскресли вновь
И божество, и вдохновенье,
И жизнь, и слезы, и любовь.

ЗИМНИЙ ВЕЧЕР   [1825]

Буря мглою небо кроет,
Вихри снежные крутя;
То, как зверь, она завоет,
То заплачет, как дитя,
То по кровле обветшалой 5
Вдруг соломой зашумит,
То, как путник запоздалый,
К нам в окошко застучит.

Наша ветхая лачужка
И печальна, и темна. 10
Что же ты, моя старушка,
Приумолкла у окна?

Years passed. The turbulent gusts of storms
Dispelled former dreams,   10
And I forgot your tender voice,
Your heavenly features.

In the numbness, the gloom of confinement.
Quietly my days dragged on,
Without godhead, without inspiration,   15
Without tears, without life, without love.

Awakening set in for my soul:
And here again *you* appeared,
Like a fleeting vision,
Like the genius of pure beauty.   20

And [my] heart beats in rapture,
And there are reborn for it afresh
Godhead, and inspiration,
And life, and tears, and love.

WINTER EVENING   [1825]

Storm with mist the heavens covers,
Snowy whirlwinds twisting;
Now like a wild beast falls roaring,
Now falls crying like a child,
Now along the wizened roof   5
Abruptly with the straw it rustles,
Now like a belated wanderer
At our window it will rap.

Our decrepit little cabin
Is (both) dismal and dark.   10
How comes it, dear old granny,
You fell silent (a little) at the window?

Или бури завываньем
Ты, мой друг, утомлена,
Или дремлешь под жужжаньем   15
Своего веретена?

Выпьем, добрая подружка
Бедной юности моей,
Выпьем с горя; где же кружка?
Сердцу будет веселей.   20
Спой мне песню, как синица
Тихо за морем жила;
Спой мне песню, как девица
За водой поутру шла.

Буря мглою небо кроет,   25
Вихри снежные крутя;
То, как зверь, она завоет,
То заплачет, как дитя.
Выпьем, добрая подружка
Бедной юности моей,   30
Выпьем с горя; где же кружка?
Сердцу будет веселей.

[1825]

Если жизнь тебя обманет,
Не печалься, не сердись!
В день уныния смирись:
День веселья, верь, настанет.

Сердце в будущем живет;   5
Настоящее уныло:
Всё мгновенно, всё пройдет;
Что пройдет, то будет мило.

By the storm's roar, off and on,
Are you numbed, my dear,
Or dozing to the buzz   15
Of your spindle?

Let us drink, kind little friend
Of my wretched youth,
Let us drink from grief; where is the jug?
The heart will be gayer.   20
Sing me the song of how the blue tit
Quietly lived beyond the sea;
Sing me the song of how the maiden
Went for water at the morn.

Storm with mist the heavens covers,   25
Snowy whirlwinds twisting;
Now like a wild beast falls roaring,
Now falls crying like a child.
Let us drink, kind little friend
Of my wretched youth,   30
Let us drink from grief; where is the jug?
The heart will be gayer.

═══════════   [1825]

If life deceives you,
Do not sorrow, do not rage!
On the day of grief submit:
The day of joy, believe, will come.

In the future lives the heart;   5
[If] the present is dismal,
All is momentary, all will pass;
What has passed, will be dear.

ВАКХИЧЕСКАЯ ПЕСНЯ [1825]

Что смолкнул веселия глас?
Раздайтесь, вакхальны припевы!
Да здравствуют нежные девы
И юные жены, любившие нас!
Полнее стакан наливайте!   5
         На звонкое дно
         В густое вино
Заветные кольца бросайте!
Подымем стаканы, содвинем их разом!
Да здравствуют музы, да здравствует разум!   10
      Ты, солнце святое, гори!
      Как эта лампада бледнеет
      Пред ясным восходом зари,
Так ложная мудрость мерцает и тлеет
      Пред солнцем бессмертным ума.   15
Да здравствует солнце, да скроется тьма!

═══════ [1825]

Цветы последние милей
Роскошных первенцев полей.
Они унылые мечтанья
Живее пробуждают в нас.
Так иногда разлуки час   5
Живее сладкого свиданья.

БУРЯ   [1825]

Ты видел деву на скале
В одежде белой над волнами,
Когда, бушуя в бурной мгле,
Играло море с берегами,

BACCHIC SONG   [1825]

Why has the voice of gaiety fallen silent?
Resound, bacchanalian refrains!
A toast to the tender maidens
And youthful women who loved us!
    Pour fuller the glass!   5
        Against the clinking bottom
        Into the thick wine
    Cast the ritual rings!
Let us raise [our] glasses, let's move them together!
A toast to the Muses, a toast to reason!   10
    Glow thou, oh, sacred sun!
    As this candelabrum pales
    Before the bright rise of the dawn,
Thus false cleverness flickers and fades
    Before the deathless sun of the mind.   15
Long live the sun, let darkness vanish!

―――――――   [1825]

The last flowers are dearer
Than the luxuriant first-blooms of the fields.
[For] melancholy musings
More vividly they wake in us.
Just so at times the hour of parting   5
Has more of life than a sweet tryst.

TEMPEST   [1825]

Saw you a maid upon a cliff
In raiment white above the breakers,
When blustering in tempestuous spray
The sea was sporting with the beaches,

Когда луч молний озарял   5
Ее всечасно блеском алым,
И ветер бился и летал
С ее летучим покрывалом?
Прекрасно море в бурной мгле   10
И небо в блесках без лазури;
Но верь мне: дева на скале
Прекрасней волн, небес и бури.

ПРИЯТЕЛЯМ   [1825]

Враги мои, покамест я ни слова...
И, кажется, мой быстрый гнев угас;
Но из виду не выпускаю вас
И выберу когда-нибудь любого:
Не избежит пронзительных когтей,   5
Как налечу нежданный, беспощадный.
Так в облаках кружится ястреб жадный
И сторожит индеек и гусей.

ПРОЗАИК И ПОЭТ   [1825]

О чем, прозаик, ты хлопочешь?
Давай мне мысль, какую хочешь:
Ее с конца я завострю,
Летучей рифмой оперю,
Взложу на тетиву тугую,   5
Послушный лук согну в дугу,
А там пошлю наудалую,
И горе нашему врагу!

When lightning's streak illumined her   5
Time and again with scarlet fulgence
And the wind struggled and flew
With her flighty covering?
Grand is the sea in tempest spray,
And the sky aflash without [its] azure;   10
Believe me, though: the maid upon the cliff
Is grander than the breakers, skies, and tempest.

TO FRIENDS   [1825]

My foes, for the time being I [say] not a word . . .
And my quick anger has, it seems, gone out;
But I'm not letting you out of [my] sight
And at some time I'll choose someone at random:
He won't escape the penetrating claws   5
As, unexpected, merciless I swoop.
Thus in the clouds circles the greedy hawk
And keeps a watch on turkey-hens and geese.

PROSE-WRITER AND POET   [1825]

For what, prose-writer, your ado and fuss?
Give me whatever thought you want:
I will sharpen it at the tip,
Fledge it with flighty rhyme,
Lay it upon the sinew taut,   5
Will bend the servile bow into an arc,
And send it home headlong,
And woe to our enemy!

———————— [1825]

Нет ни в чем вам благодати,
С счастием у вас разлад:
И прекрасны вы некстати,
И умны вы невпопад.

———————— [1825]

О муза пламенной сатиры!
Приди на мой призывный клич!
Не нужно мне гремящей лиры,
Вручи мне Ювеналов бич!
Не подражателям холодным,   5
Не переводчикам голодным,
Не безответным рифмачам
Готовлю язвы эпиграмм!
Мир вам, несчастные поэты,
Мир вам, журнальные клевреты,   10
Мир вам, смиренные глупцы!
А вы, ребята-подлецы,—
Вперед! Всю вашу сволочь буду
Я мучить казнию стыда!
Но если же кого забуду,   15
Прошу напомнить, господа!
О, сколько лиц бесстыдно-бледных,
О, сколько лбов широко-медных
Готовы от меня принять
Неизгладимую печать!   20

НА АЛЕКСАНДРА I   [1825]

Воспитанный под барабаном,
Наш царь лихим был капитаном!

———————   [1825]

Grace in anything eludes you;
Bliss and you are things apart:
You are (both) beautiful at the wrong time
And clever when it is out of place.

———————   [1825]

Oh, Muse of flaming satire!
Come upon my hail that calls you!
I do not need the thundering lyre,
Hand me the scourge of Juvenal!
Not for the cold imitators,   5
Not for the hungry translators,
Not for the rhymesters echoless
Do I prepare the sores of epigrams!
Peace unto you, luckless poets,
Peace unto you, journal minions,   10
Peace unto you, humble blockheads!
But you, my lads, the scoundrels—
Forward! All you scum I shall
Torment with the torture of shame!
But should I forget one,   15
Please remind [me], gentlemen!
Oh, how many faces shameless-sallow,
Oh, how many foreheads broad and brazen
Are ready to receive from me
The ineradicable brand!   20

ON ALEXANDER I   [1825]

Reared under the drum,
Our Tsar was a dashing commander:

Под Австерлицем он бежал,
В двенадцатом году дрожал,
Зато был фрунтовой профессор!
Но фрунт герою надоел —
Теперь коллежский он асессор
По части иностранных дел!

5

———————— [1826]

Под небом голубым страны своей родной
    Она томилась, увядала...
Увяла наконец, и верно надо мной
    Младая тень уже летала;
Но недоступная черта меж нами есть.
    Напрасно чувство возбуждал я:
Из равнодушных уст я слышал смерти весть,
    И равнодушно ей внимал я.
Так вот кого любил я пламенной душой
    С таким тяжелым напряженьем,
С такою нежною, томительной тоской,
    С таким безумством и мученьем!
Где муки, где любовь? Увы! в душе моей
    Для бедной, легковерной тени,
Для сладкой памяти невозвратимых дней
    Не нахожу ни слез, ни пени.

5

10

15

К ВЯЗЕМСКОМУ   [1826]

Так море, древний душегубец,
Воспламеняет гений твой?
Ты славишь лирой золотой
Нептуна грозного трезубец.

Не славь его. В наш гнусный век
Седой Нептун земли союзник.

5

At Austerlitz he ran,
In Eighteen-Twelve he trembled,
To make up for it he was a frontline professor.   5
But the hero got fed up with the front—
Now he is a collegiate assessor
In the department of foreign affairs.

━━━━━━━━   [1826]

Beneath the blue sky of her native land
    She suffered, wilted . . .
Faded away at last and likely over me
    The youthful shadow has already flown;
Between us, though, there is a line of no approach.   5
    In vain I tried to stir up feeling:
From lips indifferent I heard the news of death,
    And listened to it with indifference.
So this is whom I loved with soul aflame
    With such oppressive tension,   10
With such a tender wearying wretchedness,
    With such insanity and torture!
Where [are the] torments, where the love? Alas! Within my soul
    For the poor, all-too-trusting shade,
For sweet remembrance of irrevocable days   15
    I find nor tears, nor chiding.

TO VYAZEMSKY   [1826]

So the sea, ancient soul-destroyer,
Enflames your genius?
You glorify with golden lyre
Neptune's dread trident.

Do not glorify it. In our oppressive age   5
Gray-haired Neptune is earth's ally.

На всех стихиях человек —
Тиран, предатель или узник.

К ЯЗЫКОВУ   [1826]

Языков, кто тебе внушил
Твое посланье удалое?
Как ты шалишь и как ты мил,
Какой избыток чувств и сил,
Какое буйство молодое!   5
Нет, не кастальскою водой
Ты воспоил свою камену;
Пегас иную Иппокрену
Копытом вышиб пред тобой.
Она не хладной льется влагой,   10
Но пенится хмельною брагой;
Она разымчива, пьяна,
Как сей напиток благородный,
Слиянье рому и вина,
Без примеси воды негодной,   15
В Тригорском жаждою свободной
Открытый в наши времена.

ПРИЗНАНИЕ   [1826]

Я вас люблю,— хоть я бешусь,
Хоть это труд и стыд напрасный,
И в этой глупости несчастной
У ваших ног я признаюсь!

In all elements man is
Tyrant, traitor, or prisoner.

TO YAZYKOV   [1826]

Yazykov, who inspired you with
Your mettlesome message?
How you frolic, and how dear you are,
What overflow of feeling(s) and strength(s),
What youthful ebullience!   5
No, not of Castalian water
Did you give your Camoena[1] to drink;
Pegasus a different Hippocrene[2]
With [his] hoof struck up before you.
It does not flow with cool moisture,   10
But foams with intoxicating ale;
It is potent, drunken,
Like that potion noble,
A blending of rum and wine,
Without admixture of worthless water,   15
At Trigorskoe by free thirst
Discovered in our time(s).

[1] Camoenae or Camenae were soothsaying nymphs of the springs in ancient Italic folklore, equated since Livius Andronicus with the Greek Muses. The one most often cited, Egeria, came to stand in a general sense for "the Muse" who inspired the poet.
[2] Hippocrene is the source that, according to Greek legend, sprang up under the hoofbeat of Pegasus and was thought of as the fount of poetic imagination.

CONFESSION   [1826]

I love you—though I rage,
Though it is useless toil and shame,
And to this luckless folly
At your feet I confess!

Мне не к лицу и не по летам...   5
Пора, пора мне быть умней!
Но узнаю по всем приметам
Болезнь любви в душе моей:
Без вас мне скучно,— я зеваю;
При вас мне грустно,— я терплю;   10
И, мочи нет, сказать желаю,
Мой ангел, как я вас люблю!
Когда я слышу из гостиной
Ваш легкий шаг, иль платья шум,
Иль голос девственный, невинный,   15
Я вдруг теряю весь свой ум.
Вы улыбнетесь — мне отрада;
Вы отвернетесь — мне тоска;
За день мучения — награда
Мне ваша бледная рука.   20
Когда за пяльцами прилежно
Сидите вы, склонясь небрежно,
Глаза и кудри опустя,—
Я в умиленье, молча, нежно
Любуюсь вами, как дитя!..   25
Сказать ли вам мое несчастье,
Мою ревнивую печаль,
Когда гулять, порой в ненастье,
Вы собираетеся вдаль?
И ваши слезы в одиночку,   30
И речи в уголку вдвоем,
И путешествия в Опочку,
И фортепьяно вечерком?..
Алина! сжальтесь надо мною.
Не смею требовать любви.   35
Быть может, за грехи мои,
Мой ангел, я любви не стою!
Но притворитесь! Этот взгляд
Всё может выразить так чудно!
Ах, обмануть меня не трудно!..   40
Я сам обманываться рад!

It does not suit me or befit my years . . .   5
It's time, it's time for me to be more sensible!
But I recognize by all indications
The disease of love in my soul:
Without you I am bored—I yawn;
In your company I feel sad—I suffer;   10
And wish, more than I can stand, to tell you,
My angel, how much I love you!
When I hear from the drawing room
Your light step, or the rustle of [your] dress,
Or [your] girlish, innocent voice,   15
I suddenly lose all my mind.
You smile—to me it is delight;
You turn away—to me it's grief;
For a day of torment, reward
For me is your pale hand.   20
When at the embroidery frame attentively
You sit, bending forward at ease,
Eyes and ringlets cast down—
I, my heart going out to you, silently, tenderly
Rejoice in you, like a child! . . .   25
Shall I tell you [of] my unhappiness,
My jealous sorrow,
When for a walk, at times in bad weather,
You set forth into the distance?
And your tears all by yourself,   30
And words exchanged in a corner tête-à-tête,
And the trips to Opochka,
And the piano of an evening? . . .
Alina! Take pity on me;
I dare not demand love.   35
Perhaps, for my sins,
My angel, I am not worthy of love!
But pretend! That gaze
Can express anything so wondrously!
Ah, to deceive me is not hard! . . .   40
I'm glad to be deceived myself!

И. И. ПУЩИНУ   [1826]

Мой первый друг, мой друг бесценный!
И я судьбу благословил,
Когда мой двор уединенный,
Печальным снегом занесенный,
Твой колокольчик огласил.   5

Молю святое провиденье:
Да голос мой душе твоей
Дарует то же утешенье,
Да озарит он заточенье
Лучом лицейских ясных дней!   10

СТАНСЫ   [1826]

В надежде славы и добра
Гляжу вперед я без боязни:
Начало славных дней Петра
Мрачили мятежи и казни.

Но правдой он привлек сердца,   5
Но нравы укротил наукой,
И был от буйного стрельца
Пред ним отличен Долгорукой.

TO I. I. PUSHCHIN[1]   [1826]

My first friend, my friend invaluable!
I too blessed fate
When my deserted yard,
Drifted over with dismal snow,
Resounded to your little sleigh bell.   5

I implore holy Providence:
May my voice to your soul
Vouchsafe the same solace,
May it illumine your confinement
With a ray of bright Lyceum days!   10

[1] Ivan Ivanovich Pushchin had been P.'s close friend ever since they were classmates at Tsarskoe Selo (1811–17). Undeterred by P.'s latest official disgrace, Pushchin used a convenient family connection at Pskov to visit P. in January, 1825, at the nearby family estate of Mikhailovskoe, which P. inhabited under surveillance from both state and church authorities from 1824 to 1826. This was especially risky in view of Pushchin's own active role in the inner circle of the Decembrist conspiracy. The friends had a heartwarming reunion, both fearing, correctly, that under the circumstances it might be their last. Pushchin was condemned to Siberia after the Decembrist revolt, and on arriving at the remote prison camp, three years after that visit, was handed the present poem.

We owe to Pushchin an invaluable set of sensitive and penetrating memoirs covering the fourteen years of their close association.

STANZAS[1]   [1826]

In hope of glory and of bliss
I glance ahead without misgiving:
The start of Peter's glorious days
Was dark with riot and execution.

By truth, though, he attracted hearts,   5
By learning, though, he gentled manners,
Before the wanton janissary
Was honored by him Dolgoruki.[2]

[1] (On the accession of Nicholas I.)
[2] Count Vasily Lukich Dolgoruki (1672–1739) was among the first young Russians to be sent abroad by Peter I to be educated. He served for a time as his foremost ministerial counselor and was entrusted with several important embassies. His later career was both less fortunate and less savory.

Самодержавною рукой
Он смело сеял просвещенье,
Не презирал страны родной:
Он знал ее предназначенье.

То академик, то герой,
То мореплаватель, то плотник,
Он всеобъемлющей душой
На троне вечный был работник.

Семейным сходством будь же горд;
Во всем будь пращуру подобен:
Как он, неутомим и тверд,
И памятью, как он, незлобен.

ИМЕРАТОРУ НИКОЛАЮ   [1826?]

Едва царем он стал,
То разом начудесил,
Сто двадцать человек тотчас в Сибирь послал
Да пятерых повесил.

ЗИМНЯЯ ДОРОГА   [1826]

Сквозь волнистые туманы
Пробирается луна,
На печальные поляны
Льет печальный свет она.

По дороге зимней, скучной
Тройка борзая бежит,
Колокольчик однозвучный
Утомительно гремит.

With sovereign despotic hand
He boldly sowed enlightenment,   10
Did not contemn the native land:
He knew of its predestination.

Now academic sage, now hero,
Now seafarer, now carpenter,
By his all-comprehending soul   15
He was the eternal workman on the throne.

Be proud, then, of the kinship semblance;
In all be like unto the forebear:
Like him unfaltering and firm,
And in memory, like him, unspiteful.   20

TO THE EMPEROR NICHOLAS I   [1826?]

Hardly had he become tsar,
When promptly he worked wonders,
A hundred-twenty men at once sent to Siberia
And hanged five.

WINTER ROAD[1]   [1826]

Across wavering hazes
The moon is breaking through.
On the melancholy clearings
She dolorously pours her light.

Down the wintry, dismal highway   5
Runs the speedy troika,
The monotonous sleigh bell
Wearisomely tinkles.

[1] Both in metric form and lyrical atmosphere this poem oddly resembles Nikolaus
Lenau's "Der Postillon," conceived in the same general period, although there can
scarcely be any connection between the two.

Что-то слышится родное
В долгих песнях ямщика:
То разгулье удалое,
То сердечная тоска...   10

Ни огня, ни черной хаты,
Глушь и снег... Навстречу мне
Только версты полосаты   15
Попадаются одне...

Скучно, грустно... Завтра, Нина,
Завтра, к милой возвратясь,
Я забудусь у камина,
Загляжусь не наглядясь.   20

Звучно стрелка часовая
Мерный круг свой совершит,
И, докучных удаляя,
Полночь нас не разлучит.

Грустно, Нина: путь мой скучен,   25
Дремля смолкнул мой ямщик,
Колокольчик однозвучен,
Отуманен лунный лик.

ТРИ КЛЮЧА   [1827]

В степи мирской, печальной и безбрежной,
Таинственно пробились три ключа:
Ключ юности, ключ быстрый и мятежный,
Кипит, бежит, сверкая и журча.
Кастальский ключ волною вдохновенья   5
В степи мирской изгнанников поит.
Последний ключ — холодный ключ забвенья
Он слаще всех жар сердца утолит.

A familiar note one hears
In the coachman's lengthy songs: 10
Now a spirited carousal,
Now a grieving of the heart . . .

Not a light, no dusky cabin,
Hush and snow . . . As I pass,
Only milestones with their stripes   15
Come my way alone . . .

Dismal, drear . . . Tomorrow, Nina,
Tomorrow, returning to my dear one,
I shall dream before the fire,
Gaze and never gaze my fill.   20

Tunefully the hand of the clock
Will complete its measured round,
And, removing the intruders,
Midnight will not sever us.

Dismal, Nina: drear my journey,   25
Drowsing, my coachman is silent now,
Monotonous is the sleigh bell,
Beclouded the face of the moon.

THREE SPRINGS   [1827]

In the world's wasteland, dolorous and boundless,
Mysteriously have broken forth three springs:
The spring of youth, spring rapid and tumultuous,
Bubbles, runs on, aglitter and agurgle.
The spring of Castaly with swell of inspiration   5
In the world's wasteland stills the exiles' thirst.
The final spring—the cool spring of oblivion,
Slakes the heart's fever-heat more sweetly still.

АРИОН   [1827]

Нас было много на челне;
Иные парус напрягали,
Другие дружно упирали
В глубь мощны веслы. В тишине
На руль склонясь, наш кормщик умный   5
В молчанье правил грузный чёлн;
А я — беспечной веры полн,—
Пловцам я пел... Вдруг лоно волн
Измял с налету вихорь шумный...
Погиб и кормщик, и пловец! —   10
Лишь я, таинственный певец,
На берег выброшен грозою,
Я гимны прежние пою
И ризу влажную мою
Сушу на солнце под скалою.   15

ПОЭТ   [1827]

Пока не требует поэта
К священной жертве Аполлон,
В заботах суетного света
Он малодушно погружен;
Молчит его святая лира;   5
Душа вкушает хладный сон,
И меж детей ничтожных мира,
Быть может, всех ничтожней он.

Но лишь божественный глагол
До слуха чуткого коснется,   10
Душа поэта встрепенется,
Как пробудившийся орел.
Тоскует он в забавах мира,
Людской чуждается молвы,
К ногам народного кумира   15
Не клонит гордой головы;

ARION   [1827]

There were many of us in the bark;
Some were trimming the sails,
Others in harmony were plunging
The mighty oars into the deep. In calm [weather]
Bent over the rudder, our skillful helmsman   5
In silence steered the weighty bark;
And I—full of carefree trust—
I sang to the shipmates . . . Suddenly the bosom of the waves
Was ruffled with a swoop by a roaring gust . . .
Both helmsman and sailor perished!—   10
I alone, the mysterious singer,
Swept ashore by the storm,
I sing the former hymns
And dry my damp garment
In the sun at the foot of a cliff.   15

THE POET   [1827]

Until upon the poet calls
For hallowed sacrifice Apollo,
In the cares of the bustling world
He is small-mindedly absorbed;
His sacred lyre is silent;   5
[His] soul is steeped in chilly sleep,
And among the worthless children of the earth
He is perhaps the most worthless of all.

The moment, though, the word divine
Impinges on his sentient hearing,   10
The poet's soul ruffles (its feathers),
Like an awakened eagle.
He frets amid the world's amusements,
From human speech he shies away,
To the national idol's feet   15
He does not bow his proud head;

Бежит он, дикий и суровый,
И звуков и смятенья полн,
На берега пустынных волн,
В широкошумные дубровы...

20

ТАЛИСМАН   [1827]

Там, где море вечно плещет
На пустынные скалы,
Где луна теплее блещет
В сладкий час вечерней мглы,
Где, в гаремах наслаждаясь,   5
Дни проводит мусульман,
Там волшебница, ласкаясь,
Мне вручила талисман.

И, ласкаясь, говорила:
«Сохрани мой талисман: 10
В нем таинственная сила!
Он тебе любовью дан.
От недуга, от могилы,
В бурю, в грозный ураган,
Головы твоей, мой милый,   15
Не спасет мой талисман.

И богатствами Востока
Он тебя не одарит,
И поклонников пророка
Он тебе не покорит;   20
И тебя на лоно друга,
От печальных чуждых стран,
В край родной на север с юга
Не умчит мой талисман...

Но когда коварны очи   25
Очаруют вдруг тебя,

He runs, uncouth and grim,
Replete with sound and with perturbance
To shores of desolate waves,
To broadly-murmuring wildwoods . . .   20

THE TALISMAN   [1827]

Where the sea forever splashes
On deserted crags,
Where the moon more warmly glitters
At the sweet hour of evening mist,
Where, in harems his ease enjoying,   5
The Muslim whiles away his days,
There an enchantress with caresses
Handed me a talisman.

With caresses, too, she bade me:
"Guard my talisman: 10
It contains mysterious power!
Love has given it to you.
From ills of body, from the grave,
In tempest, in dread hurricane,
Your head, my dear one,   15
My talisman will not save.

"And with riches of the Orient
It will not endow you,
And adherents of the Prophet
It will not subject to you;   20
And to a friend's bosom,
From melancholy alien lands
To native shore from south to north
My talisman will not speed you . . .

"But when designing eyes   25
Of a sudden shall bewitch you,

Иль уста во мраке ночи
Поцелуют не любя —
Милый друг! от преступленья,
От сердечных новых ран,
От измены, от забвенья
Сохранит мой талисман!»

30

TO DAWE, ESQr   [1828]

Зачем твой дивный карандаш
Рисует мой арапский профиль?
Хоть ты векам его предашь,
Его освищет Мефистофель.

Рисуй Олениной черты.
В жару сердечных вдохновений,
Лишь юности и красоты
Поклонником быть должен гений.

5

ВОСПОМИНАНИЕ   [1828]

Когда для смертного умолкнет шумный день,
    И на немые стогны града
Полупрозрачная наляжет ночи тень
    И сон, дневных трудов награда,
В то время для меня влачатся в тишине
    Часы томительного бденья:

5

Or lips in the gloom of night
Shall kiss without loving—
Dear my friend! From transgression,
From new heart-wounds,   30
From betrayal, from oblivion
Will preserve my talisman!"

TO DAWE, ESQ.[1]   [1828]

Wherefore does your wondrous pencil
Draw my Moorish profile?
Though you will hand it down to the ages,
Mephistopheles will hiss it.

Draw the features of [Miss] Olenina.   5
In the glow of the heart's inspiration(s),
Only of youth and beauty
Genius ought to be adherent.

[1] George Dawe (1781–1829), English portrait painter and mezzotint engraver in
the manner of Sir Joshua Reynolds. Went to Russia and was named First Painter
to the Court of Russia by Alexander I, who had him paint about 400 portraits of
army men who served in the Napoleonic Wars. Several of Dawe's paintings hang
in the Hermitage Museum in Leningrad.

REMEMBRANCE[1]   [1828]

When for the mortal the loud day falls silent
        And on the mute squares of the city
Sinks down the half-transparent shade of night
        And sleep, reward of daily toils,—
At that time for me in the silence drag   5
        Hours of tormenting wakefulness:

[1] A continuation of this poem, to more than double its length in print, exists in a
manuscript version that shows a few single-word gaps. These, and an unexplained
reference to "two dear shades, angels given me by fate in bygone days," may explain
Pushkin's decision not to include the rest of the poem in editions printed in his life-
time.

В бездействии ночном живей горят во мне
       Змеи сердечной угрызенья;
Мечты кипят; в уме, подавленном тоской,
       Теснится тяжких дум избыток;   10
Воспоминание безмолвно предо мной
       Свой длинный развивает свиток;
И с отвращением читая жизнь мою,
       Я трепещу и проклинаю,
И горько жалуюсь, и горько слезы лью,   15
       Но строк печальных не смываю.

ТЫ И ВЫ   [1828]

Пустое *вы* сердечным *ты*
Она, обмолвясь, заменила
И все счастливые мечты
В душе влюбленной возбудила.
Пред ней задумчиво стою,   5
Свести очей с нее нет силы;
И говорю ей: как *вы* милы!
И мыслю: как *тебя* люблю!

▬▬▬▬   [1828]

Кобылица молодая,
Честь кавказского таврá,
Что ты мчишься, удалая?
И тебе пришла пора;
Не косись пугливым оком,   5
Ног на воздух не мечи,
В поле гладком и широком
Своенравно не скачи.
Погоди; тебя заставлю
Я смириться подо мной: 10
В мерный круг твой бег направлю
Укороченной уздой.

In the nocturnal idleness more briskly (burn) gnaw in me
      The heart-serpent's bites;
Fancies seethe up; in the mind weighed down by grief
      There crowds an excess of oppressive thoughts;   10
Remembrance wordlessly before me
      Unrolls her lengthy scroll;
And with revulsion reading [there] my life,
      I quail and curse
And bitterly complain, and bitterly shed tears,   15
      But cannot wipe away the grievous lines.

THOU AND YOU   [1828]

The empty *you* by the warm *thou*
She by a slip of the tongue replaced
And all happy daydreams
Stirred up in the soul in love.
Before her pensively I stand,   5
To take [my] eyes off her [I have] not the strength;
And [I] tell her: how nice of *you!*
And think: how I love *thee!*

═══════   [1828]

Young mare,
Honor of the Caucasian breed,
What are you speeding for, spirited one?
For you, too, the time has come:
Do not roll [your] skittish eye,   5
Do not fling [your] feet in the air,
In the field level and broad
Do not gallop willfully.
Wait: I shall compel you
To humble yourself beneath me: 10
Into a measured circle I shall direct your run
With a shortened bridle.

ПРЕДЧУВСТВИЕ   [1828]

Снова тучи надо мною
Собралися в тишине;
Рок завистливый бедою
Угрожает снова мне...
Сохраню ль к судьбе презренье?   5
Понесу ль навстречу ей
Непреклонность и терпенье
Гордой юности моей?

Бурной жизнью утомленный,
Равнодушно бури жду: 10
Может быть, еще спасенный,
Снова пристань я найду...
Но, предчувствуя разлуку,
Неизбежный, грозный час,
Сжать твою, мой ангел, руку   15
Я спешу в последний раз.

Ангел кроткий, безмятежный,
Тихо молви мне: *прости*,
Опечалься: взор свой нежный
Подыми иль опусти;   20
И твое воспоминанье
Заменит душе моей
Силу, гордость, упованье
И отвагу юных дней.

━━━━━━━━   [1828]

Ворон к ворону летит,
Ворон ворону кричит:
Ворон! где б нам отобедать?
Как бы нам о том проведать?

Ворон ворону в ответ: 5
Знаю, будет нам обед;

FOREBODING   [1828]

Once more clouds above me
Have gathered in silence;
Jealous destiny with trouble
Threatens me once more . . .
Will I keep contempt for fate?   5
Will I bring to meet it
The unyielding strength and patience
Of my prideful youth?

By a stormy life exhausted,
Calmly I await the storm: 10
It may be [that] once more rescued,
Anchorage again I'll find . . .
Parting, though, beforehand sensing,
[That] escapeless, dreadful hour,
I to press your hand, my angel,   15
Hasten for the last time.

Angel meek [and] unperturbing,
Speak to me a low "farewell,"
Mournful grow: your tender gaze
Lift it up or drop it low;   20
And the recollection of you
Will replace unto my soul
Vigor, pride, intoxication,
And the pluck of youthful days.

──────────   [1828]

Raven to raven flies,
Raven to raven cries:
Raven! where's to dine for us?
How shall we forage for it?

Raven to raven in reply: 5
I know there will be dinner for us;

В чистом поле под ракитой
Богатырь лежит убитый.

Кем убит и отчего,
Знает сокол лишь его,   10
Да кобылка вороная,
Да хозяйка молодая.

Сокол в рощу улетел,
На кобылку недруг сел,
А хозяйка ждет милого   15
Не убитого, живого.

━━━━━━━━━   [1828]

Город пышный, город бедный,
Дух неволи, стройный вид,
Свод небес зелено-бледный,
Скука, холод и гранит —
Всё же мне вас жаль немножко,   5
Потому что здесь порой
Ходит маленькая ножка,
Вьется локон золотой.

АНЧАР   [1828]

В пустыне чахлой и скупой,
На почве, зноем раскаленной,
Анчар, как грозный часовой,
Стоит — один во всей вселенной.

Природа жаждущих степей   5
Его в день гнева породила,

In the open field beneath a willow
A thane lies slain.

Killed by whom and for what cause,
That alone his falcon knows,   10
And his mare of raven hue
And his mistress young.

Falcon flew into the wold,
Mare was mounted by the foe,
And the mistress bides her loved one,   15
Not the slain one, but a live one.

—————————   [1828]

Gorgeous city, wretched city,
Slavedom's spirit, comely look,
Vault of heaven greenish-pallid,
Boredom, cold, and granite—
Still I grieve a bit to leave you   5
Because here from time to time
Goes a little foot a-walking,
Curls a golden ringlet.

THE UPAS TREE   [1828]

In sere and grudging wilderness,
On soil aglow with summer blazes
The Upas Tree, like a dread sentinel,
Stands—lone in all creation.

The nature of the thirsting steppes   5
Has born it on a day of wrath

И зелень мертвую ветвей
И корни ядом напоила.

Яд каплет сквозь его кору,
К полудню растопясь от зною,   10
И застывает ввечеру
Густой прозрачною смолою.

К нему и птица не летит
И тигр нейдет — лишь вихорь черный
На древо смерти набежит   15
И мчится прочь уже тлетворный.

И если туча оросит,
Блуждая, лист его дремучий,
С его ветвей уж ядовит
Стекает дождь в песок горючий.   20

Но человека человек
Послал к Анчару властным взглядом,
И тот послушно в путь потек
И к утру возвратился с ядом.

Принес он смертную смолу   25
Да ветвь с увядшими листами,
И пот по бледному челу
Струился хладными ручьями;

Принес — и ослабел и лег
Под сводом шалаша на лыки,   30
И умер бедный раб у ног
Непобедимого владыки.

А царь тем ядом напитал
Свои послушливые стрелы,
И с ними гибель разослал   35
К соседям в чуждые пределы.

And steeped the dead green of its branches
And its roots in venom.

The venom seeps across its bark,
Toward noon dissolving from the blaze,   10
And in the evening stiffens up
Into a thick transparent resin.

To it no bird will fly
Or tiger come: alone the swarthy whirlwind
Runs up upon the tree of death—   15
And rushes forth, by now death-dealing.

And if an errant cloud bedews
Its somnolent leaf,
Then from its branches, venomous now,
The rain runs down into the blazing sand.   20

But man by man
Was sent to the Upas with imperious glance,
And he obediently sped on his way
And came back with the venom by the morning.

He brought the deadly pitch   25
And a branch with withered leaves,
And sweat upon his pallid brow
Coursed down in chilly streams;

Brought it—and faltered and lay down
Beneath the vaulted tent upon the rushes,   30
And died, poor minion, at the feet
Of the unconquerable potentate.

As for the Tsar, he battened with this venom
His servile arrows,
And with them sent calamity abroad   35
On neighbors into alien parts.

[1828]

Ненастный день потух; ненастной ночи мгла
По небу стелется одеждою свинцовой;
Как привидение, за рощею сосновой
    Луна туманная взошла...
Всё мрачную тоску на душу мне наводит.   5
Далеко, там, луна в сиянии восходит;
Там воздух напоен вечерней теплотой;
Там море движется роскошной пеленой
    Под голубыми небесами...
Вот время: по горе теперь идет она   10
К брегам, потопленным шумящими волнами;
    Там, под заветными скалами,
Теперь она сидит печальна и одна...
Одна... никто пред ней не плачет, не тоскует;
Никто ее колен в забвенье не целует;   15
Одна... ничьим устам она не предает
Ни плеч, ни влажных уст, ни персей белоснежных.

. . . .
. . . .
. . . .   20

Никто ее любви небесной не достоин.
Не правда ль: ты одна... ты плачешь... я спокоен;
. . . .

Но если . . . .

[1828]

Счастлив, кто избран своенравно
Твоей тоскливою мечтой,
При ком любовью млеешь явно,
Чьи взоры властвуют тобой;
Но жалок тот, кто молчаливо,   5
Сгорая пламенем любви,
Потупя голову, ревниво
Признанья слушает твои.

———————   [1828]

The dismal day has flickered out; the dismal night's mist
Spreads over the sky like a leaden pall;
     Like a specter, behind the fir thicket
     A foggy moon has risen . . .
All [this] casts a dark gloom upon my soul.   5
Far off, over there, the moon rises in radiance;
There the air is saturated with evening warmth;
There the sea stirs like a luxurious film
     Under blue skies . . .
This is the time: now down the hill she walks   10
Toward the strand awash with rushing waves;
     There under [our] beloved crags
Now she is sitting mournful and alone.
Alone . . . nobody weeps before her, pines;
No one kisses her knees in oblivion;   15
Alone . . . to no one's lips does she surrender
[Her] shoulders, moist lips, snowy breasts.

.   .   .   .
.   .   .   .
.   .   .   .   20

No one is worthy of her heavenly love.
Is it not so: you are alone . . . you weep . . . I am at peace;
.   .   .   .

But if   .   .   .   .

———————   [1828]

Blest he who wantonly was chosen
By your fatigueful fancy,
Near whom you melt with love for all the world to see,
Whose glances lord it over you;
But wretched he who mutely,   5
Consumed with flame of love,
His head hung low, jealously,
Listens to your confessions.

━━━━━━━━━ [1829]

Я вас любил: любовь еще, быть может,
В душе моей угасла не совсем;
Но пусть она вас больше не тревожит;
Я не хочу печалить вас ничем.
Я вас любил безмолвно, безнадежно,   5
То робостью, то ревностью томим;
Я вас любил так искренно, так нежно,
Как дай вам бог любимой быть другим.

━━━━━━━━━ [1829]

Брожу ли я вдоль улиц шумных,
Вхожу ль во многолюдный храм,
Сижу ль меж юношей безумных,
Я предаюсь моим мечтам.

Я говорю: промчатся годы,   5
И сколько здесь ни видно нас,
Мы все сойдем под вечны своды —
И чей-нибудь уж близок час.

Гляжу ль на дуб уединенный,
Я мыслю: патриарх лесов   10
Переживет мой век забвенный,
Как пережил он век отцов.

Младенца ль милого ласкаю,
Уже я думаю: прости!
Тебе я место уступаю: 15
Мне время тлеть, тебе цвести.

День каждый, каждую годину
Привык я думой провождать,
Грядущей смерти годовщину
Меж их стараясь угадать.   20

[1829]

I used to love you: love has still, it may be,
Not died down altogether in my soul;
But may it not alarm you any longer;
I do not want to sadden you with aught.
I used to love you wordless, without hope,   5
With shyness now, with jealousy now racked;
I loved you so ingenuously, so dearly,
As God may grant you to be loved by another.

[1829]

Whether I wander along noisy streets
Or step into a temple dense with people,
Or sit among fervescent youth,
I give myself over to my fancies.

I say: the years will flash by,   5
And, as many of us as are to be seen here,
We all will descend beneath the eternal vaults—
And someone's hour is already near.

As I gaze upon a solitary oak,
I muse: the patriarch of the woods   10
Will outlive my forgotten age,
As it outlived [my] fathers' age.

When I caress a dear young child,
I am already thinking: farewell!
I yield my place to you: 15
It is time for me to wither, for you to flower.

Each day, each year
I have come to usher out in fancy,
Of [my] approaching death the anniversary
Intent to guess among them.   20

И где мне смерть пошлет судьбина?
В бою ли, в странствии, в волнах?
Или соседняя долина
Мой примет охладелый прах?

И хоть бесчувственному телу   25
Равно повсюду истлевать,
Но ближе к милому пределу
Мне всё б хотелось почивать.

И пусть у гробового входа
Младая будет жизнь играть,   30
И равнодушная природа
Красою вечною сиять.

К БЮСТУ ЗАВОЕВАТЕЛЯ   [1829]

Напрасно видишь тут ошибку:
Рука искусства навела
На мрамор этих уст улыбку,
А гнев на хладный лоск чела.
Недаром лик сей двуязычен.   5
Таков и был сей властелин:
К противочувствиям привычен,
В лице и в жизни арлекин.

And where will fate send me death
In battle, while roving, in the waves?
Or will the neighboring vale
Receive my dust grown-cold?[1]

And though to the unfeeling body   25
It is all one where it decays,
Yet near as may be to the dear environs
I would still like to lie at rest.

And at the entrance to the grave
May young life play,   30
And indifferent nature
Shine with everlasting beauty.

[1] This query is echoed by, among many others, Heinrich Heine when he asks
ca. 1825 in "Wo?":

> Wo wird einst des Wandermüden/ Letzte Ruhestätte sein?/ Unter Palmen in dem
> Süden?/ Unter Linden an dem Rhein?// Werd' ich wo in einer Wüste/ Einge-
> scharrt von fremder Hand?/ Oder ruh' ich an der Küste/ Eines Meeres in dem
> Sand?// Immerhin! Mich wird umgeben/ Gotteshimmel, dort wie hier,/ Und als
> Totenlampen schweben/ Nachts die Sterne über mir.

AT THE BUST OF A CONQUEROR[1]   [1829]

You're wrong to see an error here:
The hand of art has wrought
On the marble of these lips a smile,
And wrath on the chilly luster of the brow.
No wonder this face is double-tongued.   5
Such truly was this potentate:
Accustomed to conflicting feelings,
In face and in life a harlequin.

[1] Directed at Alexander I.

МОНАСТЫРЬ НА КАЗБЕКЕ   [1829]

Высоко над семьею гор,
Казбек, твой царственный шатер
Сияет вечными лучами.
Твой монастырь за облаками,
Как в небе реющий ковчег,   5
Парит, чуть видный, над горами.

    Далекий, вожделенный брег!
Туда б, сказав прости ущелью,
Подняться к вольной вышине!
Туда б, в заоблачную келью,   10
В соседство бога скрыться мне!..

ОБВАЛ   [1829]

Дробясь о мрачные скалы,
Шумят и пенятся валы,
И надо мной кричат орлы,
        И ропщет бор,
И блещут средь волнистой мглы   5
        Вершины гор.

Оттоль сорвался раз обвал,
И с тяжким грохотом упал,
И всю теснину между скал
        Загородил,   10
И Терека могущий вал
        Остановил.

Вдруг, истощась и присмирев,
О Терек, ты прервал свой рев;
Но задних волн упорный гнев   15
        Прошиб снега...

THE MONASTERY ON MT. KAZBEK   [1829]

   High above [thy] clan of mountains,
Kazbek, thy royal tent
Shines with eternal rays.
Thy monastery beyond the clouds,
Like in the skies a hovering ark,   5
Steams, barely visible above the peaks.

   Far-off, longed-for bank!
Thither, saying farewell to the gorge,
To rise up to the free height;
Thither I would, into a cell beyond the clouds,   10
Disappear to the neighborhood of God! . . .

THE SNOWSLIDE   [1829]

Shattering themselves into fragments against somber crags,
Roar and foam the waters,
And above me eagles scream,
     And the wildwood murmurs,
And there gleam amid the wave-born mist   5
     The mountain peaks.

From here a snowslide broke off once,
And with ponderous rumbling fell,
And the whole narrow space between the cliffs
     Dammed up,   10
And the Terek's mighty swell
     Arrested.

Suddenly, exhausted and calmed,
Oh, Terek, you interrupted your roar;
But the rearward waves' stubborn wrath   15
     Broke through the snows . . .

Ты затопил, освирепев,
        Свои брега.

И долго прорванный обвал
Неталой грудою лежал,   20
И Терек злой под ним бежал,
        И пылью вод
И шумной пеной орошал
        Ледяный свод.

И путь по нем широкий шел: 25
И конь скакал, и влекся вол,
И своего верблюда вёл
        Степной купец,
Где ныне мчится лишь Эол,
        Небес жилец.   30

━━━━━━━━   [1830]

Что в имени тебе моем?
Оно умрет, как шум печальный
Волны, плеснувшей в берег дальный,
Как звук ночной в лесу глухом.

Оно на памятном листке   5
Оставит мертвый след, подобный
Узору надписи надгробной
На непонятном языке.

Что в нем? Забытое давно
В волненьях новых и мятежных,   10
Твоей душе не даст оно
Воспоминаний чистых, нежных.

Но в день печали, в тишине,
Произнеси его тоскуя;

You swamped, enraged,
  Your banks.

And long the pierced-through snowslide
As an unthawing mass lay,   20
And angry Terek ran beneath it,
  And with water dust
And rushing foam bedewed
  The icy vault.

And a wide path along it went: 25
And steed cantered and ox trudged,
And his camel led
  The steppe merchant,
Where now speeds only Aeolus,
  Dweller of the heavens.   30

━━━━━━━━━━ [1830]

What is there for you in my name?[1]
It will die, like the mournful sound
Of a wave splashed-out at a distant shore,
Like a night sound in the toneless wood.

On the commemorative page   5
It will leave a dead trace, resembling
The pattern of an epitaph
In an unintelligible tongue.

What is there in it? Long forgotten
'Mid waves of feeling new and stormy,   10
It will not render to your soul
Remembrances unalloyed, tender.

But on a day of grief, in quiet,
Pronounce it as you suffer;

[1] Written in response to a request to write his name in the album of the Polish beauty, Countess Karolina Sobańska, already immortalized by the love of Mickiewicz.

Скажи: есть память обо мне,
Есть в мире сердце, где живу я...   15

━━━━━━━━ [1830]

Когда в объятия мои
Твой стройный стан я заключаю
И речи нежные любви
Тебе с восторгом расточаю,
Безмолвна, от стесненных рук   5
Освобождая стан свой гибкой,
Ты отвечаешь, милый друг,
Мне недоверчивой улыбкой;
Прилежно в памяти храня
Измен печальные преданья,   10
Ты без участья и вниманья
Уныло слушаешь меня...
Кляну коварные старанья
Преступной юности моей
И встреч условных ожиданья   15
В садах, в безмолвии ночей.
Кляну речей любовный шопот,
Стихов таинственный напев,
И ласки легковерных дев,
И слезы их, и поздний ропот.   20

ЦАРСКОСЕЛЬСКАЯ СТАТУЯ   [1830]

Урну с водой уронив, об утес ее дева разбила.
    Дева печально сидит, праздный держа черепок.
Чудо! не сякнет вода, изливаясь из урны разбитой;
    Дева, над вечной струей, вечно печальна сидит.

Say: there is memory of me,   15
There is in the world a heart in which I live.

────────   [1830]

When into my embraces
Your slender body I encompass
And tender words of love
Pour out to you with rapture,
In silence from my tightened arms   5
Freeing your supple form,
You answer me, dear friend,
With a mistrustful smile;
Earnestly in your memory storing
Betrayals' sorrowful reports,   10
Without involvement or attention
You glumly hear me out . . .
I curse the insidious endeavors
Of my red-handed youth,
And the [hours spent] awaiting trysts   15
In gardens, in the dead of night.
I curse the whispered words of love,
The secret melody of verses,
And the caress of trustful maidens,
Their tears, and their belated plaint.   20

FOUNTAIN AT TSARSKOE SELO   [1830]

Having dropped the urn of water, the maiden has
        broken it against a boulder.
    Sadly the maiden sits, holding the empty shard.
Marvel! The water does not dry up as it pours from the broken
        urn;
    Over a timeless stream, timelessly sad sits the maid.

ЗАКЛИНАНИЕ [1830]

О, если правда, что в ночи,
Когда покоятся живые,
И с неба лунные лучи
Скользят на камни гробовые,
О, если правда, что тогда   5
Пустеют тихие могилы,—
Я тень зову, я жду Леилы:
Ко мне, мой друг, сюда, сюда!

Явись, возлюбленная тень,
 Как ты была перед разлукой,   10
Бледна, хладна, как зимний день,
Искажена последней мукой.
Приди, как дальная звезда,
Как легкий звук иль дуновенье,
Иль как ужасное виденье,   15
Мне всё равно: сюда! сюда!..

Зову тебя не для того,
Чтоб укорять людей, чья злоба
Убила друга моего,
Иль чтоб изведать тайны гроба,   20
Не для того, что иногда
Сомненьем мучусь... но, тоскуя,
Хочу сказать, что всё люблю я,
Что всё я твой: сюда, сюда!

━━━━━━━━ [1830]

Для берегов отчизны дальной
Ты покидала край чужой;
В час незабвенный, в час печальный
Я долго плакал пред тобой.

CONJURY[1]   [1830]

Oh, if it is true that in the night,
When the living go to rest,
And from the heavens lunar rays
Glide on sepulchral stones,
Oh, if it is true that at that time   5
The silent graves are emptied,—
I call her shade, I wait for Leyla:
To me, my friend, come here, come here!

Appear [to me], beloved shade,
Such as you were before [our] parting,   10
As pale, as chill as winter's day,
By final agony distorted.
Come [to me] like a distant star,
Like some light sound or wafting,
Or like a dreadful apparition,   15
I do not care: come here, come here! . . .

I summon you not with a mind
To reprehend the men whose malice
Brought death upon my friend,
Or to spy out the secrets of the grave,   20
Or on the score that I at times
Am racked by doubts . . . but in my wretchedness
I want to say that I still love,
That still I'm yours: come here, come here!

[1] Barry Cornwall (pseudonym for the minor English dramatist and poet B. W. Procter, 1787–1874) published a poem with a similar title which, like other works of his, had some influence on Pushkin in this period.

───────   [1830]

For the shores of your distant country
You left the alien land;
That unforgotten hour, that mournful hour,
I long wept before you.

Мои хладеющие руки   5
Тебя старались удержать;
Томленье страшное разлуки
Мой стон молил не прерывать.

Но ты от горького лобзанья
Свои уста оторвала;   10
Из края мрачного изгнанья
Ты в край иной меня звала.
Ты говорила: «В день свиданья
Под небом вечно голубым,
В тени олив, любви лобзанья   15
Мы вновь, мой друг, соединим».

Но там, увы, где неба своды
Сияют в блеске голубом,
Где тень олив легла на воды,
Заснула ты последним сном.   20
Твоя краса, твои страданья
Исчезли в урне гробовой —
А с ними поцелуй свиданья...
Но жду его; он за тобой...

═══════════   [1831]

Перед гробницею святой
Стою с поникшею главой...
Всё спит кругом; одни лампады
Во мраке храма золотят
Столпов гранитные громады   5
И их знамен нависший ряд.

Под ними спит сей властелин,
Сей идол северных дружин,
Маститый страж страны державной,
Смиритель всех ее врагов,   10
Сей остальной из стаи славной
Екатерининских орлов.

My chiller-growing hands   5
Sought to detain you;
The terrible ordeal of parting
My groan implored [you] not to interrupt.

But you from the bitter kiss
Tore free your lips;   10
From gloomy exile's land
You called me to another land.
You kept on saying: "On the day of meeting
Beneath a sky forever blue,
In olive shade, love's kisses   15
We shall again, my friend, rejoin."

But there, alas, where vaults of heaven
Shine forth in radiance blue,
Where shade of olives rests upon the waters,
You fell into eternal sleep.   20
Your comeliness, your sufferings,
Are gone to the sepulchral urn—
And [gone] with them the kiss of meeting . . .
But I await it—as a debt you owe . . .

━━━━━━━   [1831]

Before the sacred sepulcher
I stand with lowered head . . .
All about is sleeping; alone the candelabra
Are gilding in the temple dusk
The throngs of granite pillars   5
And their standards' pendent row.

Beneath them sleeps that potentate
That idol of the northern warrior bands,
The hoary guardian of an empire land,
Subduer of its enemies all,   10
That relic of the glorious flock
Of Catherine's eagles.

В твоем гробу восторг живет!
Он русский глас нам издает;
Он нам твердит о той године, 15
Когда народной веры глас
Воззвал к святой твоей седине:
«Иди, спасай!» Ты встал — и спас...

Внемли ж и днесь наш верный глас,
Встань и спасай царя и нас, 20
О старец грозный! На мгновенье
Явись у двери гробовой,
Явись, вдохни восторг и рвенье
Полкам, оставленным тобой!

Явись и дланию своей 25
Нам укажи в толпе вождей,
Кто твой наследник, твой избранный!
Но храм — в молчанье погружен,
И тих твоей могилы бранной
Невозмутимый, вечный сон... 30

КЛЕВЕТНИКАМ РОССИИ [1831]

О чем шумите вы, народные витии?
Зачем анафемой грозите вы России?
Что возмутило вас? волнения Литвы?
Оставьте: это спор славян между собою,
Домашний, старый спор, уж взвешенный судьбою, 5
Вопрос, которого не разрешите вы.

Уже давно между собою
Враждуют эти племена;
Не раз клонилась под грозою
То их, то наша сторона. 10

In thy sepulcher lives keen ardor!
It speaks to us with Russian voice;
Relates to us of that great hour   15
When the voice of the nation's trust
Called to your sacred white-haired age:
"Come, save!" Thou didst rise—and save . . .

Then hark now, too, our trusting voice,
Rise up and save the Tsar and us,   20
Oh, grim old hero! For an instant
Appear at the sepulchral portal,
Appear, breathe ardor and élan
Into the regiments bequeathed by thee!

Appear and with thy reverend hand   25
Point out to us in the throng of leaders
Who thy successor is, thy chosen!
The temple, though—is sunk in silence,
And quiet is thy warlike tomb's
Unstirrable, eternal sleep . . .   30

TO THE SLANDERERS OF RUSSIA[1]   [1831]

What do you raise an outcry over, national bards?
Why do you threaten Russia with anathema?
What stirred you up? The throes of Lithuania?[2]
Desist: this is a strife of Slavs among themselves,
An old domestic strife, already weighed by fate,   5
An issue not to be resolved by you.

Long since among themselves
These tribes have been at war;
More than once has bent beneath the storm
Now their, now our side.   10

---

[1] This poem is Pushkin's angry reply to the clamor of indignation and calls for intervention generated in Western Europe by the brutal suppression of the Polish uprising of 1831, of which his friend Mickiewicz became the spokesman and spiritual leader abroad.

[2] Lithuania, joined with the Polish crown since 1386, often stood for Poland in poetic usage. Mickiewicz, whose home was Wilno, starts his great idyllic epic *Pan Tadeusz* with a nostalgic invocation of "Lithuania, my homeland."

Кто устоит в неравном споре:
Кичливый лях, иль верный росс?
Славянские ль ручьи сольются в русском море?
Оно ль иссякнет? вот вопрос.

Оставьте нас: вы не читали   15
Сии кровавые скрижали;
Вам непонятна, вам чужда
Сия семейная вражда;
Для вас безмолвны Кремль и Прага;
Бессмысленно прельщает вас   20
Борьбы отчаянной отвага —
И ненавидите вы нас...

За что ж? ответствуйте: за то ли,
Что на развалинах пылающей Москвы
Мы не признали наглой воли   25
Того, под кем дрожали вы?
За то ль, что в бездну повалили
Мы тяготеющий над царствами кумир
И нашей кровью искупили
Европы вольность, честь и мир?..   30

Вы грозны на словах — попробуйте на деле!
Иль старый богатырь, покойный на постеле,
Не в силах завинтить свой измаильский штык?
Иль русского царя уже бессильно слово?
Иль нам с Европой спорить ново?   35
Иль русский от побед отвык?
Иль мало нас? Или от Перми до Тавриды,
От финских хладных скал до пламенной Колхиды,
От потрясенного Кремля
До стен недвижного Китая,   40
Стальной щетиною сверкая,
Не встанет русская земля?..
Так высылайте ж нам, витии,
Своих озлобленных сынов:
Есть место им в полях России,   45
Среди нечуждых им гробов.

Who will prevail in the unequal strife:
The boastful Lekh, or the faithful Ross?[3]
Will the Slavonic streams converge in the Russian sea?
Will *it* dry up? Here is the question.

Leave us alone: you have not read   15
Those bloody tablets;
To you is unintelligible, to you is alien
This family feud;
Mute to you are the Kremlin and Praga;[4]
Unthinkingly you are beguiled   20
By the valor of a desperate struggle—
And you hate us . . .

And for what? Reply: is it because
On the ruins of blazing Moscow
We did not acknowledge the insolent will   25
Of him under whom you quaked?
Because we hurled into the abyss
The idol heavy-looming over kingdoms,
And with our blood redeemed
Europe's freedom, honor, and peace?   30

You are menacing in words—just try to be in action!
Is then the old thane, resting on his bed,
Unfit to mount his bayonet of Ismail?[5]
Or is the Russian Tsar's word powerless by now?
Or is it new to us to be at odds with Europe?   35
Or has the Russian grown unused to victories?
Are there too few of us? Or will, from Perm to Tauris,
From frigid crags of Finland to the flaming Colchis,
From the shaken Kremlin
To stagnant China's walls,   40
Flashing with steely bristle,
Not rise the Russian land?
Send then to us, oh, bards,
Your sons enraged:
There's room for them in Russia's fields,   45
'Mid graves that are not strange to them.

[3] Archaic terms for Pole and Russian, respectively.
[4] The suburb of Warsaw where the insurgents made their last desperate stand.
[5] The Turkish fortress in Bessarabia stormed by Suvorov in 1790.

ЭХО   [1831]

Ревет ли зверь в лесу глухом,
Трубит ли рог, гремит ли гром,
Поет ли дева за холмом —
　　　На всякий звук
Свой отклик в воздухе пустом   5
　　　Родишь ты вдруг.

Ты внемлешь грохоту громов
И гласу бури и валов,
И крику сельских пастухов —
　　　И шлешь ответ;   10
Тебе ж нет отзыва... Таков
　　　И ты, поэт!

КРАСАВИЦА   [1832]

Всё в ней гармония, всё диво,
Всё выше мира и страстей;
Она покоится стыдливо
В красе торжественной своей;
Она кругом себя взирает: 5
Ей нет соперниц, нет подруг;
Красавиц наших бледный круг
В ее сиянье исчезает.

Куда бы ты ни поспешал,
Хоть на любовное свиданье,   10
Какое б в сердце ни питал
Ты сокровенное мечтанье, —
Но, встретясь с ней, смущенный, ты
Вдруг остановишься невольно,
Благоговея богомольно   15
Перед святыней красоты.

ECHO[1]   [1831]

Should wild beast roar in toneless wood,
Should horn resound, should thunder peal,
Should maiden sing beyond the mound—
    To any sound
Your answer in the empty air   5
    You forthwith bear.

You hearken to the thunder's roll
And to the voice of storm and surf
And to the rustic shepherds' call—
    And send reply;   10
For you, though, no response . . . such are
    You, poet, too!

[1] The motif of this lyric appears to have been drawn from Barry Cornwall; see footnote to "Conjury."

A BEAUTY   [1832]

All in her is harmony, all marvel,
All higher than the earth and passions;
She bashfully remains sequestered
In her triumphant beauty;
She gazes about her: 5
She has no rivals, has no friends;
The pallid circle of our beauties
In her radiance vanishes.

Wherever you might have been hastening,
And if it were a lover's tryst,   10
Whatever in your heart been nursing
Of innermost private daydream—
Still, meeting her, you could, bewildered,
But willy-nilly come to halt,
Worshiping in pious awe   15
Before the sanctuary of beauty.

В АЛЬБОМ   [1832]

Долго сих листов заветных
Не касался я пером;
Виноват, в столе моем
Уж давно без строк приветных
Залежался твой альбом.   5
В именины, очень кстати,
Пожелать тебе я рад
Много всякой благодати,
Много сладостных отрад,—
На Парнасе много грома,   10
В жизни много тихих дней
И на совести твоей
Ни единого альбома
От красавиц, от друзей.

―――――   [1833]

Когда б не смутное влеченье
Чего-то жаждущей души,
Я здесь остался б — наслажденье
Вкушать в неведомой тиши:
Забыл бы всех желаний трепет,   5
Мечтою б целый мир назвал —
И всё бы слушал этот лепет,
Всё б эти ножки целовал...

―――――   [1833]

Не дай мне бог сойти с ума.
Нет, легче посох и сума;
    Нет, легче труд и глад.
Не то, чтоб разумом моим

ALBUM VERSE   [1832]

Long these intimate pages
I have not touched with [my] pen;
I apologize, in my desk
For a long time already without lines of greeting
Has your album lain and lain.   5
On [your] nameday, very opportunely,
I am glad to wish you
Much of every kind of blessing,
Many sweet comforts,
On Parnassus plenty of thunder,   10
In life plenty of quiet days,
And on your conscience
Not a single album
From fair ladies, from friends.

———————   [1833]

Were it not for the troubled urging
Of a soul athirst for who knows what,
I would stay here—delight to taste
In [this] unnoted quietude:
I would forget all wishing's flutter,   5
Would call a fancy all the world—
And would forever hark this lisping,
Forever kiss these little feet.

———————   [1833]

God grant that I not lose my mind.
No, easier were the staff and bag;
    No, easier toil and want.
It is not that my reason

Я дорожил; не то, чтоб с ним   5
    Расстаться был не рад:

Когда б оставили меня
На воле, как бы резво я
    Пустился в темный лес!
Я пел бы в пламенном бреду,   10
Я забывался бы в чаду
    Нестройных, чудных грез.

И я б заслушивался волн,
И я глядел бы, счастья полн,
    В пустые небеса;   15
И силен, волен был бы я,
Как вихорь, роющий поля,
    Ломающий леса.

Да вот беда: сойди с ума,
И страшен будешь как чума,   20
    Как раз тебя запрут,
Посадят на цепь дурака
И сквозь решетку как зверка
    Дразнить тебя придут.

А ночью слышать буду я   25
Не голос яркий соловья,
    Не шум глухой дубров—
А крик товарищей моих,
Да брань смотрителей ночных,
    Да визг, да звон оков.   30

[1835]

Юношу, горько рыдая, ревнивая дева бранила;
    К ней на плечо преклонен, юноша вдруг задремал.
Дева тотчас умолкла, сон его легкий лелея,
    И улыбалась ему, тихие слезы лия.

I treasure; not that with it   5
   I would not gladly part:

Were they to leave me
At liberty, how eagerly would I
   Make for the darkling wood!
In flaming frenzy would I sing,   10
Forget myself within a haze
   Of shapeless, wondrous dreams.

And I would hark my fill of waves,
And I would gaze, with gladness filled,
   Into the empty skies;   15
And strong were I, and free were I
   Like to the whirlwind gashing fields,
    [And] breaking forests down.

But here's the rub: go off your mind,
And men will dread you like the plague,   20
   [And] straightway lock you up,
Will put the madman on a chain
And, through the screen like some small beast,
   Will come to harass you.

And in the night I shall not hear   25
The nightingale's clear voice,
   Nor oak groves' murmurous rustle—
But my companions' cries,
And the night warders' curses,
   And shrieks, and clanging chains.   30

━━━━━━━━━━   [1835]

Bitterly sobbing, the jealous maiden was chiding the youth;
   Cradled against her shoulder, the youth of a sudden dozed off.
The maiden at once fell silent, lulling his light slumber,
   And was smiling at him, shedding quiet tears.

[1835]

Я думал, сердце позабыло
Способность легкую страдать,
Я говорил: тому, что было,
Уж не бывать! уж не бывать!
Прошли восторги, и печали,
И легковерные мечты...
Но вот опять затрепетали
Пред мощной властью красоты.

5

[Между 1827 и 1836]

Она глядит на вас так нежно,
Она лепечет так небрежно,
Она так тонко весела,
Ее глаза так полны чувством,
Вечор она с таким искусством
Из-под накрытого стола
Мне свою ножку подала!

5

(ИЗ ПИНДЕМОНТИ)   [1836]

Не дорого ценю я громкие права,
От коих не одна кружится голова.
Я не ропщу о том, что отказали боги
Мне в сладкой участи оспоривать налоги,
Или мешать царям друг с другом воевать;
И мало горя мне, свободно ли печать
Морочит олухов, иль чуткая цензура
В журнальных замыслах стесняет балагура.
Всё это, видите ль, *слова, слова, слова.* [1]
Иные, лучшие, мне дороги права;
Иная, лучшая, потребна мне свобода;

5

10

═══════════   [1835]

I thought my heart had quite forgotten
Its easy aptitude for pain,
I used to say: what was before
Shall be no more! shall be no more!
Gone are the raptures, and the sorrows,   5
And dreams too easily believed . . .
But here again they're set aquiver
At beauty's sovereign command.

═══════════   [Between 1827 and 1836]

   She gazes at you so tenderly,
She babbles away so carelessly,
She is so wittily gay,
Her eyes are so full of feeling,
Last night she with such deftness   5
From under the laid table
Gave me her little foot [to caress]!

FROM PINDEMONTE[1]   [1836]

I do not greatly value [those] loud rights
From which more than one head is spinning.
I do not mutter at the gods' having denied me
The sweet participation in disputing taxes
Or interfering with the kings at war with one another;   5
And it's small grief to me whether the Press is free
To mystify the numskulls, or a sensitive censorship
Does cramp some wag in journalistic schemes;
All this, you see, is "words, words, words."
Other [and] better rights are dear to me;   10
Another, better freedom do I need:

[1] Italian poet (1753–1828), to whom Pushkin ascribed this ode to privacy solely in order to hoodwink the censorship.

Зависеть от царя, зависеть от народа —
Не всё ли нам равно? Бог с ними.
Никому
Отчета не давать, себе лишь самому
Служить и угождать; для власти, для ливреи   15
Не гнуть ни совести, ни помыслов, ни шеи;
По прихоти своей скитаться здесь и там,
Дивясь божественным природы красотам,
И пред созданьями искусств и вдохновенья
Трепеща радостно в восторгах умиленья,   20
Вот счастье! вот права...

Be subject to a king, be subject to a nation—
Is it not all the same to us? Let them be. To nobody
To be accountable, oneself alone
To serve and please; to power, to a livery   15
Not [have to] bend nor conscience, nor ideas, nor neck;
By one's own whim to wander here and there,
Marveling at Nature's godlike beauties,
And before works of art and inspiration
Joyfully tremulous in transports of emotion: 20
There [is] happiness! There [are] rights . . .

Поэмы, Сказки

и Баллады

ЦАРЬ НИКИТА И СОРОК ЕГО ДОЧЕРЕЙ [1822]

Царь Никита жил когда-то
Праздно, весело, богато,
Не творил добра, ни зла,
И земля его цвела.
Царь трудился по немногу,   5
Кушал, пил, молился богу
И от разных матерей
Прижил сорок дочерей,
Сорок девушек прелестных,
Сорок ангелов небесных,   10
Милых сердцем и душой.
Что за ножка — боже мой,
А головка, темный волос,
Чудо — глазки, чудо — голос,
Ум — с ума свести бы мог.   15
Словом, с головы до ног
Душу, сердце всё пленяло.
Одного не доставало.
Да чего же одного?
Так, безделки, ничего.   20
Ничего иль очень мало,
Всё равно — не доставало.
Как бы это изъяснить,
Чтоб совсем не рассердить
Богомольной важной дуры,   25
Слишком чопорной цензуры?
Как быть?… Помоги мне, бог!
У царевен между ног…

Narrative Poems, Fairy Tales, and Ballads

TSAR NIKITA AND HIS FORTY DAUGHTERS   [1822]

Tsar Nikita lived once-upon-a-time
Idly, gaily, richly
Did not wreak good, or evil:
And his land bloomed.
He busied himself a little at a time: 5
Ate, drank, prayed to God,
And from various mothers
Came to have forty daughters,
Forty charming girls,
Forty heavenly angels,   10
Dear of heart and soul,
What little [foot] feet—my Lord!—
And little head, dark hair,
A marvel the eyes, a marvel the voice!
[Their] mind could make [you] lose [your] mind;   15
In a word, from head to foot [feet]
Everything captivated the soul, the heart;
One thing was missing
But what one thing, come?
As I say, a trifle, nothing—   20
Nothing or very little,
Still—it was missing.
How [is one] to clear this up
So as not to exasperate completely
That pious dignified dunce,   25
All too blue-nosed censorship?
How manage, God help me!—
Between the princesses' legs . . .

Нет, уж это слишком ясно
И для скромности опасно,—   30
Так иначе как-нибудь:
Я люблю в Венере грудь,
Губки, ножку особливо,
Но любовное огниво,
Цель желанья моего…   35
Что такое?… Ничего!…
Ничего, иль очень мало…
И того-то не бывало
У царевен молодых,
Шаловливых и живых.   40
Их чудесное рожденье
Привело в недоуменье
Все придворные сердца.
Грустно было для отца
И для матерей печальных…   45
А от бабок повивальных
Как узнал о том народ—
Всякий тут разинул рот,
Ахал, охал, дивовался,
А иной, хоть и смеялся,   50
Да тихонько, чтобы в путь
До Нерчинска не махнуть.
Царь созвал своих придворных,
Нянек, мамушек покорных—
Им держал такой приказ: 55
„Если кто-нибудь из вас
Дочерей греху научит,
Или мыслить их приучит,
Или только намекнет,
Что у них недостает,   60
Иль двусмысленное скажет,
Или кукиш им покажет,—
То—шутить я не привык—
Бабам вырежу язык,
А мужчинам нечто хуже,   65
Что порой бывает туже“.
Царь был строг, но справедлив,
А приказ красноречив;
Всяк со страхом поклонился,

No, even this is too clear
And dangerous for modesty—   30
So [let's get at it] some other way:
I love Venus' bosom,
[Her] little lips, little feet especially;
But love's focus—
The goal of my desire . . .   35
What is it? . . . Nothing! . . .
Nothing, or very little . . .
And that's just what was not there
With the young princesses
Frolicsome and lively.   40
Their outlandish birth
Threw into consternation
All hearts at court
It was sad for the father
And for the woebegone mothers . . .   45
And from the swaddling women
When the people found out about this—
Everyone gaped at it,
Oh'ed, oh'ed, marveled
And though one or the other laughed   50
Still [they did it] very quietly, in order not to be
Packed off to Nerchinsk.[1]
The Tsar summoned his courtiers,
The abashed nannies, mommies,
And pronounced a command as follows: 55
"If any one of you
Shall teach [my] daughters sinful things
Or induce them to (think) wonder
Or shall merely hint at
What is amiss with them,   60
Or say something ambiguous,
Or show [them] a finger[2]
Then—I am not in the habit of joking—
[If they are] ladies I shall cut out [their] tongue[s].
And [if they are] men, something worse,   65
A thing that at times gets stiffer!"
The Tsar was strict, but just,
And [his] command was eloquent.
Everyone bowed in fear,

[1] A place of deportation deep in Siberia.
[2] The Russian version of this forthright international gesture is called *kukiš*.

Остеречься всяк решился,   70
Ухо всяк держал востро
И хранил свое добро.
Жены бодные боялись,
Чтоб мужья не проболтались;
Втайне думали мужья: 75
„Провинись, жена моя!“
(Видно, сердцем были гневны).
Подросли мои царевны.
Жаль их стало. Царь — в совет;
Изложил там свой предмет: 80
Так и так—довольно ясно,
Тихо, шопотом, негласно,
Осторожнее от слуг.
Призадумались бояры,
Как лечить такой недуг.   85
Вот один советник старый
Поклонился всем — и вдруг
В лысый лоб рукою брякнул
И царю он так вавакнул:
„О, премудрый государь!   90
Не взыщи мою ты дерзость,
Если про плотскую мерзость
Расскажу, что было встарь.
Мне была знакома сводня
(Где она? и чем сегодня?   95
Верно тем же, чем была).
Баба ведьмою слыла,
Всем недугам пособляла,
Немощь членов исцеляла.
Вот ее бы разыскать;   100
Ведьма дело всё поправит:
А что надо—то и вставит“.

—„Так за ней сейчас послать!“
Восклицает царь Никита,
Брови сдвинувши сердито: 105
—„Тотчас ведьму отыскать!
Если ж нас она обманет,
Чего надо не достанет,
На бобах нас проведет,

Everyone resolved to take heed   70
Everyone pricked up his ears
And guarded his welfare.
Poor wives were afraid
That their husbands might blurt [it] out;
Husbands thought in private: 75
[If only] my wife fell into guilt! . . .
(One can see they were wroth at heart.)
My princesses grew up,
One came to pity them. The Tsar [went] into council,
Set forth his topic there   80
Thus and so, rather clearly,
Quickly, in a whisper, not aloud,
Discreetly [so as to keep it] from the servants.
The nobles fell into a study
How to heal such a defect.   85
Presently one old councillor
Bowed to everyone, and suddenly
Gave a ringing tap to his bald head
And blah-blah'ed to the Tsar thus:
"Oh most wise sovereign!   90
Do not turn upon my impertinence
If about a carnal coarseness
I tell that took place of old.
I used to know a procuress;
(Where is she, and what, today? . . .   95
Probably the same that she was.)
She was held to be a witch
All maladies she relieved,
Weakness of limbs she cured.
Now she would be the one to seek out.   100
She will remedy the whole business,
And will insert what is needed all right."

"Send for her at once, then,"
Pronounces Tsar Nikita,
His brows knitted angrily,   105
"Seek the sorceress out!
But if she should deceive us,
Not furnish what is needful
(Walk us on beans), play us a trick,

Или с умыслом солжет,—   110
Будь не царь я, а бездельник,
Если в чистый понедельник
Сжечь колдунью не велю:
И тем небо умолю“.

      Вот секретно, осторожно,   115
По курьерской подорожной
И во все земли концы
Были посланы гонцы.
Они скачут, всюду рыщут
И царю колдунью ищут.   120
Год проходит и другой—
Нету вести никакой.
Наконец один ретивый
Вдруг напал на след счастливый.
Он заехал в темный лес   125
(Видно, вел его сам бес),
Видит он: в лесу избушка,
Ведьма в ней живет, старушка.
Как он был царев посол,
То к ней прямо и вошел,   130
Поклонился ведьме смело,
Изложил царево дело:
Как царевны рождены
И чего все лишены.
Ведьма мигом всё смекнула…   135
В дверь гонца она толкнула,
Так примолвив: „Уходи
Поскорей и без оглядки,
Не то—бойся лихорадки…
Через три дня приходи   140
За посылкой и ответом,
Только помни—чуть с рассветом.“
После ведьма заперлась,
Уголечком запаслась,
Трое суток ворожила,   145
Так что беса приманила.
Чтоб отправить во дворец,
Сам принес он ей ларец,

Or by design tell a lie,—   110
Let me be a rascal and ne'er-do-well
If on Lenten Monday
I do not order the sorceress to be burnt,
And (with this I implore Heaven) of this let Heaven be witness."

Now secretly, cautiously,   115
With unrestricted travel passes
And to all corners of the earth
Messengers were sent:
They gallop everywhere, scamper,
And seek the witch for the Tsar.   120
A year passes and another,
But there is no news whatever.
At last one zealous one
Suddenly hit upon a lucky trail.
He rode into the dark forest   125
(Evidently the Devil himself was leading him),
He sees a little cabin in the wood,
In it lives the old witch-woman;
Since he [was] the Tsar's envoy,
He went straight in to her.   130
He bowed boldly to the witch,
Explained to her the Tsar's concern,
How the princesses had been born,
And what they were all deprived of.
The witch took it all in at once . . .   135
Pushed the messenger out through the door,
Saying the while, "Go away,
With all speed and without looking back,
Or else fear the fever.
In three days' time you come   140
For a package and an answer,
Just remember, right at dawn."
Then the witch locked herself in,
Got herself a little supply of coal,
For three days and nights cast spells,   145
So that she (lured to herself) conjured up the Devil.
To despatch to the palace,
He himself brought her a casket

Полный грешными вещами,
Обожаемыми нами.　　　　　　　　　　　150
Там их было всех сортов,
Всех размеров, всех цветов,
Всё отборные, с кудрями…
Ведьма все перебрала,
Сорок лучших оточла,　　　　　　　　　155
Их в салфетку завернула
И на ключ в ларец замкнула,
С ним отправила гонца,
Дав на путь серебреца.
Едет он. Заря зарделась…　　　　　　　160
Отдых сделать захотелось,
Захотелось закусить,
Жажду водкой утолить:
Он был малый аккуратный,
Всем запасся в путь обратный.　　　　165
Вот коня он разнуздал
И покойно кушать стал.
Конь пасется. Он мечтает,
Как его царь вознесет,
Графом, князем назовет.　　　　　　　170
Что же ларчик заключает?
Что царю в нем ведьма шлет?
В щелку смотрит: нет, не видно —
Заперт плотно. Как обидно!
Любопытство страх берет　　　　　　　175
И всего его тревожит.
Ухо он к замку приложит —
Ничего не чует слух;
Нюхает — знакомый дух…
Тьфу ты пропасть! что за чудо?　　　180
Посмотреть ей-ей не худо.
И не вытерпел гонец…
Но лишь отпер он ларец,
Птички — порх и улетели,
И кругом на сучьях сели　　　　　　　185
И хвостами завертели.
Наш гонец давай их звать,
Сухарями их прельщать:

Full of the sinful things
Adored by us.   150
There were all sorts of them there,
All sizes, all colors.
All select ones, all with curls . . .
The witch looked them over,
Counted off the forty best ones,   155
Wrapped them in a napkin
And locked them into the casket.
With it she despatched the messenger,
After giving him a piece of silver for the way.
He rides—the sunset started glowing . . .   160
He felt like taking a rest,
Felt like having a bite,
Slaking his thirst with vodka.
He was a methodical fellow,
Had provided himself with everything for the return trip;   165
Now he unbridled his horse
And started to eat in peace.
The charger is grazing; he is daydreaming
About how the Tsar will elevate him,
Appoint him count, prince.   170
Now what could the little casket contain?
What is the witch sending the Tsar in it?
Looking into the crack—nothing to be seen,
It is tightly locked . . . what a nuisance!
Curiosity takes [him] something dreadful   175
And troubles his whole person.
He lays his ear to the lock,
[His] hearing perceives nothing;
Sniffs—familiar scent!
What-the-devil queer business is this?   180
It wouldn't be half bad if I took a look;
And the messenger could not resist . . .
But hardly had he opened the casket,
[And] The little birds flew off in a swarm,
And settled on branches thereabouts   185
And flirted their tails.
Did he cry, did he call them,
Did he lure them with bits of dry bread!

Крошки сыплет—всё напрасно
(Видно кормятся не тем):   190
На сучках им петь прекрасно,
А в ларце сидеть зачем?
Вот тащится вдоль дороги,
Вся согнувшися дугой,
Баба старая с клюкой.   195
Наш гонец ей бухнул в ноги:
„Пропаду я с головой!
Помоги, будь мать родная!
Посмотри, беда какая:
Не могу их изловить!   200
Как же горю пособить?"
Вверх старуха посмотрела,
Плюнула и прошипела:
„Поступил ты хоть и скверно,
Но не плачься, не тужи…   205
Ты им только покажи—
Сами все слетят наверно".
„Ну, спасибо!" он сказал…
И лишь только показал—
Птички вмиг к нему слетели   210
И квартирой овладели.
Чтоб беды не знать другой,
Он без дальних отговорок
Тотчас их под ключ все сорок
И отправился домой.   215
Как княжны их получили,
Прямо в клетки посадили.
Царь на радости такой
Задал тотчас пир горой:
Семь дней сряду пировали,   220
Целый месяц отдыхали;
Царь совет весь наградил,
Да и ведьму не забыл:
Из кунсткамеры в подарок
Ей послал в спирту огарок,   225
(Тот, который всех дивил),
Две ехидны, два скелета
Из того же кабинета…

He strews crumbs—all in vain
(Evidently this is not what they feed on).   190
They have an excellent time singing on the branches,
What should they sit in the casket for?
There plods along the road
All bent (bowlike) double
An old woman on a (crook) crooked stick.   195
Our messenger, flop, [throws himself] to her feet:
"(I am going to be lost with my head)
    My head is at stake,
Help, be [my native mother] like a real mother to me!
Look what sort of trouble it is:
I cannot catch them;   200
How on earth relieve the misery?"
The old woman looked up,
Spat and hissed:
"Although you have behaved badly,
Still, don't complain, don't fret . . .   205
Just you show them—
They will all fly down on their own, likely."
"Why, thanks!" he said;
And hardly had he shown—
The birdies in a flash flew down to him   210
And took up [their] quarters;
Lest he get into more trouble,
Without lengthy excuses
He [clapped] all forty of them under [lock and] key
And set off for home.   215
When the princesses received them,
Straightaway [they] set them into [their] cages.
The Tsar at such a joy[ous event]
At once gave a (mountain) whale of a feast.
Seven days in a row they feasted,   220
A whole month they rested;
The Tsar rewarded the whole Council,
And did not forget the witch either:
From the museum as a gift
He sent her a candle-end in spirits   225
(The one which amazed everyone),
Two adders, two skeletons
Out of the same cabinet;

Награжден был и гонец.
Вот и сказочки конец.

Многие меня поносят
И теперь пожалуй спросят
Глупо так зачем шучу?
Что за дело им? Хочу!

The messenger also was rewarded—
And this is the end of the whole tale.   230

Many will abuse me,
And will perhaps ask now
Why I make such a silly joke!
What business is it of theirs? I want to!

ЦЫГАНЫ   [1824]

Цыганы шумною толпой
По Бессарабии кочуют.
Они сегодня над рекой
В шатрах изодранных ночуют.
Как вольность, весел их ночлег   5
И мирный сон под небесами;
Между колесами телег,
Полузавешанных коврами,
Горит огонь; семья кругом
Готовит ужин; в чистом поле   10
Пасутся кони; за шатром
Ручной медведь лежит на воле.
Все живо посреди степей:
Заботы мирные семей,
Готовых с утром в путь недальний,   15
И песни жен, и крик детей,
И звон походной наковальни.
Но вот на табор кочевой
Нисходит сонное молчанье,
И слышно в тишине степной   20
Лишь лай собак да коней ржанье.
Огни везде погашены.
Спокойно всё: луна сияет
Одна с небесной вышины
И тихий табор озаряет.   25
В шатре одном старик не спит;
Он перед углями сидит,
Согретый их последним жаром,
И в поле дальнее глядит,
Ночным подернутое паром.   30
Его молоденькая дочь
Пошла гулять в пустынном поле.
Она привыкла к резвой воле,
Она придет; но вот уж ночь,
И скоро месяц уж покинет   35
Небес далеких облака,—
Земфиры нет как нет; и стынет
Убогий ужин старика.

THE GYPSIES   [1824]

The Gypsies in a noisy throng
Roam about Bessarabia.
Today on a river bank they
Spend the night in [their] tattered tents.
Like freedom, gay is their night's camp   5
And peaceful [their] sleep beneath the heavens;
Between the wheels of the wagons,
Half-hung-over with rugs,
Burns the fire; the family around [it]
Cooks supper; in the bare field   10
Graze the horses; behind the tent
A tame bear lies at liberty.
All is lively amid the steppes:
The peaceful cares of the families,
Ready [to be off] by morning on the short [day's] trek,   15
And women's songs, and children's shouting
And the ring of the traveling anvil.
But presently upon the nomad train
Descends sleepy silence,
And one can hear in the steppe quiet   20
But the barking of dogs and the neighing of horses.
The lights everywhere are extinguished,
Quiet is all, the moon gleams
Alone from the heavenly height
And sheds her twilight over the quiet encampment.   25
In one tent an old man is awake;
He is sitting in front of the embers,
Warmed by their last glow;
And gazes at the distant field[s],
[Which are] covered by the mist of night.   30
His young daughter
Has gone to ramble in the deserted field[s]
She is inured to frisky freedom,
She will come [back]; but here it is night already,
And soon the moon will have left   35
The distant heaven's clouds—
Zemfira is missing as before; and
The old man's poor supper is growing cold.

Но вот она. За нею следом
По степи юноша спешит;   40
Цыгану вовсе он неведом.
«Отец мой,— дева говорит,—
Веду я гостя; за курганом
Его в пустыне я нашла
И в табор нà ночь зазвала.   45
Он хочет быть как мы цыганом;
Его преследует закон,
Но я ему подругой буду.
Его зовут Алеко — он
Готов идти за мною всюду».   50

Старик

Я рад. Останься до утра
Под сенью нашего шатра
Или пробудь у нас и доле,
Как ты захочешь. Я готов
С тобой делить и хлеб и кров.   55
Будь наш — привыкни к нашей доле,
Бродящей бедности и воле —
А завтра с утренней зарей
В одной телеге мы поедем;
Примись за промысел любой: 60
Железо куй иль песни пой
И селы обходи с медведем.

Алеко

Я остаюсь.

Земфира

            Он будет мой —
Кто ж от меня его отгонит?
Но поздно... месяц молодой   65
Зашел; поля покрыты мглой,
И сон меня невольно клонит...

———

But here she is. Following behind her
Over the steppe a young man hurries;   40
To the gypsy he is quite unknown.
"My father," says the maiden,
"I am bringing a guest, behind the mound
In the wasteland I found him
And called him to the camp for the night.   45
He wants to be a gypsy like us;
He is pursued by the law,
But I will be his love.
His name is Aleko—he
Is ready to follow me everywhere."   50

Old Man

I am glad. Stay till morning
Under the shelter of our tent
Or else make a longer stay with us,
As you wish. I am ready
To share with you both bread and roof.   55
Be one of us—get used to our lot,
Wandering poverty and freedom—
And tomorrow by dawn
We shall get under way in the same wagon;
Take up any pursuit you like: 60
Forge iron and sing songs
And make the rounds of the villages with the bear.

Aleko

I am staying!

Zemfira

He shall be mine:
Who is there to drive him from me?
But it is late . . . the young moon   65
Has set; the fields are covered with mist,
And I can't help being (bowed) overcome by sleep . . .

———

Светло. Старик тихонько бродит
Вокруг безмолвного шатра.
«Вставай, Земфира: солнце всходит,   70
Проснись, мой гость! пора, пора!..
Оставьте, дети, ложе неги!..»
И с шумом высыпал народ;
Шатры разобраны; телеги
Готовы двинуться в поход.   75
Всё вместе тронулось — и вот
Толпа валит в пустых равнинах.
Ослы в перекидных корзинах
Детей играющих несут;
Мужья и братья, жены, девы,   80
И стар и млад вослед идут;
Крик, шум, цыганские припевы,
Медведя рев, его цепей
Нетерпеливое бряцанье,
Лохмотьев ярких пестрота,   85
Детей и старцев нагота,
Собак и лай, и завыванье,
Волынки говор, скрып телег,
Всё скудно, дико, всё нестройно,
Но всё так живо-неспокойно,   90
Так чуждо мертвых наших нег,
Так чуждо этой жизни праздной,
Как песнь рабов однообразной!

———

Уныло юноша глядел
На опустелую равнину   95
И грусти тайную причину
Истолковать себе не смел.
С ним черноокая Земфира,
Теперь он вольный житель мира,
И солнце весело над ним   100
Полуденной красою блещет;
Что ж сердце юноши трепещет?
Какой заботой он томим?

Птичка божия не знает
Ни заботы, ни труда;   105

It is light. The old man is quietly wandering
Around the silent tent.
"Get up, Zemfira: the sun is rising,   70
Wake up, my guest, it's time, it's time!
Leave, children, the couch of bliss!"
And noisily the tribe came pouring out;
The tents were taken down; the wagons
[Were] ready to get moving on the trek.   75
Everything started off at one time—and here is
The throng pressing [on] in the empty plains.
Asses carry in throw-over [-the-back] baskets
Playing children;
Husbands and brothers, wives, maidens,   80
Both old and young follow along;
Shouting, noise, gypsy airs,
The bear's roar, his chains'
Impatient jangling,
The motley of bold-colored rags,   85
The children's and old men's nakedness,
Dogs' barking and yelping,
The bagpipe's voice, the wagons' creak,
All wretched, wild, all disorderly,
But all so briskly-restless   90
So foreign to our deathly pleasures
So foreign to this idle life
[That is] monotonous as the song of slaves!

———

Moodily the young man gazed
At the deserted plain   95
And [his] sorrow's secret cause
Dares not interpret to himself.
Black-eyed Zemfira is with him,
He is now a free dweller of the world,
And the sun gaily above him   100
In its noonday beauty gleams;
Why then does the young man's heart quake?
By what care is he oppressed?

God's little bird does not know
Either care or toil;   105

Хлопотливо не свивает
Долговечного гнезда;
В долгу ночь на ветке дремлет;
Солнце красное взойдет,
Птичка гласу бога внемлет,   110
Встрепенется и поет.
За весной, красой природы,
Лето знойное пройдет —
И туман и непогоды
Осень поздняя несет: 115
Людям скучно, людям горе;
Птичка в дальные страны,
В теплый край, за сине море
Улетает до весны.

Подобно птичке беззаботной,   120
И он, изгнанник перелетный,
Гнезда надежного не знал
И ни к чему не привыкал.
Ему везде была дорога,
Везде была ночлега сень;   125
Проснувшись поутру, свой день
Он отдавал на волю бога,
И жизни не могла тревога
Смутить его сердечну лень.
Его порой волшебной славы   130
Манила дальная звезда;
Нежданно роскошь и забавы
К нему являлись иногда;
Над одинокой головою
И гром нередко грохотал;   135
Но он беспечно под грозою
И в вёдро ясное дремал.
И жил, не признавая власти
Судьбы коварной и слепой;
Но боже! как играли страсти   140
Его послушною душой!
С каким волнением кипели
В его измученной груди!
Давно ль, надолго ль усмирели?
Они проснутся: погоди!   145

Does not bustlingly weave
A long-enduring nest;
In the long night on a twig it slumbers;
Let the fair sun rise,
And the little bird harks the voice of God,   110
Ruffles its feathers and sings.
After spring, the glory of nature,
Glowing summer will pass—
And fog and bad weather
Late autumn brings: 115
People find it irksome, to people it is distress;
The little bird to far-off countries
To a warm land beyond the blue sea
Flies off until the spring.

Like the carefree little bird,   120
He, too, exile of swift passage,
Did not know a steady nest
And did not grow used to anything.
To him everywhere was a road,
Everywhere was shelter for a night's stay;   125
Having woken in the morning, his day
He would give over to the will of God,
And life's alarms could not
Trouble his heart's indolence.
At times, of magic fame   130
The far-off star would lure him;
Unlooked-for luxury and amusements
Came his way sometimes;
Over his lonely head
Thunder, too, rumbled more than once;   135
But carefree beneath the storm
And under clear skies he slumbered;
And he lived, not taking cognizance of the power
Of Fate designing and blind;
But God! how the passions played   140
With his pliable soul!
With what turmoil they seethed
In his tormented breast!
Long since, for long have they abated?
They will wake up: wait!   145

————

Земфира

Скажи, мой друг: ты не жалеешь
О том, что бросил навсегда?

Алеко

Что ж бросил я?

Земфира

       Ты разумеешь:
Людей отчизны, города.

Алеко

О чем жалеть? Когда б ты знала,   150
Когда бы ты воображала
Неволю душных городов!
Там люди, в кучах за оградой,
Не дышат утренней прохладой,
Ни вешним запахом лугов;   155
Любви стыдятся, мысли гонят,
Торгуют волею своей,
Главы пред идолами клонят
И просят денег да цепей.
Что бросил я? Измен волненье,   160
Предрассуждений приговор,
Толпы безумное гоненье
Или блистательный позор.

Земфира

Но там огромные палаты,
Там разноцветные ковры,   165
Там игры, шумные пиры,
Уборы дев там так богаты!..

Алеко

Что шум веселий городских?
Где нет любви, там нет веселий.

———

ZEMFIRA

Tell [me], my friend: you don't regret
What you have given up forever?

ALEKO

What have I given up?

ZEMFIRA

        You understand:
The people of [your] homeland, the cities.

ALEKO

What is there to regret? If you knew,   150
If you could imagine
The servitude of stifling towns!
There people in throngs behind a barrier
Do not breathe the morning cool,
Nor the vernal perfume of meadows;   155
Of love they are ashamed, thought they persecute,
They trade their freedom,
Bow their heads before idols
And ask for money and for chains.
What have I given up? The heart-stir of betrayals,   160
The verdict of preconceived opinions,
The mob's mindless hue and cry,
Or glittering vice.

ZEMFIRA

But there are vast halls there,
There are carpets of many colors,   165
There are games, clamorous feasts,
The girls' dresses are so rich there—!

ALEKO

What of the noise of city pleasures?
Where love is not, there are no pleasures.

А девы... Как ты лучше их 170
И без нарядов дорогих,
Без жемчугов, без ожерелий!
Не изменись, мой нежный друг!
А я... одно мое желанье
С тобой делить любовь, досуг 175
И добровольное изгнанье!

Старик

Ты любишь нас, хоть и рожден
Среди богатого народа.
Но не всегда мила свобода
Тому, кто к неге приучен. 180
Меж нами есть одно преданье:
Царем когда-то сослан был
Полудня житель к нам в изгнанье.
(Я прежде знал, но позабыл
Его мудреное прозванье.) 185
Он был уже летами стар,
Но млад и жив душой незлобной —
Имел он песен дивный дар
И голос, шуму вод подобный —
И полюбили все его, 190
И жил он на брегах Дуная,
Не обижая никого,
Людей рассказами пленяя;
Не разумел он ничего,
И слаб, и робок был, как дети; 195
Чужие люди за него
Зверей и рыб ловили в сети;
Как мерзла быстрая река
И зимни вихри бушевали,
Пушистой кожей покрывали 200
Они святого старика;
Но он к заботам жизни бедной
Привыкнуть никогда не мог;
Скитался он иссохший, бледный,
Он говорил, что гневный бог 205
Его карал за преступленье...
Он ждал: придет ли избавленье.

And the girls . . . How much better you are than they   170
Even without costly finery,
Without pearls, without necklaces!
Do not change, my tender love!
And I—my one desire
[Is] to share with you love, leisure,   175
And voluntary exile!

OLD MAN

  You like us, though you were born
Amid a rich nation.
But not always dear is freedom
To one inured to a soft life.   180
There is a certain story handed down among us:
By the Emperor there once was deported
A dweller of the South[1] into exile with us.
(I used to know, but have forgotten
His outlandish name.)   185
He was already old in years,
Yet young and lively in his guileless soul—
He had the wondrous gift of song
And a voice like the sound of rushing waters—
And all grew fond of him,   190
And he lived on the banks of the Danube,
Giving no offense to anyone,
Charming the people with [his] tales;
He did not understand anything,
And was weak and timid, as children are;   195
Strangers for him
Caught game and fish in nets;
When the swift river froze
And the wintry gusts raged,
With fluffy fur they covered   200
The saintly old man;
But he to the concern of [our] poor life
Never could accustom himself;
He wandered, withered, pale,
He used to say that an angry God   205
Was punishing him for a transgression . . .
He waited for deliverance to come.

---

[1] The legend alludes to Ovid, the Roman poet banished by Augustus in A.D. 8
to Tomi on the Black Sea, not far from Bessarabia, the setting of *The Gypsies*
and Pushkin's own temporary place of exile.

И всё несчастный тосковал,
Бродя по берегам Дуная,
Да горьки слезы проливал,   210
Свой дальный град воспоминая;
И завещал он, умирая,
Чтобы на юг перенесли
Его тоскующие кости,
И смертью — чуждой сей земли   215
Неуспокоенные гости!

Алеко

Так вот судьба твоих сынов,
О Рим, о громкая держава!..
Певец любви, певец богов,
Скажи мне, что такое слава?   220
Могильный гул, хвалебный глас,
Из рода в роды звук бегущий?
Или под сенью дымной кущи
Цыгана дикого рассказ?

———

Прошло два лета. Так же бродят   225
Цыганы мирною толпой;
Везде по-прежнему находят
Гостеприимство и покой.
Презрев оковы просвещенья,
Алеко волен, как они;   230
Он без забот и сожаленья
Ведет кочующие дни.
Всё тот же он; семья всё та же;
Он, прежних лет не помня даже,
К бытью цыганскому привык.   235
Он любит их ночлегов сени,
И упоенье вечной лени,
И бедный, звучный их язык.
Медведь, беглец родной берлоги,
Косматый гость его шатра,   240
В селеньях, вдоль степной дороги,
Близ молдаванского двора
Перед толпою осторожной

And constantly the luckless man grieved,
Roving by the banks of the Danube,
And shed bitter tears,   210
Recalling his far-off city,
And, dying, he ordained
That they transfer to the South
His sorrowing bones,
This alien soil's   215
Guests unappeased even by death!

ALEKO

Is this, then, the fate of your sons,
Oh, Rome, oh (loud) far-famed power . . .
Singer of love, singer of gods,
Tell me, what is glory?   220
A hollow sound from the grave, a voice in praise,
From generation to generation on-speeding sound?
Or under the shade of a smoky shelter
A wild gypsy's tale?

Two years passed. In the same way wander   225
The gypsies in peaceful throng;
Everywhere as before they find
Hospitality and rest.
Having spurned the shackles of enlightenment,
Aleko is free like them;   230
Without cares or regret
He passes the roving days.
He is the same still, the family is the same still;
Former years not remembering even,
He has grown inured to the gypsy way of life.   235
He is fond of the shelter of their night's encampments,
And the intoxication of everlasting leisureliness,
And their frugal tuneful tongue.
The bear, fugitive from its native lair,
Shaggy guest of his tent,   240
In the settlement along the prairie road,
Near a Moldavian homestead
Before a cautious crowd

И тяжко пляшет, и ревет,
И цепь докучную грызет;   245
На посох опершись дорожный,
Старик лениво в бубны бьет,
Алеко с пеньем зверя водит,
Земфира поселян обходит
И дань их вольную берет.   250
Настанет ночь; они все трое
Варят нежатое пшено;
Старик уснул... и всё в покое,
В шатре и тихо, и темно.

———

     Старик на вешнем солнце греет   255
Уж остывающую кровь;
У люльки дочь поет любовь.
Алеко внемлет и бледнеет.

Земфира

     Старый муж, грозный муж,
Режь меня, жги меня: 260
Я тверда; не боюсь
Ни ножа, ни огня.

     Ненавижу тебя,
Презираю тебя;
Я другого люблю,   265
Умираю любя.

Алеко

Молчи. Мне пенье надоело,
Я диких песен не люблю.

Земфира

     Не любишь? мне какое дело!
Я песню для себя пою.   270

     Режь меня, жги меня;
Не скажу ничего;

Ponderously dances and roars
And gnaws at the irksome chain;   245
Leaning on his wayfarer's staff,
The old man unhurriedly strikes the tambourine,
Aleko sings and leads the beast around,
Zemfira makes the round of the villagers
And gathers their voluntary tribute.   250
Night falls; all three they
Cook the gleaned millet;
The old man has gone to sleep—and all is at peace.
In the tent it is quiet and dark.

———

The old man in the spring sunshine warms   255
His already cooling blood;
By the cradle [his] daughter sings [of] love.
Aleko listens and turns pale.

ZEMFIRA

Old husband, grim husband,
Slash me, burn me: 260
I am firm; I fear
Neither knife nor fire.

I hate you,
I despise you;
I love another,   265
Am dying of love.

ALEKO

Be quiet. I am sick of [your] singing,
I do not like [those] barbarous songs.

ZEMFIRA

You don't? What do I care!
I am singing the song for myself.   270

Slash me, burn me
I won't say anything

Старый муж, грозный муж,
Не узнаешь его.

Он свежее весны,   275
Жарче летнего дня;
Как он молод и смел!
Как он любит меня!

Как ласкала его
Я в ночной тишине!   280
Как смеялись тогда
Мы твоей седине!

Алеко

Молчи, Земфира! я доволен...

Земфира

Так понял песню ты мою?

Алеко

Земфира!

Земфира

       Ты сердиться волен,   285
Я песню про тебя пою.
(Уходит и поет: «Старый муж» и проч.)

Старик

   Так, помню, помню — песня эта
Во время наше сложена,
Уже давно в забаву света
Поется меж людей она.   290
Кочуя на степях Кагула,
Ее, бывало, в зимню ночь
Моя певала Мариула,
Перед огнем качая дочь.
В уме моем минувши лета   295
Час от часу темней, темней;
Но заронилась песня эта
Глубоко в памяти моей.

Old husband, grim husband,
You shall not find him out.

He is fresher than spring,   275
Hotter than summer's day;
How he is young and bold!
How he loves me!

How I caressed him
In the still of the night,   280
How we laughed then
At your gray hair!

ALEKO

Be quiet, Zemfira! Enough . . .

ZEMFIRA

So you have understood my song?

ALEKO

Zemfira!

ZEMFIRA

Be angry if you like,   285
I am singing the song about you.
Goes off singing "Old husband," etc.

OLD MAN

Yes, I remember, I remember—This song
Was made up in our time;
It has long, to entertain the public,
Been sung among the people.   290
Roaming in the Kaǧul steppes,
My Mariula used to sing it
Once in a while of a winter night,
In front of the fire, dandling her daughter.
In my mind the bygone years   295
Hour by hour [grow] darker, darker;
But that song has settled
Deep in my memory.

———

Всё тихо; ночь. Луной украшен
Лазурный юга небосклон.   300
Старик Земфирой пробужден:
«О мой отец! Алеко страшен.
Послушай: сквозь тяжелый сон
И стонет, и рыдает он».

Старик

Не тронь его. Храни молчанье.   305
Слыхал я русское преданье:
Теперь полунощной порой
У спящего теснит дыханье
Домашний дух; перед зарей
Уходит он. Сиди со мной.   310

Земфира

Отец мой! шепчет он: Земфира!

Старик

Тебя он ищет и во сне:
Ты для него дороже мира.

Земфира

Его любовь постыла мне.
Мне скучно; сердце воли просит —   315
Уж я... Но тише! слышишь? он
Другое имя произносит...

Старик

Чье имя?

Земфира

Слышишь? хриплый стон
И скрежет ярый!.. Как ужасно!..
Я разбужу его...

All is quiet; it is night. The moon adorns
The azure southern firmament;   300
The old man is awakened by Zemfira:
"Oh my father! Aleko frightens [me]
Listen: through [his] heavy sleep
He groans and sobs."

OLD MAN

Do not touch him. Keep silent.   305
I have heard of an old Russian belief:
Now at the midnight hour
A sleeper's breathing is stifled
By a domestic spirit; before dawn
It goes away. Sit with me.   310

ZEMFIRA

Father mine! He whispers: "Zemfira!"

OLD MAN

You he seeks even in sleep:
To him you are dearer than [all] the world.

ZEMFIRA

His love has turned stale to me.
I am bored; [my] heart asks freedom—   315
Already I . . . but hush! you hear? he
Utters another name . . .

OLD MAN

Whose name?

ZEMFIRA

                    You hear? A hoarse groan
And violent gnashing . . . ! How horrible!
I will wake him . . .

Старик

Напрасно,   320
Ночного духа не гони —
Уйдет и сам...

Земфира

Он повернулся,
Привстал, зовет меня... проснулся —
Иду к нему, — прощай, усни.

Алеко

Где ты была?

Земфира

С отцом сидела: 325
Какой-то дух тебя томил;
Во сне душа твоя терпела
Мученья; ты меня страшил:
Ты, сонный, скрежетал зубами
И звал меня.

Алеко

Мне снилась ты.   330
Я видел, будто между нами...
Я видел страшные мечты!

Земфира

Не верь лукавым сновиденьям.

Алеко

Ах, я не верю ничему:
Ни снам, ни сладким увереньям,   335
Ни даже сердцу твоему.

———

Old Man

No use,　　　　　　　　　　　　　　320
Do not chase off the night spirit,
It will leave of itself . . .

Zemfira

He has turned over,
Has half-risen, is calling me . . . He has woken up
I am going to him—farewell, go to sleep.

Aleko

Where have you been?

Zemfira

I sat with Father.　　　　　　　325
Some spirit was plaguing you;
In [your] sleep your soul suffered
Torments; you frightened me:
In [your] sleep you ground your teeth
And called me.

Aleko

I dreamt of you.　　　　　　　　330
I dreamed that between us . . .
I had dreadful dreams!

Zemfira

Do not believe deceptive dreams.

Aleko

Ah, I believe nothing:
Neither dreams, nor sweet assurances,　　　335
Nor even your heart.

———

Старик

О чем, безумец молодой,
О чем вздыхаешь ты всечасно?
Здесь люди вольны, небо ясно,
И жены славятся красой.   340
Не плачь: тоска тебя погубит.

Алеко

Отец, она меня не любит.

Старик

Утешься, друг: она дитя.
Твое унынье безрассудно:
Ты любишь горестно и трудно,   345
А сердце женское — шутя.
Взгляни: под отдаленным сводом
Гуляет вольная луна;
На всю природу мимоходом
Равно сиянье льет она.   350
Заглянет в облако любое,
Его так пышно озарит —
И вот — уж перешла в другое;
И то недолго посетит.
Кто место в небе ей укажет,   355
Примолвя: там остановись.
Кто сердцу юной девы скажет:
Люби одно, не изменись.
Утешься.

Алеко

Как она любила!
Как, нежно преклонясь ко мне,   360
Она в пустынной тишине
Часы ночные проводила!
Веселья детского полна,
Как часто милым лепетаньем
Иль упоительным лобзаньем   365
Мою задумчивость она

OLD MAN

What, young hothead,
What do you sigh for all the time?
Here men are free, the sky is clear,
And women famed for beauty.   340
Weep not: grief will undo you.

ALEKO

Father, she does not love me.

OLD MAN

Console yourself, friend: she is a child.
Your sorrowing is unreasonable:
You love with bitterness and travail,   345
A woman's heart—in fun.
Behold: beneath the far-off vault
Wanders the moon;
Upon all nature in her passing
Evenly she pours her radiance.   350
She will look in at random on a cloud,
Will illumine it so splendidly—
And lo—has passed on to another;
And it, too, she will visit not for long.
Who will appoint to her a place in heaven   355
And say: there you shall come to rest!
Who shall tell a youthful maiden's heart:
Love one thing only, do not change?
Console yourself.

ALEKO

How she loved!
How tenderly bent toward me,   360
Did she in the silence of the wilderness
While away the hours of night!
Full of childish gaiety,
How often with [her] dear babbling
Or her intoxicating kiss   365
She contrived to dispel in a moment

В минуту разогнать умела!..
И что ж? Земфира неверна?
Моя Земфира охладела!..

Старик

Послушай: расскажу тебе   370
Я повесть о самом себе.
Давно, давно, когда Дунаю
Не угрожал еще москаль
(Вот видишь, я припоминаю,
Алеко, старую печаль),   375
Тогда боялись мы султана,
А правил Буджаком паша
С высоких башен Аккермана —
Я молод был; моя душа
В то время радостно кипела;   380
И ни одна в кудрях моих
Еще сединка не белела —
Между красавиц молодых
Одна была... и долго ею
Как солнцем любовался я   385
И наконец назвал моею...

Ах, быстро молодость моя
Звездой падучею мелькнула!
Но ты, пора любви, минула
Еще быстрее: только год   390
Меня любила Мариула.

Однажды близ Кагульских вод
Мы чуждый табор повстречали;
Цыганы те, свои шатры
Разбив близ наших у горы,   395
Две ночи вместе ночевали.
Они ушли на третью ночь,—
И, б勿ся маленькую дочь,
Ушла за ними Мариула.
Я мирно спал — заря блеснула,   400
Проснулся я, подруги нет!
Ищу, зову — пропал и след...

My thoughtful mood . . . !
And [now] what? Zemfira faithless . . . !
My Zemfira grown cold . . . !

OLD MAN

Listen: I will tell you   370
A story about myself.
Long, long ago, when the Danube
Was not yet menaced by the Moskal[2]—
(There, you see, I am recalling,
Aleko, an old grievance.)   375
At that time we feared the Sultan,
And the Budzhak[3] was ruled by a pasha
From the lofty towers of Ak-Kerman—
I was young; my soul
In those days was joyfully astir;   380
And amid my curls
Not a single touch of white shone as yet;
Among the fair young girls
There was one . . . and long
I took delight in her as in the sun,   385
And in the end called her my own . . .

Ah, swiftly my youth
Like a falling star flashed by!
But you, season of love, passed
More swiftly still: only a year   390
Did Mariula love me.

Once near the waters of Kağul
We fell in with an unknown band;
Those gypsies, having pitched their tents
Close to ours by a hillside,   395
Spent two nights together [with us].
They went off on the third night—
And abandoning [our] little daughter,
Mariula went off after them.
I was peacefully asleep; the dawn glinted,   400
I woke up, my love was gone!
I search, I call—all trace was lost.

[2] Derogatory Slavic, especially Polish, term for "Muscovite."
[3] The Budzhak (Turkish: *bucak*, "corner," probably from the angle between the Prut and the Danube) is the extensive *puszta*-like prairieland of southern Bessarabia.

Тоскуя, плакала Земфира,
И я заплакал — с этих пор
Постыли мне все девы мира;   405
Меж ими никогда мой взор
Не выбирал себе подруги —
И одинокие досуги
Уже ни с кем я не делил.

Алеко

Да как же ты не поспешил   410
Тотчас вослед неблагодарной
И хищникам и ей коварной,
Кинжала в сердце не вонзил?

Старик

К чему? вольнее птицы младость;
Кто в силах удержать любовь?   415
Чредою всем дается радость;
Что было, то не будет вновь.

Алеко

Я не таков. Нет, я не споря
От прав моих не откажусь!
Или хоть мщеньем наслажусь.   420
О нет! когда б над бездной моря
Нашел я спящего врага,
Клянусь, и тут моя нога
Не пощадила бы злодея;
Я в волны моря, не бледнея,   425
И беззащитного б толкнул;
Внезапный ужас пробужденья
Свирепым смехом упрекнул,
И долго мне его паденья
Смешон и сладок был бы гул.   430

———

Молодой цыган

Еще одно... одно лобзанье...

Zemfira pined and cried,
I broke down and cried too; ever since
All the world's maids have grown distasteful to me;   405
Never did my glance among them
Seek itself out a lover,
And [my] lonesome leisure
I have not shared with anyone since.

ALEKO

But how is it that you did not hurry   410
Forthwith after the ungrateful woman
And did not plunge a dagger into the hearts
Of the robbers and the treacherous woman?

OLD MAN

To what end? Freer than a bird is youth;
Who has the power to restrain love?   415
To each in his turn joy is granted;
What has been will not be again.

ALEKO

I am not like that. No, I will not without contest
Renounce my rights!
Or at least I will enjoy revenge.   420
Oh, no! If over the bottomless depth of the sea
I found [my] enemy asleep,
I swear, even there my foot
Would not spare the villain;
Into the waves of the sea, unblanching,   425
Would I thrust him, helpless as he was;
The sudden horror of his waking
With savage laughter I would upbraid,
And long would the rushing sound of his fall
Make me laugh and exult.   430

———

YOUNG GYPSY

One more . . . one more kiss . . .

Земфира
Пора: мой муж ревнив и зол.

Цыган
Одно... но доле!.. на прощанье.

Земфира
Прощай, покамест не пришел.

Цыган
Скажи — когда ж опять свиданье?   435

Земфира
Сегодня, как зайдет луна.
Там за курганом над могилой...

Цыган
Обманет! не придет она!

Земфира
Вот он! беги!.. Приду, мой милый.

———

Алеко спит: в его уме   440
Виденье смутное играет;
Он с криком пробудясь во тьме,
Ревниво руку простирает;
Но обробелая рука
Покровы хладные хватает —   445
Его подруга далека...
Он с трепетом привстал и внемлет...
Всё тихо — страх его объемлет,
По нем текут и жар и хлад;
Встает он, из шатра выходит,   450
Вокруг телег, ужасен, бродит;
Спокойно всё; поля молчат;

ZEMFIRA

It is time: my husband is jealous and angry.

GYPSY

Just one—but longer! For good-byes.

ZEMFIRA

Farewell, before he comes.

GYPSY

Say—when shall we meet again?   435

ZEMFIRA

Tonight, when the moon rises.
There, beyond the mound above the grave . . .

GYPSY

She will deceive [me]! She will not come!

ZEMFIRA

Here he is! Run! . . . I will come, my dear.

———

Aleko is asleep. Within his mind   440
A turbid fancy is at play;
Waking up with a shout in the gloom,
He jealously reaches out with his hand;
But grown hesitant, his hand
Grasps cold covers—   445
His beloved is far away . . .
With a shudder he has half-risen and listens:
All is quiet—terror clutches him,
[Waves of] heat and cold run over him;
He gets up, goes out of the tent,   450
Stalks, fearful [to behold], about the wagons;
All is calm; the fields are silent,

Темно; луна зашла в туманы,
Чуть брезжит звезд неверный свет,
Чуть по росе приметный след   455
Ведет за дальные курганы:
Нетерпеливо он идет,
Куда зловещий след ведет.

    Могила на краю дороги
Вдали белеет перед ним...   460
Туда слабеющие ноги
Влачит, предчувствием томим,
Дрожат уста, дрожат колени,
Идет... и вдруг... иль это сон?
Вдруг видит близкие две тени   465
И близкий шепот слышит он —
Над обесславленной могилой.

1-й голос

Пора...

2-й голос

Постой...

1-й голос

    Пора, мой милый.

2-й голос

Нет, нет, постой, дождемся дня.

1-й голос

Уж поздно.

2-й голос

    Как ты робко любишь.   470
Минуту!

It is dark; the moon has passed into the fogs,
The stars' uncertain light barely glimmers.
A barely discernible trail in the dew   455
Leads beyond the far-off mounds:
Impatiently he strides
Where the ill-boding trail leads.

   A tomb by the edge of the path
Shines whitely in the distance before him . . .   460
There [his] faltering feet
He drags, haunted by a presentiment;
His lips tremble, his knees tremble,
He walks [on] . . . and suddenly . . . or is it a dream?
Suddenly he sees two nearby shadows   465
And nearby whispering he hears.
Upon the desecrated tomb.

FIRST VOICE

It's time . . .

SECOND VOICE

Stay . . .

FIRST VOICE

It's time, my dear.

SECOND VOICE

No, no, stay, let's await the day.

FIRST VOICE

It's late already.

SECOND VOICE

How timidly you love.   470
[One] minute [more]!

1-й голос
Ты меня погубишь.

2-й голос
Минуту!

1-й голос
Если без меня
Проснется муж?..

Алеко
Проснулся я.
Куда вы! не спешите оба;
Вам хорошо и здесь у гроба.   475

Земфира
Мой друг, беги, беги...

Алеко
Постой!
Куда, красавец молодой?
Лежи!
(*Вонзает в него нож.*)

Земфира
Алеко!

Цыган
Умираю...

Земфира
Алеко, ты убьешь его!   480
Взгляни: ты весь обрызган кровью!
О, что ты сделал?

Алеко
Ничего.
Теперь дыши его любовью.

FIRST VOICE

You will ruin me.

SECOND VOICE

[One] minute!

FIRST VOICE

What if while I am gone
My husband should wake up . . . ?

ALEKO

He is awake.
Where are you off to? Don't hurry, you two;
You are in a good place right here by the grave.   475

ZEMFIRA

My love, run, run . . .

ALEKO

Stay!
Where away, young gallant?
Lie there!
            Thrusts a knife into him.

ZEMFIRA

Aleko!

GYPSY

I am dying . . .

ZEMFIRA

Aleko, you will kill him!   480
Look: you are all bespattered with blood!
Oh, what have you done?

ALEKO

Never mind.
Now breathe [of] his love.

Земфира

Нет, полно, не боюсь тебя! —
Твои угрозы презираю,
Твое убийство проклинаю...

485

Алеко

Умри ж и ты!

(Поражает ее.)

Земфира

Умру любя...

———

Восток, денницей озаренный,
Сиял. Алеко за холмом,
С ножом в руках, окровавленный,
Сидел на камне гробовом.
Два трупа перед ним лежали;
Убийца страшен был лицом.
Цыганы робко окружали
Его встревоженной толпой.
Могилу в стороне копали.
Шли жены скорбной чередой
И в очи мертвых целовали.
Старик-отец один сидел
И на погибшую глядел
В немом бездействии печали;
Подняли трупы, понесли
И в лоно хладное земли
Чету младую положили.
Алеко издали смотрел
На всё... когда же их закрыли
Последней горстию земной,
Он молча, медленно склонился
И с камня на траву свалился.

490

495

500

505

Тогда старик, приближась, рек:
«Оставь нас, гордый человек!

510

ZEMFIRA

No, enough, I am not afraid of you!
Your threats I spurn,   485
Your murder I curse . . .

ALEKO

Die, then, you too!

Stabs her.

ZEMFIRA

I die in love . . .

————

The east, illumined by the morning star,
Was gleaming. Aleko, beyond the mound,
Knife in hand(s), bloodied,   490
Sat on the tombstone.
Two corpses lay before him,
The murderer was terrible of aspect.
The gypsies timidly surrounded
Him in an abashed throng.   495
Off on one side they were digging a grave.
The women came in sorrowing procession
And kissed the dead [couple] on the eyes.
The old father sat alone
And gazed at the dead girl   500
In the numb torpor of grief;
They lifted the bodies up, carried them off,
And into the chill lap of the earth
Laid the youthful couple.
Aleko from afar watched   505
It all . . . but when they had covered them
With the last handful of earth,
He silently, slowly leaned forward
And fell heavily from the stone onto the grass.

Then the old man approached and spoke: 510
"Leave us, prideful man!

Мы дики; нет у нас законов.
Мы не терзаем, не казним—
Не нужно крови нам и стонов,—
Но жить с убийцей не хотим...   515
Ты не рожден для дикой доли,
Ты для себя лишь хочешь воли;
Ужасен нам твой будет глас:
Мы робки и добры душою,
Ты зол и смел,— оставь же нас,   520
Прости, да будет мир с тобою».

Сказал — и шумною толпою
Поднялся табор кочевой
С долины страшного ночлега.
И скоро всё в дали степной   525
Сокрылось; лишь одна телега,
Убогим крытая ковром,
Стояла в поле роковом.
Так иногда перед зимою,
Туманной, утренней порою,   530
Когда подъемлется с полей
Станица поздних журавлей
И с криком вдаль на юг несется,
Пронзенный гибельным свинцом,
Один печально остается,   535
Повиснув раненым крылом.
Настала ночь; в телеге темной
Огня никто не разложил,
Никто под крышею подъемной
До утра сном не опочил.   540

ЭПИЛОГ

Волшебной силой песнопенья
В туманной памяти моей
Так оживляются виденья
То светлых, то печальных дней.

В стране, где долго, долго брани   545
Ужасный гул не умолкал,

We are savages; we have no laws,
We do not torture, do not put [men] to death—
We have no need of blood and groans—
But live with a murderer we will not . . .   515
You were not born for the life of the wild,
You for yourself alone crave freedom;
Dreadful will be your voice for us:
We are timid and good of soul,
You are fierce and bold—leave us then;   520
Farewell, may peace be with you."

   He spoke—and in a noisy throng
Rose the nomadic camp
From the vale of the dreadful night's stay.
And soon all had vanished   525
In the distance of the steppes. A single wagon,
Covered with a poor rug,
Stood in the fateful field.
Thus sometimes before winter,
At a foggy time of morning,   530
When there rises from the fields
A flock of belated cranes
And with screaming soars afar to the south,
Pierced by the fatal lead,
One will sadly remain behind,   535
Its wounded wing hanging.
Night came on; in the dark wagon
No one laid a fire,
No one under the folding hood
Rested in sleep until morning.   540

EPILOGUE

   By the magic power of song
In my hazy memory
Visions thus revive
Now of sunny, now of mournful days.

   In the land where long, long the dread   545
Clamor of arms never fell silent,

Где повелительные грани
Стамбулу русский указал,
Где старый наш орел двуглавый
Еще шумит минувшей славой,   550
Встречал я посреди степей
Над рубежами древних станов
Телеги мирные цыганов,
Смиренной вольности детей.
За их ленивыми толпами   555
В пустынях часто я бродил,
Простую пищу их делил
И засыпал пред их огнями.
В походах медленных любил
Их песен радостные гулы —   560
И долго милой Мариулы
Я имя нежное твердил.

   Но счастья нет и между вами,
Природы бедные сыны!..
И под издранными шатрами   565
Живут мучительные сны.
И ваши сени кочевые
В пустынях не спаслись от бед,
И всюду страсти роковые,
И от судеб защиты нет.   570

Where the Russian marked for Stambul
His imperious borders,
Where our old double-headed eagle
Still rustles with its bygone glory,   550
I used to meet amid the steppes
On the boundaries of ancient forts
The peaceful wagons of the gypsies
Children of lowly freedom.
Behind their leisurely swarms   555
In the wildernesses I often roamed,
Their simple fare I shared
And fell asleep before their fires.
On [those] slow treks I loved
Their songs' joyous ring—   560
And for a long time sweet Mariula's
Tender name I spoke over and over.

    But there is no happiness even among you,
Nature's poor sons . . . !
Even beneath tattered tents   565
Dwell tormenting dreams,
Even your nomadic shelters
In the wilderness have not escaped misfortunes
And everywhere are fateful passions,
And against the Fates there is no defense.   570

ЖЕНИХ   [1825]

Три дня купеческая дочь
  Наташа пропадала;
Она на двор на третью ночь
  Без памяти вбежала.
С вопросами отец и мать   5
К Наташе стали приступать.
  Наташа их не слышит,
  Дрожит и еле дышит.

Тужила мать, тужил отец,
  И долго приступали,
И отступились наконец,   10
  А тайны не узнали.
Наташа стала, как была,
Опять румяна, весела,
  Опять пошла с сестрами
  Сидеть за воротами.   15

Раз у тесовых у ворот,
  С подружками своими,
Сидела девица — и вот
  Промчалась перед ними
Лихая тройка с молодцом.   20
Конями, крытыми ковром,
  В санях он стоя правит,
  И гонит всех, и давит.

Он, поровнявшись, поглядел,   25
  Наташа поглядела,
Он вихрем мимо пролетел,
  Наташа помертвела.
Стремглав домой она бежит.
«Он! он! узнала! — говорит, —   30
  Он, точно он! держите,
  Друзья мои, спасите!»

Печально слушает семья,
  Качая головою;

THE BRIDEGROOM   [1825]

Three days the merchant's daughter,
   Natasha, had been missing;
On the third night she came
   Running into the house, distracted.
With questions [her] father and mother   5
Began to ply Natasha.
   Natasha does not hear them,
   Trembles and barely breathes.

Her mother grieved, her father grieved,
   And long insisted,   10
And in the end desisted,
   And did not learn the secret.
Natasha turned, as she had been,
Rosy again [and] merry,
   Again went with [her] sisters   15
   To sit outside the gate.

Once at the shingled (at the) gate,
   With her girl friends
Sat the maiden—and lo,
   There flashed past before them   20
A dashing troika with a fine lad.
The horses, covered with a rug,
   He drives standing in the sleigh,
   And scatters all and runs over [all].

Having drawn level, he glanced,   25
   Natasha glanced,
He like the whirlwind sped past,
   Natasha was petrified.
Headlong she runs home.
"[It's] he, [it's] he! I recognized [him]!" she says,   30
   "He, he indeed! Hold him,
   My friends, save me!"

In sorrow her family listens,
   Shaking [their] head[s];

Отец ей: «Милая моя,
   Откройся предо мною,
Обидел кто тебя, скажи,
Хоть только след нам укажи».   35
   Наташа плачет снова
   И более ни слова.   40

Наутро сваха к ним на двор
   Нежданная приходит.
Наташу хвалит, разговор
   С отцом ее заводит:
«У вас товар, у нас купец;   45
Собою парень молодец,
   И статный, и проворный,
   Не вздорный, не зазорный.

Богат, умен, ни перед кем
   Не кланяется в пояс,
А как боярин между тем   50
   Живет, не беспокоясь;
А подарит невесте вдруг
И лисью шубу, и жемчуг,
   И перстни золотые,   55
   И платья парчевые.

Катаясь, видел он вчера
   Ее за воротами;
Не по рукам ли, да с двора,
   Да в церковь с образами?»   60
Она сидит за пирогом,
Да речь ведет обиняком,

   А бедная невеста
   Себе не видит места.

«Согласен, — говорит отец; —   65
   Ступай благополучно,
Моя Наташа, под венец:
   Одной в светелке скучно.
Не век девицей вековать,
Не всё касатке распевать,   70

[Her] father [says] to her: "My dear one,   35
  Open [your heart] before me.
[If] someone has offended you, tell [me],
Show us but a trace."
  Natasha is weeping again.
  And not a word more [did she speak].   40

In the morning a marriage-broker woman
  Comes to their place unexpectedly.
[She] praises Natasha, a conversation
  With her father [she] begins:
"You have the goods, we have a buyer;   45
The lad is a fine young fellow
  (Both) well-made and lissome,
  Not quarrelsome, not dissolute.

"He's rich, he's clever, not before anyone
  Does he bow to the waist,   50
And like a nobleman at that
  He lives without a care;
And he is apt to give [his] bride
(Both) a fox-fur coat, and a pearl,
  And gold rings,   55
  And brocaded dresses.

"Driving about, he saw her
  Yesterday outside the gate;
[Shall we] not shake hands, and [be] off,
  And [go] to the church with the ikons?"   60
She sits having cake,
And beats around the bush,
  While the poor bride-to-be
  Is in a quandary.

"I agree," says [her] father;   65
  "Step with good luck,
My Natasha, under the wreath:
  [To sit] alone in the upper room is dull.
[It is] not [right] for a maiden to live [her] span [as a maiden],
Not for the swallow always to sing,   70

Пора гнездо устроить,
Чтоб детушек покоить».

Наташа к стенке уперлась
   И слово молвить хочет —
Вдруг зарыдала, затряслась,   75
   И плачет и хохочет.
В смятенье сваха к ней бежит,
Водой студеною поит
   И льет остаток чаши
   На голову Наташи.   80

Крушится, охает семья.
   Опомнилась Наташа
И говорит: «Послушна я,
   Святая воля ваша.
Зовите жениха на пир,   85
Пеките хлебы на весь мир,
   На славу мед варите,
   Да суд на пир зовите».

«Изволь, Наташа, ангел мой!
   Готов тебе в забаву   90
Я жизнь отдать!» — И пир горой;
   Пекут, варят на славу.
Вот гости честные нашли,
За стол невесту повели;
   Поют подружки, плачут,   95
   А вот и сани скачут.

Вот и жених — и все за стол.
   Звенят, гремят стаканы;
Заздравный ковш кругом пошел;
   Всё шумно, гости пьяны.   100

Жених

«А что же, милые друзья,
Невеста красная моя
   Не пьет, не ест, не служит:
   О чем невеста тужит?»

It is time to build a nest,
So as to nurture little children."

Natasha has leaned back against the wall
   And is about to speak—
Of a sudden she gave a sob, and a shudder,   75
   And weeps and laughs loudly.
In dismay the broker-woman runs up to her,
Gives her well water to drink
   And pours the rest of the tumbler
   On Natasha's head.   80

The family is distressed [and] moans.
   Natasha has come to her senses.
And says: "I obey,
   Sacred is your will.
Call [my] betrothed to the feast,   85
Bake loaves for all the world,
   Brew a mead worth remembering,
   And call the law to the feast."

"You name it, Natasha, my angel!
   I am ready for your delight   90
To give my life!"—And a mountainous feast [is prepared];
   They bake [and] cook to make a brave show.
Here worthy guests galore have come,
The bride has been led to table;
   The bridesmaids sing [and] cry,   95
   And here the sleigh [and team] comes galloping.

And here is the bridegroom—and all [sit down] to table.
   The glasses ring [and] clatter,
The toasting bowl went round;
   All is noisy, the guests are drunk.   100

BRIDEGROOM

"Why is it, dear friends,
My fair bride
   Is not drinking, not eating, not serving;
   What is [my] bride fretting about?"

Невеста жениху в ответ: 105
 «Откроюсь наудачу.
Душе моей покоя нет,
 И день и ночь я плачу.
Недобрый сон меня крушит».
Отец ей: «Что ж твой сон гласит? 110
 Скажи нам, что такое,
 Дитя мое родное?»

«Мне снилось,— говорит она,—
 Зашла я в лес дремучий,
И было поздно; чуть луна   115
 Светила из-за тучи;
С тропинки сбилась я; в глуши
Не слышно было ни души,
 И сосны лишь да ели
 Вершинами шумели.   120

И вдруг, как будто наяву,
 Изба передо мною.
Я к ней, стучу — молчат. Зобу —
 Ответа нет; с мольбою
Дверь отворила я. Вхожу — 125
В избе свеча горит; гляжу —
 Везде сребро да злато,
 Всё светло и богато».

Жених

«А чем же худ, скажи, твой сон?
 Знать, жить тебе богато». 130

Невеста

«Постой, сударь, не кончен он.
 На серебро, на злато,
На сукна, коврики, парчу,
На новгородскую камчу
 Я молча любовалась   135
 И диву дивовалась.

The bride [says] to the bridegroom in reply: 105
   "I will tell all as best I can.
There is no peace for my soul,
   And day and night I weep:
An evil dream afflicts me."
The father [says] to her: "Well, what does your dream say?   110
   Tell us, what is it,
   My own baby?"

"I dreamed," she says,
   "I had gone into a dense forest,
And it was late; barely the moon   115
   Shone from behind a cloud;
I had strayed from the path: in the toneless depth
Not a soul was to be heard,
   And pines alone and firs
   Rustled with their crowns.   120

"And suddenly, as if I were awake,
   A hut [rose] before me.
I [go up] to it, knock—silence. I call—
   There is no answer; with a prayer
I opened the door. I enter—   125
In the hut a candle burns; I look—
   Everywhere [is] silver and gold,
   All is bright and rich."

BRIDEGROOM

"But what is bad, tell [me], about your dream?
   It means you are going to live in wealth."   130

BRIDE

"Stay, sir, it is not finished.
   Upon the silver, on the gold,
Upon the cloths, the rugs, brocade,
Upon the silk from Novgorod
   I feasted silently my eyes   135
   And wondered at the marvel.

Вдруг слышу крик и конский топ...
   Подъехали к крылечку.
Я поскорее дверью хлоп
   И спряталась за печку.   140
Вот слышу много голосов...
Взошли двенадцать молодцов,
   И с ними голубица
   Красавица-девица.

Взошли толпой, не поклонясь,   145
   Икон не замечая;
За стол садятся, не молясь
   И шапок не снимая.
На первом месте брат большой,
По праву руку брат меньшой,   150
   По леву голубица
   Красавица-девица.

Крик, хохот, песни шум и звон,
   Разгульное похмелье...»

Жених

«А чем же худ, скажи, твой сон?   155
   Вещает он веселье».

Невеста

«Постой, сударь, не кончен он.
Идет похмелье, гром и звон,
   Пир весело бушует,
   Лишь девица горюет.   160

Сидит, молчит, ни ест, ни пьет
   И током слезы точит,
А старший брат свой нож берет,
   Присвистывая точит;
Глядит на девицу-красу,   165
И вдруг хватает за косу,
   Злодей девицу губит,
   Ей праву руку рубит».

"Suddenly I hear a shout and horses' hoofbeat . . .
  Someone has ridden up to the porch.
I quickly up and slam the door
  And hide behind the stove.   140
Now I hear a lot of voices . . .
Twelve fine lads have entered,
  And with them a dear girl,
  A maiden fair and pure.

"They came thronging in, without bowing,   145
  Not noticing the ikons;
They sat down to table, without praying
  Or taking off their caps.
At the head the (big) eldest brother [sits],
On [his] right hand the (smaller) younger brother,   150
  On [his] left the dear girl,
  The maiden fair and pure.

"Shouting, laughter, songs, din, and clatter,
  Uproarious carousal . . ."

BRIDEGROOM

"But what's so bad, tell [me], about your dream?   155
  It bodes a wedding feast."

BRIDE

"Stay, sir, it is not finished.
On go carousing, roar, and clang,
  The feast [is] boisterous with merriment,
  Alone the maiden sorrows.   160

She sits, is silent, neither eats nor drinks,
  And streams with stream of tears,
Then the eldest brother takes his knife,
  [And] whets [it], whistling the while;
Looks at the maiden fair,   165
And of a sudden seizes [her] by the braid,
  The villain kills the maiden,
  Cuts off her right hand."

«Ну, это,— говорит жених,—
    Прямая небылица!   170
Но не тужи, твой сон не лих,
    Поверь, душа-девица».
Она глядит ему в лицо.
«А это с чьей руки кольцо?»
    Вдруг молвила невеста,   175
    И все привстали с места.

Кольцо катится и звенит,
    Жених дрожит, бледнея;
Смутились гости.— Суд гласит:
    «Держи, вязать злодея!»   180
Злодей окован, обличен
И скоро смертию казнен.
    Прославилась Наташа!
    И вся тут песня наша.

"Why, this," the bridegroom says,
   "Is downright nonsense!   170
But do not fret, your dream is not evil,
   Believe [me], maiden love."
She looks him in the face.
"And from whose hand [does] this ring [come]?"
   The bride says of a sudden,   175
   And all have half-risen from [their] place[s].

The ring rolls and clinks,
   The bridegroom, blanching, trembles;
The guests [stand] bewildered.—The law bids:
   "Halt, bind the villain!"   180
The villain is put in irons, convicted,
And presently put to death.
   Glory has come to Natasha!
   And here our song is done.

ГРАФ НУЛИН   [1825]

Пора, пора! рога трубят;
Псари в охотничьих уборах
Чем свет уж на конях сидят,
Борзые прыгают на сворах.
Выходит барин на крыльцо,   5
Всё, подбочась, обозревает;
Его довольное лицо
Приятной важностью сияет.
Чекмень затянутый на нем,
Турецкий нож за кушаком,   10
За пазухой во фляжке ром,
И рог на бронзовой цепочке.
В ночном чепце, в одном платочке,
Глазами сонными жена
Сердито смотрит из окна   15
На сбор, на псарную тревогу...
Вот мужу подвели коня;
Он холку хвать и в стремя ногу,
Кричит жене: не жди меня!
И выезжает на дорогу.   20

В последних числах сентября
(Презренной прозой говоря)
В деревне скучно: грязь, ненастье,
Осенний ветер, мелкий снег
Да вой волков.— Но то-то счастье   25
Охотнику! Не зная нег,
В отъезжем поле он гарцует,
Везде находит свой ночлег,
Бранится, мокнет и пирует
Опустошительный набег.   30

А что же делает супруга
Одна в отсутствии супруга?
Занятий мало ль есть у ней:
Грибы солить, кормить гусей,
Заказывать обед и ужин,   35
В анбар и в погреб заглянуть,—

COUNT NULIN   [1825]

It's time, it's time! the horns blare;
The whippers in hunting costumes
By [first] light already sit on their horses;
The borzois leap at the leashes.
The squire steps out onto the porch,   5
Surveys everything, arms akimbo;
His contented face
Shines with pleasant [self-] importance.
He wears a trim Cossack coat,
A Turkish knife tucked in his sash,   10
In his bosom, rum in a little flask,
And a horn on a little bronze chain.
With nightcap on, wearing just a little shawl,
[His] wife with sleepy eyes
Crossly looks out of the window   15
At the assembly, at the bustle of huntsmen.
Here they have led up the husband's horse;
He lays hold of the withers—and foot into stirrup,
Shouts to the wife: "Don't wait for me!"
And rides out on [his] way.   20

In the final days of September
(Speaking in disdained prose)
It's dreary in the country, mud, foul weather,
Autumn wind, fine snow,
And the howl of wolves. But this very thing is happiness   25
To the huntsman! A stranger to soft luxury,
In a remote field he prances,
Finds anywhere his night's billet,
Grumbles, gets soaked, and exults in
The devastating assault.   30

But what does the spouse do,
Alone in her spouse's absence?
Does she lack for employment?
Mushrooms to pickle, geese to feed,
Dinner and supper to order,   35
Storeroom and cellar to look into.

Хозяйки глаз повсюду нужен:
Он вмиг заметит что-нибудь.

К несчастью, героиня наша...
(Ах! я забыл ей имя дать.   40
Муж просто звал ее: Наташа,
Но мы — мы будет называть
Наталья Павлобна) к несчастью,
Наталья Павловна совсем
Своей хозяйственною частью   45
Не занималася, затем,
Что не в отеческом законе
Она воспитана была,
А в благородном пансионе
У эмигрантки Фальбала.   50

Она сидит перед окном.
Пред ней открыт четвертый том
Сентиментального романа:
Любовь Элизы и Армана,
Иль переписка двух семей —   55
Роман классический, старинный,
Отменно длинный, длинный, длинный,
Нравоучительный и чинный,
Без романтических затей.

Наталья Павловна сначала   60
Его внимательно читала,
Но скоро как-то развлеклась
Перед окном возникшей дракой
Козла с дворовою собакой
И ею тихо занялась.   65
Кругом мальчишки хохотали.
Меж тем печально, под окном,
Индейки с криком выступали
Вослед за мокрым петухом.
Три утки полоскались в луже;   70
Шла баба через грязный двор
Белье повесить на забор;
Погода становилась хуже —

The housewife's eye is needed everywhere:
It is quick to notice something.

    Unfortunately, our heroine
(Oh, I forgot to give her name!   40
Her husband simply called her Natasha,
But we—we shall call [her]
Natalia Pavlovna), unfortunately
Natalia Pavlovna altogether
With her housekeeping rôle   45
Did not occupy herself, for the reason
That not by the patriarchal code
She had been brought up,
But in a boarding school for gentlewomen
At the émigré lady's [Mme] Falbalat.   50

    She sits by the window;
Open before her [lies] the fourth volume
Of the sentimental novel:
The Love of Eliza and Armand,
Or, A Correspondence Between Two Families—   55
A novel classical, old-fashioned,
Exceedingly long, long, long,
Edifying and worthy,
Without romantic conceits.

    Natalia Pavlovna had at first   60
Been reading it attentively,
But soon she was distracted somehow
By a tussle which had developed before her window
Of a billy goat with a yard dog,
And to this she quietly gave her attention.   65
Round about little boys were guffawing;
Meanwhile under the window mournfully
Turkey-hens appeared with clucking
Following a wet rooster;
Three ducks splashed in a puddle;   70
A peasant woman walked across the muddy yard
To hang up laundry on the fence;
The weather was worsening:

Казалось, снег идти хотел...
Вдруг колокольчик зазвенел.   75

Кто долго жил в глуши печальной,
Друзья, тот, верно, знает сам,
Как сильно колокольчик дальный
Порой волнует сердце нам.
Не друг ли едет запоздалый,   80
Товарищ юности удалой?..
Уж не она ли?.. Боже мой!
Вот ближе, ближе... сердце бьется...
Но мимо, мимо звук несется,
Слабей... и смолкнул за горой.   85

Наталья Павловна к балкону
Бежит, обрадована звону,
Глядит и видит: за рекой,
У мельницы, коляска скачет.
Вот на мосту — к нам точно! нет;   90
Поворотила влево. Вслед
Она глядит и чуть не плачет.

Но вдруг — о радость! косогор —
Коляска на бок. — «Филька, Васька!
Кто там? скорей! вон там коляска.   95
Сейчас везти ее на двор
И барина просить обедать!
Да жив ли он?.. беги проведать,
Скорей, скорей!..»
                            Слуга бежит.
Наталья Павловна спешит   100
Взбить пышный локон, шаль накинуть,
Задернуть завес, стул подвинуть,
И ждет. «Да скоро ль, мой творец?»
Вот едут, едут наконец.
Забрызганный в дороге дальной,   105
Опасно раненый, печальный
Кой-как тащится экипаж.
Вслед барин молодой хромает.
Слуга-француз не унывает
И говорит: allons, courage!   110

It looked as if it were getting ready to snow . . .
Suddenly a little sleigh bell rang out.   75

He who has long lived in the dreary deep countryside,
Friends, surely knows himself
How strongly a far-away sleigh bell
Sometimes agitates our heart.
Is it not a belated friend coming,   80
Companion of [one's] spirited youth? . . .
Could it be she, by any chance? . . . My God!
Here [it comes] nearer, nearer. The heart beats.
But past, past floats the sound,
[Gets] fainter . . . and has died away beyond the mountain.   85

Natalia Pavlovna to the balcony
Runs, joyful at the sound,
Looks and sees: beyond the river,
By the mill, a carriage is rolling,
Here it is on the bridge—straight toward us . . . no,   90
It has turned left. She follows it
With her eye and almost cries.

But suddenly . . . oh joy! a slant;
The carriage capsizes. "Filka! Vaska!
Who is there? Quickly! Over there's a carriage: 95
Bring it into the yard at once
And ask the master for dinner!
Is he even alive? . . . Run and find out!
Faster, faster!"
                    The servant runs.
Natalia Pavlovna hastens   100
To whip up a splendid curl, put on a shawl,
Draw the curtain, move up a chair,
And waits: will it be soon, my Creator!
Here they come driving up at last.
Bespattered on the long road,   105
Gravely wounded, a melancholy
Coach drags along somehow;
In its train limps a young gentleman.
The French servant does not fret
And says: *"Allons, courage!"*   110

Вот у крыльца; вот в сени входят.
Покаместь барину теперь
Покой особенный отводят
И настежь отворяют дверь,
Пока Picard шумит, хлопочет   115
И барин одеваться хочет,
Сказать ли вам, кто он таков?
Граф Нулин из чужих краев,
Где промотал он в вихре моды
Свои грядущие доходы.   120
Себя казать, как чудный зверь,
В Петрополь едет он теперь
С запасом фраков и жилетов,
Шляп, вееров, плащей, корсетов,
Булавок, запонок, лорнетов,   125
Цветных платков, чулков à jour,
С ужасной книжкою Гизота,
С тетрадью злых карикатур,
С романом новым Вальтер-Скотта,
С bon-mots парижского двора,   130
С последней песней Беранжера,
С мотивами Россини, Пера,
Et cetera, et cetera.

Уж стол накрыт. Давно пора;
Хозяйка ждет нетерпеливо.   135
Дверь отворилась. Входит граф;
Наталья Павловна, привстав,
Осведомляется учтиво,
Каков он? что нога его?
Граф отвечает: ничего.   140
Идут за стол. Вот он садится,
К ней подвигает свой прибор
И начинает разговор:
Святую Русь бранит, дивится,
Как можно жить в ее снегах,   145
Жалеет о Париже страх...

Now they are at the porch; now they enter the hall.
For the time being to the gentleman now
They assign a special room
And throw open the door wide;
While Picard noisily bustles,   115
And the gentleman is about to dress,
Shall I tell you what kind of person he is?
Count Nulin from foreign parts,
Where he has wasted in the whirlwind of fashion
His future revenues;   120
To show himself, like a fabled beast,
He now travels to Petropolis
With a supply of dress suits and waistcoats,
Hats, fans, cloaks, corsets,
Pins, cuff links, lorgnettes,   125
Flowered handkerchiefs, socks *à la mode,*
With a dreadful little book by Guizot,[1]
With a portfolio of malicious cartoons,
With a new novel by Walter Scott,
With *bons mots* of the Paris court,   130
With the latest song of Béranger's,[2]
With motifs of Rossini, Paer,[3]
Et cetera, et cetera.

The table is already laid; it has long been time;
The hostess waits impatiently;   135
The door has opened, the Count comes in;
Natalia Pavlovna, half-rising,
Inquires politely,
How he feels? What about his leg?
The Count replies: All right.   140
They go to table; now he sits down,
Directs his instrument at her
And begins the conversation:
He scolds Holy Russia, wonders
How one can live in her snows,   145
Dreadfully misses Paris.

[1] François Guizot (1787–1874), French conservative statesman and historian, elected to the Academy. "Little books" were not Guizot's forte; some of his studies and memoirs run from eight to thirty-one volumes.

[2] Pierre Jean de Béranger (1780–1857), most popular writer of *chansons* of the century.

[3] Ferdinando Paer (1771–1839), Italian composer (Venice, Vienna, Dresden, Paris) of over forty operas.

«А что театр?» — О! сиротеет,
C'est bien mauvais, ça fait pitié .
Тальма совсем оглох, слабеет,
И мамзель Марс — увы! стареет...   150
Зато Потье, le grand Potier!
Он славу прежнюю в народе
Доныне поддержал один».
«Какой писатель нынче в моде?»
— Всё d'Arlincourt| и Ламартин.—   155
«У нас им также подражают».
— Нет? право? так у нас умы
Уж развиваться начинают?
Дай бог, чтоб просветились мы!—
«Как тальи носят?» — Очень низко,   160
Почти до... вот, по этих пор.
Позвольте видеть ваш убор...
Так: рюши, банты... здесь узор...
Всё это к моде очень близко.—
«Мы получаем «Телеграф».   165
— Ага! Хотите ли послушать
Прелестный водевиль? — И граф
Поет. «Да, граф, извольте ж кушать».
— Я сыт и так.—
           Изо стола
Встают. Хозяйка молодая   170
Черезвычайно весела;
Граф, о Париже забывая,
Дивится: как она мила!
Проходит вечер неприметно;
Граф сам не свой. Хозяйки взор   175
То выражается приветно,
То вдруг потуплен безответно...
Глядишь — и полночь вдруг на двор.
Давно храпит слуга в передней,
Давно поет петух соседний,   180

"What about the theatre?" "Oh, being orphaned!
C'est bien mauvais, ça fait pitié.
Talma[4] has become completely deaf, is growing feebler,
And Mlle Mars,[5] alas, is aging.   150
Potier,[6] on the other hand, *le grand Potier!*
His former fame in the nation
He alone has maintained to the present."
"What writer is in fashion nowadays?"
"It's all d'Arlincourt[7] and Lamartine."   155
"With us, too, they are being imitated."
"You don't say! Really? So minds with us
Begin already to develop.
God grant we may become enlightened!"
"How are waistlines worn?" "Very low,   160
Almost to . . . here, up to this time.
Allow me to see your toilette . . .
Yes: ruches, ribbons . . . the tracery here . . .
All this is very close to the fashion."
"We get the *Telegraph.*"   165
"I see! . . . Would you like to listen
To a charming vaudeville?" And the Count
Sings. "But, Count, be good enough to eat."
"I have had enough anyway . . ."
                                    From table
They rise. The young hostess   170
Is in an exceedingly gay mood;
The Count, forgetting about Paris,
Is astonished how nice she is.
The evening passes imperceptibly;
The Count is not at ease; the hostess' gaze   175
Now expresses itself invitingly,
Now suddenly has turned unresponsively dull.
You look—and of a sudden it's midnight outside.
The footman in the hall has long been snoring,
The neighbor's cock has long been crowing,   180

[4] François Joseph Talma (1763–1826), brilliant tragedian (French classical drama and Shakespeare); chosen by Napoleon to play before a *parterre de rois* at Erfurt in 1808.

[5] Stage name of Anne Françoise Hippolyte Boutet (1779–1847), celebrated Paris actress, active for forty-seven years, like Talma a favorite of Napoleon's.

[6] Charles Potier (1775–1838), veteran Paris actor of the time, father of the prominent vaudeville playwright of the forties by the same name.

[7] Charles Victor Prévot, Vicomte d'Arlincourt (1789–1856), French poet, dramatist, and historical novelist.

В чугунну доску сторож бьет;
В гостиной свечки догорели.
Наталья Павловна встает:
«Пора, прощайте: ждут постели.
Приятный сон»... С досадой встав,   185
Полувлюбленный нежный граф
Целует руку ей. И что же?
Куда кокетство не ведет?
Проказница — прости ей, боже! —
Тихонько графу руку жмет.   190

Наталья Павловна раздета;
Стоит Параша перед ней.
Друзья мои, Параша эта
Наперсница ее затей;
Шьет, моет, вести переносит,   195
Изношенных капотов просит,
Порою с барином шалит,
Порой на барина кричит,
И лжет пред барыней отважно.
Теперь она толкует важно   200
О графе, о делах его,
Не пропускает ничего,
Бог весть, разведать как успела.
Но госпожа ей, наконец,
Сказала: «полно, надоела!»   205
Спросила кофту и чепец.
Легла и выйти вон велела.

Своим французом между тем
И граф раздет уже совсем.
Ложится он, сигару просит,   210
Monsieur Picard ему приносит
Графин, серебряный стакан,
Сигару, бронзовый светильник,
Щипцы с пружиною, будильник
И неразрезанный роман.   215

В постеле лежа, Вальтер-Скотта
Глазами пробегает он.

The watchman beats the iron plate;
In the sitting room the tapers have burned down.
Natalia Pavlovna gets up:
"It's time, good-bye! The beds are waiting.
Pleasant sleep! . . ." Rising with chagrin,   185
The half-enamored tender Count
Kisses her hand. And what then?
Where does flirtatiousness not lead?
The prankish girl—forgive her, God!—
Softly presses the Count's hand.   190

    Natalia Pavlovna is undressed;
Before her stands Parasha.
My friends, this Parasha
Is the confidante of her designs;
She sews, washes, carries news,   195
Asks for outworn housecoats,
At times frolics with the Master,
At times screams at the Master,
And boldly lies to the Mistress.
Now she discourses gravely   200
About the Count, about his affairs,
Does not leave out anything—
God knows how she managed to find out.
But the lady at last
Told her: "Enough, I am sick of it!"   205
Asked for her night-robe and cap,
Lay down, and ordered her to go on out.

    By his Frenchman in the meantime
The Count, too, has already been quite undressed.
He goes to bed, asks for a cigar,   210
Monsieur Picard brings him
A decanter, a silver beaker,
The cigar, a bronze candlestick,
Tweezers with a spring, an alarm clock
And an uncut novel.   215

    Lying in bed, Walter Scott
He skims over with his eyes.

Но граф душевно развлечен...
Неугомонная забота
Его тревожит; мыслит он: 220
«Неужто вправду я влюблен?
Что, если можно?.. вот забавно!
Однако ж это было б славно.
Я, кажется, хозяйке мил»,—
И Нулин свечку погасил.   225

Несносный жар его объемлет,
Не спится графу — бес не дремлет
И дразнит грешною мечтой
В нем чувства. Пылкий наш герой
Воображает очень живо   230
Хозяйки взор красноречивый,
Довольно круглый, полный стан,
Приятный голос, прямо женский,
Лица румянец деревенский —
Здоровье краше всех румян.   235
Он помнит кончик ножки нежной,
Он помнит: точно, точно так!
Она ему рукой небрежной
Пожала руку; он дурак,
Он должен бы остаться с нею —   240
Ловить минутную затею.
Но время не ушло. Теперь
Отворена, конечно, дверь...
И тотчас, на плеча накинув
Свой пестрый шелковый халат   245
И стул в потемках опрокинув.
В надежде сладостных наград,
К Лукреции Тарквиний новый
Отправился, на всё готовый.

Так иногда лукавый кот,   250
Жеманный баловень служанки,
За мышью крадется с лежанки:
Украдкой, медленно идет,
Полузажмурясь подступает,
Свернется в ком, хвостом играет,   255

But the Count is distracted in his mind:
A restless worry
Troubles him; he thinks: 220
Could I indeed be in love?
What if it were possible? . . . Here's an amusing thing;
Still, it would be splendid after all;
The hostess seems to find me nice—
And Nulin extinguished the taper. 225

An unbearable fever possesses him,
The Count can't sleep—the Devil is wakeful
And teases with a sinful daydream
The feelings in him. Our fiery hero
Imagines very vividly 230
The hostess' eloquent gaze,
[Her] rather rounded, full figure,
Pleasant voice, truly womanly,
The rustic high color of the face—
Health redder than any rouge. 235
He remembers the tip of the tender little foot,
He remembers—exactly, exactly so—
With a careless hand she had
Pressed his hand; he was a fool,
He should have stayed with her, 240
Caught the momentary impulse.
But the time had not passed: now
The door, of course, would be open—
And forthwith, throwing over his shoulders
His silken robe of many colors, 245
And upsetting a chair in the darkness,
In the hope of sweet rewards,
To Lucretia the new Tarquin
Set forth, ready for anything.

Thus sometimes a crafty cat, 250
The dainty darling of the maid,
Will steal off the stove bench after a mouse:
Stealthily, slowly he walks,
Moves up with eyes half-closed,
Turns into a ball, twitches his tail, 255

Разинет когти хитрых лап
И вдруг бедняжку цап-царап.

    Влюбленный граф в потемках бродит,
Дорогу ощупью находит.
Желаньем пламенным томим,   260
Едва дыханье переводит,
Трепещет, если пол под ним
Вдруг заскрыпит... Вот он подходит
К заветной двери и слегка
Жмет ручку медную замка;   265
Дверь тихо, тихо уступает...
Он смотрит: лампа чуть горит
И бледно спальню освещает;
Хозяйка мирно почивает
Иль притворяется, что спит.   270

    Он входит, медлит, отступает —
И вдруг упал к ее ногам...
Она... Теперь, с их позволенья,
Прошу я петербургских дам
Представить ужас пробужденья   275
Натальи Павловны моей
И разрешить, что делать ей?

    Она, открыв глаза большие,
Глядит на графа — наш герой
Ей сыплет чувства выписные   280
И дерзновенною рукой
Коснуться хочет одеяла,
Совсем смутив ее сначала...
Но тут опомнилась она,
И, гнева гордого полна,   285
А впрочем, может быть, и страха,
Она Тарквинию с размаха
Дает — пощечину. Да, да,
Пощечину, да ведь какую!

    Сгорел граф Нулин от стыда,   290
Обиду проглотив такую.

Unsheathes the claws of his cunning paws,
And suddenly, scritch-scratch [onto] the poor thing.

    The enamored Count wanders in the darkness,
Finds the way by groping,
By flaming desire tormented,   260
Scarcely takes time to breathe,
Trembles when the floor under him
Suddenly creaks. Now he approaches
The private door and lightly
Presses the brass handle of the lock;   265
The door quietly, quietly yields;
He looks: a lamp is barely alight
And dimly illuminates the bedroom;
The mistress peacefully reposes,
Or pretends to be asleep.   270

    He enters, searches, retreats—
And suddenly has fallen to her feet.
She . . . Now, with their permission,
I ask the ladies of Petersburg
To picture the horror at awakening   275
Of my Natalia Pavlovna
And to decide what she is to do.

    She, opening her eyes wide,
Looks at the Count—our hero
Pours out exotic[8] feelings to her   280
And with emboldened hand
Is about to touch the blanket,
Taking her completely aback at first . . .
But suddenly she comes to her senses,
And full of proud anger,   285
And besides of terror, too, perhaps,
She hauls off and gives Tarquin
A slap, yes, yes!
A slap, and what a [slap], what's more!

    Count Nulin flared up from shame,   290
To have swallowed such an insult;

[8] The somewhat archaic Russian adjective literally means "imported, procured by special order from far off," here denoting "exquisite, artificial, foreign, la-di-da."

Не знаю, чем бы кончил он,
Досадой страшною пылая,
Но шпиц косматый, вдруг залая,
Прервал Параши крепкий сон.   295
Услышав граф ее походку
И проклиная свой ночлег
И своенравную красотку,
В постыдный обратился бег.

    Как он, хозяйка и Параша   300
Проводят остальную ночь,
Воображайте. Воля ваша,
Я не намерен вам помочь.

    Восстав поутру молчаливо,
Граф одевается лениво,   305
Отделкой розовых ногтей
Зевая занялся небрежно,
И галстук вяжет неприлежно,
И мокрой щеткою своей
Не гладит стриженых кудрей.   310
О чем он думает — не знаю;
Но вот его позвали к чаю.
Что делать? Граф, преодолев
Неловкий стыд и тайный гнев,
Идет.

    Проказница младая,   315
Насмешливый потупя взор
И губки алые кусая,
Заводит скромно разговор
О том, о сем. Сперва смущенный,
Но постепенно ободренный,   320
С улыбкой отвечает он.
Получаса не проходило,
Уж он и шутит очень мило,
И чуть ли снова не влюблен.
Вдруг шум в передней. Входят. Кто же?   325
«Наташа, здравствуй».
          — Ах, мой боже...

I don't know what lengths he might have gone to,
Burning with terrible resentment,
But the shaggy Pomeranian, suddenly starting to bark,
Interrupted Parasha's sound sleep.   295
The Count, hearing her footsteps,
And cursing his night's billet
And the wayward little beauty,
Turned to ignominious flight.

    How he, the mistress, and Parasha   300
Spend the remainder of the night
Imagine as you please!
I don't intend to help you.

    Having risen in the morning in a taciturn mood,
The Count dresses lazily,   305
With manicure of his rosy nails
Lackadaisically he has started occupying himself, yawning,
And inattentively ties his necktie,
And with his moist brush
Does not smooth his trimmed locks.   310
What he thinks about I do not know;
But here they have called him to tea.
What to do? The Count, overcoming
His awkward embarrassment and secret anger,
Goes.

    The young scamp,   315
Veiling her mocking gaze
And biting her crimson little lips,
Modestly carries on a conversation
About this and that. At first confused,
But gradually emboldened,   320
He answers her with a smile.
A half hour has not passed,
And he already even jokes very affably,
And is all but in love again.
Suddenly a noise in the hall. Someone enters. Who can it be?   325
"Natasha, hallo!"
        "Oh, good heavens!

Граф, вот мой муж. Душа моя,
Граф Нулин.—
           «Рад сердечно я...
Какая скверная погода!
У кузницы я видел ваш   330
Совсем готовый экипаж...
Наташа! там у огорода
Мы затравили русака...
Эй! водки! Граф, прошу отведать:
Прислали нам издалека.   335
Вы с нами будете обедать?»
— Не знаю, право, я спешу.—
«И, полно, граф, я вас прошу.
Жена и я, гостям мы рады.
Нет, граф, останьтесь!»
                 Но с досады   340
И все надежды потеряв,
Упрямится печальный граф.
Уж подкрепив себя стаканом,
Пикар кряхтит за чемоданом.
Уже к коляске двое слуг   345
Несут привинчивать сундук.
К крыльцу подвезена коляска,
Пикар всё скоро уложил,
И граф уехал... Тем и сказка
Могла бы кончиться, друзья;   350
Но слова два прибавлю я.

    Когда коляска ускакала,
Жена всё мужу рассказала
И подвиг графа моего
Всему соседству описала.   355
Но кто же более всего
С Натальей Павловной смеялся?
Не угадать вам. Почему ж?
Муж? — как не так! совсем не муж.
Он очень этим оскорблялся,   360
Он говорил, что граф дурак,
Молокосос; что если так,
То графа он визжать заставит,

Count, this is my husband. Darling,
Count Nulin."
                    ' "I am sincerely pleased.
What miserable weather!
By the blacksmith's shop I saw your   330
Coach completely ready.
Natasha! By the orchard there
We tracked down a brown hare.
Hey, vodka! Count, please sample [it]:
They sent it to us from far away.   335
You will have dinner with us?"
"I don't know, really, I am in a hurry."
"Oh, no more of that, Count, I beg you.
My wife and I are fond of guests.
No, Count, do stay!"
                    But out of resentment,   340
And having lost all hopes,
The gloomy Count is stubborn.
Having already fortified himself with a glass,
Picard [toils] groaning with a suitcase,
Already to the carriage two footmen   345
Carry the trunk to screw [it] down.
The carriage is brought up to the porch,
Picard soon has everything stowed,
And the Count has departed. . . . And with this the tale
Might have ended, friends;   350
But I will add a few words.

   When the carriage had rolled away,
The wife told the husband everything,
And my count's exploit
Described to the whole neighborhood.   355
But who was it that most of all
Laughed with Natalia Pavlovna?
You cannot guess it. "Why so?
The husband?" Why, all wrong. Not the husband at all.
He took great offense at this,   360
He said that the Count was a fool,
A young pup; that if this was so,
He would make the Count squeal,

Что псами он его затравит.
Смеялся Лидин, их сосед,
Помещик двадцати трех лет.

    Теперь мы можем справедливо
Сказать, что в наши времена
Супругу верная жена,
Друзья мои, совсем не диво.

365

370

That he would sic his hounds at him.
It was Lidin, their neighbor, who laughed,   365
A squire twenty-three-years old.

   Now we may with justice
Say that in our time
A wife faithful to her husband,
My friends, is not at all a wonder.   370

СКАЗКА О ЦАРЕ САЛТАНЕ, О СЫНЕ ЕГО СЛАВНОМ И МОГУЧЕМ БОГАТЫРЕ КНЯЗЕ ГВИДОНЕ САЛТАНОВИЧЕ И О ПРЕКРАСНОЙ ЦАРЕВНЕ ЛЕБЕДИ   [1831]

Три девицы под окном
Пряли поздно вечерком.
«Кабы я была царица,—
Говорит одна девица,—
То на весь крещеный мир   5
Приготовила б я пир».
«Кабы я была царица,—
Говорит ее сестрица,—
То на весь бы мир одна
Наткала я полотна».   10
«Кабы я была царица,—
Третья молвила сестрица,—
Я б для батюшки-царя
Родила богатыря».

Только вымолвить успела,   15
Дверь тихонько заскрыпела,
И в светлицу входит царь,
Стороны той государь.
Во всё время разговора
Он стоял позадь забора;   20
Речь последней по всему
Полюбилася ему.
«Здравствуй, красная девица,—
Говорит он,— будь царица
И роди богатыря   25
Мне к исходу сентября.
Вы ж, голубушки-сестрицы,
Выбирайтесь из светлицы,
Поезжайте вслед за мной,
Вслед за мной и за сестрой: 30
Будь одна из вас ткачиха,
А другая повариха».

В сени вышел царь-отец.
Все пустились во дворец.

THE TALE OF TSAR SALTAN,
OF HIS SON, THE FAMED AND MIGHTY HERO
DUKE GUIDON SALTANOVICH,
AND OF THE PASSING FAIR PRINCESS SWAN   [1831]

Three maidens under the window
Were spinning late of an evening.
"If I were Queen,"
Says one maiden,
"Then for all of Christendom   5
I should prepare a feast."
"If I were Queen,"
Says her sister,
"Then for the whole world I alone
Would weave a pile of linen."   10
"If I were Queen,"
Spoke the third sister,
"I for [our] Father Tsar
Would bear a hero."

Barely had she finished speaking,   15
[When] the door softly creaked,
And into the chamber comes the Tsar,
That country's sovereign.
During all the conversation
He had stood behind the enclosure;   20
The last one's speech of all else
Had found favor with him.
"Hail, fair maiden,"
Says he, "be Queen
And bear a hero   25
To me by the end of September.
As for you, sisters, little doves,
Come forth from the chamber,
Follow in my train,
In mine and [your] sister's: 30
Let the one of you be weaver,
And the other cook."

Out into the hall went Father Tsar.
All started for the palace.

Царь недолго собирался: 35
В тот же вечер обвенчался.
Царь Салтан за пир честной
Сел с царицей молодой;
А потом честные гости
На кровать слоновой кости   40
Положили молодых
И оставили одних.
В кухне злится повариха,
Плачет у станка ткачиха,
И завидуют оне   45
Государевой жене.
А царица молодая,
Дела вдаль не отлагая,
С первой ночи понесла.

В те-поры война была.   50
Царь Салтан, с женой простяся,
На добра-коня садяся,
Ей наказывал себя
Поберечь, его любя.
Между тем как он далёко   55
Бьется долго и жестоко,
Наступает срок родин;
Сына бог им дал в аршин,
И царица над ребенком,
Как орлица над орленком;   60
Шлет с письмом она гонца,
Чтоб обрадовать отца.
А ткачиха с поварихой,
С сватьей бабой Бабарихой,
Извести ее хотят,   65
Перенять гонца велят;
Сами шлют гонца другого
Вот с чем от слова до слова:
«Родила царица в ночь
Не то сына, не то дочь;   70
Не мышонка, не лягушку,
А неведому зверюшку».

The Tsar was not long preparing: 35
That same evening [he] had the wedding.
Tsar Saltan to the solemn banquet
Sat down with the young Queen;
And then the guests of honor
On a bed of ivory   40
Laid the young couple
And left [them] alone.
In the kitchen rages the cook,
Weeps the weaver at the loom,
And they envy   45
The sovereign's wife.
But the young Queen,
Not putting off the business to a distant time,
From the first night started bearing.

    At that time there was a war.   50
Tsar Saltan, taking leave of [his] wife,
Mounting [his] goodly steed,
Instructed her
To take care of herself, as she loved him.
While he far away   55
Fights long and fiercely,
It comes the time of childbirth;
A son God gave him, an ell long,
And the Queen [watched] over the child
Like a she-eagle over [her] eaglet;   60
She sends a courier with a letter,
In order to gladden the father.
But the weaver and cook,
With the marriage broker Babarikha,
Want to undo her,   65
Have the courier taken up;
Themselves send another courier
With this [message] word for word:
"The Queen has born at night
Not a son, not a daughter;   70
Not a little mouse, not a frog,
But an unknown little creature."

Как услышал царь-отец,
Что донес ему гонец,
В гневе начал он чудесить   75
И гонца хотел повесить;
Но, смягчившись на сей раз,
Дал гонцу такой приказ:
«Ждать царева возвращенья
Для законного решенья».   80

    Едет с грамотой гонец,
И приехал наконец.
А ткачиха с поварихой,
С сватьей бабой Бабарихой,
Обобрать его велят;   85
Допьяна гонца поят
И в суму его пустую
Суют грамоту другую —
И привез гонец хмельной
В тот же день приказ такой: 90
«Царь велит своим боярам,
Времени не тратя даром,
И царицу и приплод
Тайно бросить в бездну вод».
Делать нечего: бояре,   95
Потужив о государе
И царице молодой,
В спальню к ней пришли толпой.
Объявили царску волю —
Ей и сыну злую долю,   100
Прочитали вслух указ,
И царицу в тот же час
В бочку с сыном посадили,
Засмолили, покатили
И пустили в Окиян —   105
Так велел-де царь Салтан.

    В синем небе звезды блещут,
В синем море волны хлещут;
Туча по небу идет,
Бочка по морю плывет.   110
Словно горькая вдовица,

When the Father Tsar heard
What the courier reported to him,
In [his] wrath he started raving   75
And wanted to hang the courier;
But, relenting for this time,
[He] gave the courier the following order:
"Let the Tsar's return be awaited
For a judicial decision."   80

    Rides the courier with the screed,
And arrived in the end.
But the weaver and cook,
With the broker-woman Babarikha,
Have him snatched up;   85
They ply the courier with drink until he is drunk
And into his empty pouch
Shove another screed—
And the drunken courier brought
That same day the following order: 90
"The Tsar commands his boyars,
Without wasting time,
Both the Queen and her offspring
Secretly to cast into the waters' depth."
There's no help for it: the boyars,   95
Grieved over the sovereign
And the young Queen,
Came into her bedchamber in a throng.
They announced the Tsar's will—
Evil lot for her and [her] son,   100
Read out aloud the decree,
And put the Queen that very hour
Into a barrel with [her] son,
Tarred [it] up, rolled [it] off
And let [it] go into the Ocean—   105
Thus, they thought, Tsar Saltan had ordered.

    In the dark-blue sky stars glitter,
In the dark-blue sea waves plash;
A cloud wanders over the sky,
The barrel swims on the sea.   110
Like a bitter widow,

Плачет, бьется в ней царица;
И растет ребенок там
Не по дням, а по часам.
День прошел, царица вопит...   115
А дитя волну торопит:
«Ты, волна моя, волна!
Ты гульлива и вольна;
Плещешь ты, куда захочешь,
Ты морские камни точишь,   120
Топишь берег ты земли,
Подымаешь корабли —
Не губи ты нашу душу:
Выплесни ты нас на сушу!»
И послушалась волна: 125
Тут же на берег она
Бочку вынесла легонько
И отхлынула тихонько.
Мать с младенцем спасена;
Землю чувствует она.   130
Но из бочки кто их вынет?
Бог неужто их покинет?
Сын на ножки поднялся,
В дно головкой уперся,
Понатужился немножко: 135
«Как бы здесь на двор окошко
Нам проделать?» — молвил он,
Вышиб дно и вышел вон.

    Мать и сын теперь на воле;
Видят холм в широком поле,   140
Море синее кругом,
Дуб зеленый над холмом.
Сын подумал: добрый ужин
Был бы нам, однако, нужен.
Ломит он у дуба сук   145
И в тугой сгибает лук,
Со креста снурок шелковый
Натянул на лук дубовый,
Тонку тросточку сломил,
Стрелкой легкой завострил   150

The Queen weeps, struggles in it;
And the child grows there
Not by days, but by hours.
The day has gone by, the Queen wails . . . 115
But the babe hurries on the wave:
"You, wave, my wave!
You are footloose and free;
You ramble where you want,
You roll the rocks of the sea, 120
You flood the shore of the land,
Lift up ships—
Do not make us perish:
Wash us onto the dry land!"
And the wave obeyed: 125
Forthwith ashore it
Washed up the barrel very gently
And went plashing off quietly.
Mother and baby are saved;
She feels land. 130
But who will take them out of the barrel?
Will God by any chance get them moving?
The son rose to his little feet,
Braced himself against the bottom with his little head,
Strained a little bit: 135
"How about our breaking through a window
Here to the outside?" he said,
Burst the bottom out and went on out.

　Mother and son are now at liberty;
They see a knoll in the broad field, 140
The dark-blue sea around,
A green oak tree on the knoll.
The son thought: a good supper
Would be useful to us, after all.
He breaks a branch off the oak 145
And bends it into a stout bow,
From [his] cross the silken cord
He strung to the oaken bow,
Broke off a thin little twig,
Sharpened it into a light arrow 150

И пошел на край долины
У моря искать дичины.

      К морю лишь подходит он,
Вот и слышит будто стон...
Видно, нá море не тихо;   155
Смотрит — видит дело лихо:
Бьется лебедь средь зыбей,
Коршун носится над ней;
Та бедняжка так и плещет,
Воду вкруг мутит и хлещет...   160
Тот уж когти распустил,
Клёв кровавый навострил...
Но как раз стрела запела,
В шею коршуна задела —
Коршун в море кровь пролил,   165
Лук царевич опустил;
Смотрит: коршун в море тонет
И не птичьим криком стонет,
Лебедь около плывет,
Злого коршуна клюет,   170
Гибель близкую торопит,
Бьет крылом и в море топит —
И царевичу потом
Молвит русским языком:
«Ты, царевич, мой спаситель,   175
Мой могучий избавитель,
Не тужи, что за меня
Есть не будешь ты три дня,
Что стрела пропала в море;
Это горе — всё не горе.   180
Отплачу тебе добром,
Сослужу тебе потом:
Ты не лебедь ведь избавил,
Девицу в живых оставил;
Ты не коршуна убил,   185
Чародея подстрелил.
Ввек тебя я не забуду:
Ты найдешь меня повсюду,
А теперь ты воротись,
Не горюй и спать ложись».   190

And started for the border of the valley
To search for game by the seaside.

Just as he reaches the sea,
Lo, he hears as if a groan . . .
Evidently, it is not quiet at sea;   155
He looks—sees an evil business:
A swan is struggling amid the wave-troughs,
A kite floats over her;
She, poor thing, splashes ever so hard,
Churns and lashes the water about [her] . . .   160
That one has already spread forth [his] talons,
Whetted his bloody beak . . .
But of a sudden the arrow sang out,
Struck the kite in the neck—
The kite spilled blood into the sea,   165
The Prince dropped the bow;
He looks: the kite is drowning in the sea
And groans with an unbirdlike cry,
The swan swims nearby,
Pecks the wicked kite,   170
Speeds [his] near perdition,
Beats [him] with [his] wing and drowns [him] in the sea—
And to the Prince then
Speaks in the Russian tongue:
"You, Prince, my savior,   175
My mighty redeemer,
Grieve not that in exchange for me
You will not eat for three days,
That the arrow was lost in the sea;
This sorrow—[is] no sorrow at all.   180
I shall repay you with good,
Will serve you hereafter:
You see, it was no swan you saved,
A maiden [you] kept among the living;
Not a kite you killed,   185
Shot down a warlock.
For life I shall not forget you:
You will find me everywhere,
But now turn back,
Fret not, and go to bed."   190

Улетела лебедь-птица,
А царевич и царица,
Целый день проведши так,
Лечь решились натощак.—
Вот открыл царевич очи;   195
Отрясая грезы ночи
И дивясь, перед собой
Видит город он большой,
Стены с частыми зубцами,
И за белыми стенами   200
Блещут маковки церквей
И святых монастырей.—
Он скорей царицу будит;
Та как ахнет!.. «То ли будет? —
Говорит он,— вижу я: 205
Лебедь тешится моя».
Мать и сын идут ко граду.
Лишь ступили за ограду,
Оглушительный трезвон
Поднялся со всех сторон: 210
К ним народ навстречу валит,
Хор церковный бога хвалит;
В колымагах золотых
Пышный двор встречает их;
Все их громко величают   215
И царевича венчают
Княжей шапкой, и главой
Возглашают над собой;
И среди своей столицы,
С разрешения царицы,   220
В тот же день стал княжить он
И нарекся: князь Гвидон.

Ветер на море гуляет
И кораблик подгоняет;
Он бежит себе в волнах   225
На раздутых парусах.
Корабельщики дивятся,
На кораблике толпятся,
На знакомом острову
Чудо видят наяву: 230

The swan-bird flew off,
And the Prince and Queen,
Having spent the whole day thus,
Decided to go to bed on an empty stomach.
Now the Prince has opened [his] eyes;   195
Shaking off the fancies of the night
And marveling, before him
He sees a great city,
Walls with frequent crenellations,
And behind the white walls   200
Gleam the onion domes of churches
And of holy monasteries.
He quickly wakes the Queen;
How she exclaims! . . . "Is this what lies ahead?"
Says he, "I see: 205
My swan is busying herself."
Mother and son walk to the city.
Hardly have they crossed the barrier,
[When] a deafening peal of bells
Arose from all sides: 210
People throng to meet them,
A church choir praises God;
In heavy golden coaches
A splendid court meets them;
All exalt them loudly   215
And crown the Prince
With a ducal cap, and as head
Proclaim [him] over themselves;
And within his capital city,
By the Queen's permission,   220
That same day he began to reign
And styled himself: Duke Guidon.

The wind roams on the sea
And drives up a little ship;
It runs along in the waves   225
With bulging sails.
The ship's company marvel,
Crowd together in the little ship,
On the familiar island
They see a wonder in plain sight: 230

Город новый златоглавый,
Пристань с крепкою заставой,
Пушки с пристани палят,
Кораблю пристать велят.
Пристают к заставе гости;   235
Князь Гвидон зовет их в гости,
Их он кормит и поит
И ответ держать велит:
«Чем вы, гости, торг ведете
И куда теперь плывете?»   240
Корабельщики в ответ:
«Мы объехали весь свет,
Торговали соболями,
Черно-бурыми лисами;
А теперь нам вышел срок,   245
Едем прямо на восток,
Мимо острова Буяна,
В царство славного Салтана...»
Князь им вымолвил тогда:
«Добрый путь вам, господа,   250
По морю по Окияну
К славному царю Салтану;
От меня ему поклон».
Гости в путь, а князь Гвидон
С берега душой печальной   255
Провожает бег их дальный;
Глядь — поверх текучих вод
Лебедь белая плывет.
«Здравствуй, князь ты мой прекрасный!
Что ты тих, как день ненастный?   260
Опечалился чему?» —
Говорит она ему.
Князь печально отвечает:
«Грусть-тоска меня съедает
Одолела молодца: 265
Видеть я б хотел отца».
Лебедь князю: «Вот в чем горе!
Ну, послушай: хочешь в море
Полететь за кораблем?
Будь же, князь, ты комаром».   270
И крылами замахала,

A new city golden-topped,
A pier with a strong breakwater,
Cannons fire from the pier,
Bid the ship put in.
The merchants make fast to the breakwater;   235
Duke Guidon bids them be his guests,
Gives them food as well as drink
And commands them to give account:
"What, merchants, are you trading in,
And where are you sailing now?"   240
The sailors in reply:
"We have sailed the whole world round,
Traded in sables,
Black-and-russet foxes;
And now our term is up,   245
We are sailing due east,
Past the island of Buyan,
To the kingdom of the famed Saltan . . ."
The Duke spoke to them then:
"A good passage to you, gentlemen,   250
Across the ocean sea
To the famous Tsar Saltan;
Greetings to him from me."
The traders go on [their] way, but Duke Guidon
From the shore, [his] soul distressed,   255
Traces their far-off course;
Behold—atop the streaming seas
The white swan swims.
"Hail, you fairest Prince of mine!
Why are you still, like a dismal day?   260
Has something saddened you?"
She says to him.
The Duke replies sadly:
"Sadness-sorrow gnaws me,
Has overwhelmed the spirited lad: 265
I should like to see [my] father."
The swan to the Prince: "So this is [your] grief!
Well, listen: would you like to fly
To sea after the ship?
Be then, Prince, a gnat."   270
And she beat her wings,

Воду с шумом расплескала
И обрызгала его
С головы до ног всего.
Тут он в точку уменьшился,   275
Комаром оборотился,
Полетел и запищал,
Судно на море догнал,
Потихоньку опустился
На корабль — и в щель забился.   280

   Ветер весело шумит,
Судно весело бежит
Мимо острова Буяна,
К царству славного Салтана,
И желанная страна   285
Вот уж издали видна.
Вот на берег вышли гости;
Царь Салтан зовет их в гости,
И за ними во дворец
Полетел наш удалец.   290
Видит: весь сияя в злате,
Царь Салтан сидит в палате
На престоле и в венце,
С грустной думой на лице;
А ткачиха с поварихой,   295
С сватьей бабой Бабарихой,
Около царя сидят
И в глаза ему глядят.
Царь Салтан гостей сажает
За свой стол и вопрошает: 300
«Ой вы, гости-господа,
Долго ль ездили? куда?
Ладно ль за морем, иль худо?
И какое в свете чудо?»
Корабельщики в ответ: 305
«Мы объехали весь свет;
За морем житье не худо,
В свете ж вот какое чудо:
В море остров был крутой,
Не привальный, не жилой;   310

Noisily churned up the water
And splashed him
From head to foot all over.
Then he diminished to a dot,   275
Turned into a gnat,
Flew off and shrilled,
Caught up with the vessel at sea,
Very quietly dropped down
On the ship—and tucked himself into a crack.   280

   The wind rushes merrily,
The vessel merrily runs
Past the island of Buyan,
To the realm of famed Saltan,
And the desired land   285
Here is already in sight from afar.
Here the merchants have gone ashore;
Tsar Saltan bids them be his guests,
And after them to the palace
Flew our bold lad.   290
He sees: all shining in gold,
Tsar Saltan sits in the chamber of state
On the throne and in [his] crown
With sad musing on his face;
And the weaver and cook,   295
With the broker-woman Babarikha,
Sit near the Tsar
And look him in the eyes.
Tsar Saltan seats the merchants
At his table and questions [them]:   300
"Ho, you, merchant gentlemen,
Have you fared long? Whither?
Are things fair overseas or foul?
And what wonder in the world?"
The sailors in reply: 305
"We have sailed the whole world round;
Life overseas is fair enough,
Here is what kind of wonder [is] in the world:
Was at sea a craggy island,
Harborless and uninhabited;   310

Он лежал пустой равниной;
Рос на нем дубок единый;
А теперь стоит на нем
Новый город со дворцом,
С златоглавыми церквами,   315
С теремами и садами,
А сидит в нем князь Гвидон;
Он прислал тебе поклон».
Царь Салтан дивится чуду;
Молвит он: «Коль жив я буду,   320
Чудный остров навещу,
У Гвидона погощу».
А ткачиха с поварихой,
С сватьей бабой Бабарихой,
Не хотят его пустить   325
Чудный остров навестить.
«Уж диковинка, ну право,—
Подмигнув другим лукаво,
Повариха говорит,—
Город у моря стоит!   330
Знайте, вот что не безделка:
Ель в лесу, под елью белка,
Белка песенки поет
И орешки всё грызет,
А орешки не простые,   335
Всё скорлупки золотые,
Ядра — чистый изумруд;
Вот что чудом-то зовут».
Чуду царь Салтан дивится,
А комар-то злится, злится —   340
И впился комар как раз
Тетке прямо в правый глаз.
Повариха побледнела,
Обмерла и окривела.
Слуги, сватья и сестра   345
С криком ловят комара.
«Распроклятая ты мошка!
Мы тебя!..» А он в окошко,
Да спокойно в свой удел
Через море полетел.   350

It lay as an empty plateau;
There grew on it a single young oak tree;
But now there stands on it
A new city with a palace,
With golden-topped churches,   315
With donjon chambers and gardens,
And there resides in it Duke Guidon;
He sent you greetings."
Tsar Saltan marvels at the wonder;
Says he: "If I live [long enough],   320
I shall visit the wondrous island,
Be Guidon's guest."
But the weaver and cook,
With the broker-woman Babarikha,
Do not want to let him   325
Visit the wondrous island.
"There's an outlandish thing, yes indeed,"
With a sly wink to the others
Says the cook,
"A city stands by the sea!   330
Know, here's what's not a trifle:
A spruce in the wood, beneath the spruce a squirrel,
The squirrel sings songs
And keeps gnawing little nuts,
And the little nuts aren't plain ones,   335
All golden the little shells,
The kernels—pure emerald;
Here is what is called a marvel."
Tsar Saltan wonders at the marvel,
But the gnat is raging, raging—   340
And all at once the gnat dug his stinger
Straight into the aunt's right eye.
The cook blanched,
Stiffened, and turned crooked.
The servants, the broker, and the sister   345
With an outcry chase the gnat.
"You accursed midge!
We [will get] you! . . ." But he through the window,
And calmly to his realm
Flew across the sea.   350

Снова князь у моря ходит,
С синя моря глаз не сводит;
Глядь — поверх текучих вод
Лебедь белая плывет.
«Здравствуй, князь ты мой прекрасный!   355
Что ж ты тих, как день ненастный?
Опечалился чему?» —
Говорит она ему.
Князь Гвидон ей отвечает:
«Грусть-тоска меня съедает;   360
Чудо чудное завесть
Мне б хотелось. Где-то есть
Ель в лесу, под елью белка;
Диво, право, не безделка —
Белка песенки поет,   365
Да орешки всё грызет,
А орешки не простые,
Всё скорлупки золотые,
Ядра — чистый изумруд;
Но, быть может, люди врут».   370
Князю лебедь отвечает:
«Свет о белке правду бает;
Это чудо знаю я;
Полно, князь, душа моя,
Не печалься; рада службу   375
Оказать тебе я в дружбу».
С ободрённою душой
Князь пошел себе домой;
Лишь ступил на двор широкой —
Что ж? — под елкою высокой,   380
Видит, белочка при всех
Золотой грызет орех,
Изумрудец вынимает,
А скорлупку собирает,
Кучки равные кладет   385
И с присвисточкой поет
При честном при всем народе:
Во саду ли, в огороде.
Изумился князь Гвидон.
«Ну, спасибо,— молвил он,—   390
Ай да лебедь — дай ей боже.

Again the Duke walks by the sea,
From the dark-blue sea does not turn his eye;
Behold—atop the streaming seas
Swims the white swan.
"Hail, you fairest Prince of mine!   355
Why are you quiet, like a dismal day?
Has something saddened you?"
She says to him.
Duke Guidon replies to her:
"Sadness-sorrow gnaws me;   360
A wonder of wonders I should like
To carry off. Somewhere there is
A spruce in the wood, beneath the spruce a squirrel;
A marvel, truly, not a trifle—
The squirrel sings songs,   365
And keeps gnawing little nuts,
And the little nuts aren't plain ones,
All golden the little shells,
The kernels—pure emerald;
But, it may be, people lie."   370
To the Duke the swan replies:
"The world tells truth about the squirrel;
This marvel I know;
Enough [said], Prince, my dear,
Do not grieve; I am glad a service   375
To render you for friendship."
With his soul heartened,
The Duke betook himself home;
Hardly had he entered the wide courtyard—
What? Under a tall spruce,   380
He sees, a little squirrel, for all to see,
Gnaws a golden nut,
Takes out an emerald stone,
And gathers the shell,
Lays even piles   385
And sings, with a little whistling to accompany it,
For all the honest folk to hear:
"If in garden or in orchard."
Duke Guidon was amazed.
"Well, thank you," he said,   390
"There's a swan for you—God give her

Что и мне, веселье то же».
Князь для белочки потом
Выстроил хрустальный дом,
Караул к нему приставил   395
И притом дьяка заставил
Строгий счет орехам весть.
Князю прибыль, белке честь.

  Ветер по морю гуляет
И кораблик подгоняет;   400
Он бежит себе в волнах
На поднятых парусах
Мимо острова крутого,
Мимо города большого;
Пушки с пристани палят,   405
Кораблю пристать велят.
Пристают к заставе гости;
Князь Гвидон зовет их в гости,
Их и кормит и поит
И ответ держать велит: 410
«Чем вы, гости, торг ведете
И куда теперь плывете?»
Корабельщики в ответ:
«Мы объехали весь свет,
Торговали мы конями,   415
Всё донскими жеребцами,
А теперь нам вышел срок —
И лежит нам путь далек:
Мимо острова Буяна,
В царство славного Салтана...»   420
Говорит им князь тогда:
«Добрый путь вам, господа,
По морю по Окияну
К славному царю Салтану;
Да скажите: князь Гвидон   425
Шлет царю-де свой поклон».

  Гости князю поклонились,
Вышли вон и в путь пустились.
К морю князь — а лебедь там
Уж гуляет по волнам.   430

The same joy as to me."
The Duke for the little squirrel then
Fashioned a crystal house,
Set a guard on it   395
And moreover had a clerk
Keep strict count of the nuts;
For the Duke, profit, for the squirrel, honor.

   The wind roams over the sea
And drives up a little ship;   400
It runs along in the waves
Under full sail(s)
Past the craggy island,
Past the great city:
Cannons fire from the pier,   405
Command the ship to put in.
The merchants make fast to the breakwater;
Duke Guidon bids them be his guests,
Gives them food as well as drink
And commands them to give account: 410
"What, merchants, do you trade in,
And whither are you sailing now?"
The sailors in reply:
"We have sailed the whole world round,
We traded in steeds,   415
Ponies all from the Donland,
And now our term has run out—
And a long way lies [before] us:
Past the island of Buyan,
To the realm of famed Saltan . . ."   420
The Duke tells them then:
"A good passage to you, gentlemen,
Over the ocean sea
To the famed Tsar Saltan;
And say: Duke Guidon   425
Sends the Tsar his greeting."

   The merchants bowed to the Prince,
Went on out and got under way.
The Duke [went] to the sea—and the swan there
Already cruises over the waves.   430

Молит князь: душа-де просит,
Так и тянет и уносит...
Вот опять она его
Вмиг обрызгала всего:
В муху князь оборотился,   435
Полетел и опустился
Между моря и небес
На корабль — и в щель залез.

Ветер весело шумит,
Судно весело бежит   440
Мимо острова Буяна,
В царство славного Салтана —
И желанная страна
Вот уж издали видна;
Вот на берег вышли гости;   445
Царь Салтан зовет их в гости,
И за ними во дворец
Полетел наш удалец.
Видит: весь сияя в злате,
Царь Салтан сидит в палате   450
На престоле и в венце,
С грустной думой на лице.
А ткачиха с Бабарихой
Да с кривою поварихой
Около царя сидят,   455
Злыми жабами глядят.
Царь Салтан гостей сажает
За свой стол и вопрошает:
«Ой вы, гости-господа,
Долго ль ездили? куда?   460
Ладно ль за морем, иль худо,
И какое в свете чудо?»
Корабельщики в ответ:
«Мы объехали весь свет;
За морем житье не худо;   465
В свете ж вот какое чудо:
Остров на море лежит,
Град на острове стоит
С златоглавыми церквами,
С теремами да садами;   470

Begs the Duke: [his] soul is asking,
Drawing [him] ever so and carrying away . . .
So again she instantly
Splashed him all over:
To a fly the Duke was changed,   435
Flew off and dropped down
Between the sea and the heavens
Onto the ship—and crawled into a crack.

   The wind rushes merrily,
The vessel runs merrily
Past the island of Buyan,   440
To the realm of famed Saltan—
And the desired land
Here already is in sight from afar;
Now the merchants went ashore;   445
Tsar Saltan bids them be his guests,
And behind them to the palace
Flew our bold lad.
He sees: all shining in gold,
Tsar Saltan sits in the chamber of state   450
On the throne and in [his] crown,
With sad musing on his face.
But the weaver and Babarikha
And the crooked cook
Sit near the Tsar,   455
Stare like wicked toads.
Tsar Saltan seats the merchants
At his table and questions:
"Ho, you, merchant gentlemen,
Have you fared long? Whither?   460
Are things fair overseas or foul,
And what wonder in the world?"
The sailors in reply:
"We have sailed the whole world round;
Life across the sea is fair enough;   465
Here is what wonder [is] in the world:
On the sea there lies an island,
On the island stands a city
With golden-topped churches,
With donjon chambers and gardens;   470

Ель растет перед дворцом,
А под ней хрустальный дом;
Белка там живет ручная,
Да затейница какая!
Белка песенки поет   475
Да орешки всё грызет,
А орешки не простые,
Всё скорлупки золотые,
Ядра — чистый изумруд;
Слуги белку стерегут,   480
Служат ей прислугой разной —
И приставлен дьяк приказный
Строгий счет орехам весть;
Отдает ей войско честь;
Из скорлупок льют монету   485
Да пускают в ход по свету;
Девки сыплют изумруд
В кладовые да под спуд;
Все в том острове богаты,
Изоб нет, везде палаты;   490
А сидит в нем князь Гвидон;
Он прислал тебе поклон».
Царь Салтан дивится чуду.
«Если только жив я буду,
Чудный остров навещу,   495
У Гвидона погощу».
А ткачиха с поварихой,
С сватьей бабой Бабарихой,
Не хотят его пустить
Чудный остров навестить.   500
Усмехнувшись исподтиха,
Говорит царю ткачиха:
«Что тут дивного? ну, вот!
Белка камушки грызет,
Мечет золото и в груды   505
Загребает изумруды;
Этим нас не удивишь,
Правду ль, нет ли говоришь.
В свете есть иное диво:
Море вздуется бурливо,   510
Закипит, подымет вой,

A spruce grows in front of the palace,
And beneath it is a crystal house;
There a squirrel lives, a tame one,
And what a trickster it is!
The squirrel sings songs   475
And keeps gnawing little nuts,
And the nuts not plain ones,
All golden the little shells,
The kernels—pure emerald;
Servants guard the squirrel,   480
Serve it with all manner of service—
And attached is a state clerk
To keep strict count of the nuts;
The army salutes it;
Out of the little shells they cast coin   485
And put it in circulation around the world;
Maidens pour the emeralds
Into storehouses and stow them away;
Everyone on this island is rich,
There are no cottages, everywhere mansions;   490
And there resides on it Duke Guidon;
He sent you greeting[s]."
Tsar Saltan marvels at the wonder.
"If only I live [long enough],
I shall visit the wonder island,   495
Be Guidon's guest."
But the weaver and cook,
And the broker-woman Babarikha,
Do not want to let him
Visit the wondrous island.   500
Smiling slyly,
Says the weaver to the Tsar:
"What is [so] wonderful here? Well, there it is!
A squirrel gnaws pebbles,
Sweeps up gold, and into piles   505
Rakes up emeralds;
With that you won't amaze us,
Whether you speak truth or not.
There's another marvel in the world:
The sea blusters stormily,   510
Boils up, raises a roar,

Хлынет на берег пустой,
Разольется в шумном беге,
И очутятся на бреге,
В чешуе, как жар горя,   515
Тридцать три богатыря,
Все красавцы удалые,
Великаны молодые,
Все равны, как на подбор,
С ними дядька Черномор.   520
Это диво, так уж диво,
Можно молвить справедливо!»
Гости умные молчат,
Спорить с нею не хотят.
Диву царь Салтан дивится,   525
А Гвидон-то злится, злится...
Зажужжал он и как раз
Тетке сел на левый глаз,
И ткачиха побледнела:
«Ай!» — и тут же окривела;   530
Все кричат: «Лови, лови,
Да дави ее, дави...
Вот ужо! постой немножко,
Погоди...» А князь в окошко,
Да спокойно в свой удел   535
Через море прилетел.

    Князь у синя моря ходит,
С синя моря глаз не сводит;
Глядь — поверх текучих вод
Лебедь белая плывет.   540
«Здравствуй, князь ты мой прекрасный!
Что ты тих, как день ненастный?
Опечалился чему?» —
Говорит она ему.
Князь Гвидон ей отвечает: 545
«Грусть-тоска меня съедает —
Диво б дивное хотел
Перенесть я в мой удел».
«А какое ж это диво?»
«Где-то вздуется бурливо   550

Surges up an empty shore,
Flows apart in rushing run,
And there emerge on the shore,
In coat of mail, glowing like fire,   515
Thirty-three heroes,
All handsome bold lads,
Young giants,
All alike, as for a muster,
With them Uncle Chernomor.   520
Talk of marvels, that's a marvel,
One may say with justice!"
The wise visiting merchants are silent,
Do not want to quarrel with her.
Tsar Saltan marvels at the marvel,   525
But Guidon, he rages, rages . . .
He gave a buzz and directly
Lighted on [his] aunt's left eye,
And the weaver turned pale:
"Ai!" and turned crooked on the spot;   530
All cry: "Catch, catch,
And swat it, swat . . .
Just you wait! Hold on a little,
Stay . . ." But the Duke [is off] through the window,
And calmly to his realm   535
Across the sea came flying.

    The Duke walks by the dark-blue sea,
From the dark-blue sea does not turn his eyes;
Behold—across the streaming seas
Swims the white swan.   540
"Hail, you fairest Prince of mine!
Why are you still, like a dismal day?
Are you grieved by something?"
She says to him.
Duke Guidon replies to her: 545
"Sadness-sorrow gnaws me—
A marvel of marvels I would like
To carry off into my realm."
"Why, what marvel is that?"
"Somewhere blusters stormily   550

Окиян, подымет вой,
Хлынет на берег пустой,
Расплеснется в шумном беге,
И очутятся на бреге,
В чешуе, как жар горя,   555
Тридцать три богатыря,
Все красавцы молодые,
Великаны удалые,
Все равны, как на подбор,
С ними дядька Черномор».   560
Князю лебедь отвечает:
«Вот что, князь, тебя смущает?
Не тужи, душа моя,
Это чудо знаю я.
Эти витязи морские   565
Мне ведь братья все родные.
Не печалься же, ступай,
В гости братцев поджидай».

     Князь пошел, забывши горе,
Сел на башню, и на море   570
Стал глядеть он; море вдруг
Всколыхалося вокруг,
Расплескалось в шумном беге
И оставило на бреге
Тридцать три богатыря;   575
В чешуе, как жар горя,
Идут витязи четами,
И, блистая сединами,
Дядька впереди идет
И ко граду их ведет.   580
С башни князь Гвидон сбегает,
Дорогих гостей встречает;
Второпях народ бежит;
Дядька князю говорит:
«Лебедь нас к тебе послала   585
И наказом наказала
Славный город твой хранить
И дозором обходить.
Мы отныне ежеденно
Вместе будем непременно   590

The ocean, raises a roar,
Surges up an empty shore,
Flashes apart in rushing run,
And there emerge on the beach,
In a coat of mail, like fire glowing,   555
Thirty-three heroes,
All handsome young lads,
Spirited giants,
All alike, as for a muster,
With them uncle Chernomor."   560
To the Duke the swan replies:
"Is this, Prince, what troubles you?
Do not grieve, my dear,
This wonder I know.
These knights of the sea   565
Are all my own brothers, you see.
Do not sorrow, then, make haste,
Presently await [my] brothers' visit."

   The Duke went off, grief forgotten,
Mounted the tower, and at the sea   570
He started gazing; suddenly the sea
Started heaving all about,
Plashed apart in rushing run
And left on the beach
Thirty-three heroes;   575
In coat of mail, like fire glowing,
Stride the knights in pairs,
And, silver hair flashing,
Uncle strides ahead
And leads them to the city.   580
Down from the tower runs Duke Guidon,
Goes to meet the dear guests;
In a hurry run the people;
The Uncle tells the Duke:
"The swan has sent us to you   585
And with bidding bade us
To guard your famous city
And patrol it as a watch.
We from now on every day
Shall together without fail   590

У высоких стен твоих
Выходить из вод морских,
Так увидимся мы вскоре,
А теперь пора нам в море;
Тяжек воздух нам земли».   595
Все потом домой ушли.

   Ветер по морю гуляет
И кораблик подгоняет;
Он бежит себе в волнах
На поднятых парусах   600
Мимо острова крутого,
Мимо города большого;
Пушки с пристани палят,
Кораблю пристать велят.
Пристают к заставе гости;   605
Князь Гвидон зовет их в гости,
Их и кормит и поит
И ответ держать велит:
«Чем вы, гости, торг ведете?
И куда теперь плывете?»   610
Корабельщики в ответ:
«Мы объехали весь свет;
Торговали мы булатом,
Чистым серебром и златом,
И теперь нам вышел срок;   615
А лежит нам путь далек,
Мимо острова Буяна,
В царство славного Салтана».
Говорит им князь тогда:
«Добрый путь вам, господа,   620
По морю по Окияну
К славному царю Салтану.
Да скажите ж: князь Гвидон
Шлет-де свой царю поклон».

   Гости князю поклонились,   625
Вышли вон и в путь пустились.
К морю князь, а лебедь там
Уж гуляет по волнам.

By your high walls
Come out of the waters of the sea,
So we shall see each other shortly,
But now it's time for us [to return] to sea;
Burdensome to us is the air of earth."   595
All then went off home.

    The wind roams over the sea
And drives up a little ship;
It runs its course in the waves
Under full sail(s)   600
Past the craggy island,
Past the great city;
Cannons fire from the pier,
Command the ship to put in.
The merchants make fast to the breakwater.   605
Duke Guidon bids them be his guests,
Gives them food as well as drink
And commands to give account:
"What, merchants, do you trade in?
And whither are you sailing now?"   610
The sailors in reply:
"We have sailed the whole world round;
We traded in Damask steel,
Pure silver and gold,
And now our term has run out;   615
But a long way lies [before] us,
Past the island of Buyan,
To the realm of famed Saltan."
Thereupon the Duke tells them:
"A good passage to you, gentlemen,   620
Over the ocean sea
To the famous Tsar Saltan.
And be sure to say: Duke Guidon
Sends his greeting to the Tsar."

    The merchants bowed to the Duke,   625
Went on out and got under way.
To the sea [went] the Duke, and the swan there
Already cruises over the waves.

Князь опять: душа-де просит...
Так и тянет и уносит... 630
И опять она его
Вмиг обрызгала всего.
Тут он очень уменьшился,
Шмелем князь оборотился,
Полетел и зажужжал; 635
Судно на море догнал,
Потихоньку опустился
На корму — и в щель забился.

Ветер весело шумит,
Судно весело бежит 640
Мимо острова Буяна,
В царство славного Салтана,
И желанная страна
Вот уж издали видна.
Вот на берег вышли гости. 645
Царь Салтан зовет их в гости,
И за ними во дворец
Полетел наш удалец.
Видит, весь сияя в злате,
Царь Салтан сидит в палате 650
На престоле и в венце,
С грустной думой на лице.
А ткачиха с поварихой,
С сватьей бабой Бабарихой,
Около царя сидят — 655
Четырьмя все три глядят.
Царь Салтан гостей сажает
За свой стол и вопрошает:
«Ой вы, гости-господа,
Долго ль ездили? куда? 660
Ладно ль за морем, иль худо?
И какое в свете чудо?»
Корабельщики в ответ:
«Мы объехали весь свет;
За морем житье не худо; 665
В свете ж вот какое чудо:
Остров на море лежит,

The Duke again: his soul is asking . . .
Draws [him] ever so and carries away . . .   630
And again she
In a flash splashed him all over.
At once he shrank very much,
The Duke turned into a bumblebee,
Flew off and gave a buzz;   635
The vessel at sea [he] overtook,
Very quietly dropped down
Onto the stern—and tucked himself into a crack.

   The wind rushes merrily,
The vessel runs merrily   640
Past the island of Buyan,
To the realm of famed Saltan,
And the desired land
Now already is in sight from afar.
Now the merchants went ashore.   645
Tsar Saltan bids them be his guests,
And behind them to the palace
Flew our bold lad.
He sees, all shining in gold,
Tsar Saltan sits in the chamber of state   650
On the throne and in [his] crown,
With sad musing on his face.
But the weaver and cook,
And the broker-woman Babarikha,
Sit near the Tsar—   655
With four [eyes] all three look.
Tsar Saltan seats the merchants
At his table and questions:
"Ho, you, merchant gentlemen,
Have you fared long? Whither?   660
Fair or foul things overseas?
And what wonder in the world?"
The sailors in reply:
"We have sailed the whole world round;
Life across the sea is fair enough;   665
And here's what wonder's in the world:
There's an island lies at sea,

Град на острове стоит,
Каждый день идет там диво:
Море вздуется бурливо,   670
Закипит, подымет вой,
Хлынет на берег пустой,
Расплеснется в скором беге —
И останутся на бреге
Тридцать три богатыря,   675
В чешуе златой горя,
Все красавцы молодые,
Великаны удалые,
Все равны, как на подбор;
Старый дядька Черномор   680
С ними из моря выходит
И попарно их выводит,
Чтобы остров тот хранить
И дозором обходить —
И той стражи нет надежней,   685
Ни храбрее, ни прилежней.
А сидит там князь Гвидон;
Он прислал тебе поклон».
Царь Салтан дивится чуду.
«Коли жив я только буду,   690
Чудный остров навещу
И у князя погощу».
Повариха и ткачиха
Ни гугу — но Бабариха,
Усмехнувшись, говорит: 695
«Кто нас этим удивит?
Люди из моря выходят
И себе дозором бродят!
Правду ль бают, или лгут,
Дива я не вижу тут.   700
В свете есть такие ль дива?
Вот идет молва правдива:
За морем царевна есть,
Что не можно глаз отвесть;
Днем свет божий затмевает,   705
Ночью землю освещает,
Месяц под косой блестит,
А во лбу звезда горит.

On the island stands a city,
Every day a marvel goes on there:
The sea blusters stormily,   670
Boils up, raises a roar,
Surges up the empty shore,
Breaks with splashing in swift run—
And there will be left ashore
Thirty-three heroes,   675
In golden armor glowing.
All are handsome young lads,
Spirited giants,
All alike as for a muster;
Old uncle Chernomor   680
Comes out of the sea with them
And leads them out in pairs,
To guard that island
And patrol [it] as a watch—
And than that guard none is more reliable,   685
Nor more valiant, nor more diligent.
And resides there Duke Guidon;
He has sent you greeting[s]."
Tsar Saltan marvels at the wonder.
"If only I live,   690
I shall visit the wondrous island
And be the Duke's guest."
The cook and weaver
Not a murmur—but Babarikha,
Says with a smile: 695
"Who is going to amaze us with that?
Men come out of the sea
And amble about as a watch!
Whether truth they tell or lie,
I don't see a marvel here.   700
Is that the kind of marvel that's in the world?
Here is a true saying goes about:
Beyond the sea there is a princess
That one cannot take one's eyes off:
By day she dims God's light,   705
By night lights up the earth,
The moon gleams under her braid,
And on her brow glows a star.

А сама-то величава,
Выплывает, будто пава;   710
А как речь-то говорит,
Словно реченька журчит.
Молвить можно справедливо —
Это диво, так уж диво»,
Гости умные молчат: 715
Спорить с бабой не хотят.
Чуду царь Салтан дивится —
А царевич хоть и злится,
Но жалеет он очей
Старой бабушки своей;   720
Он над ней жужжит, кружится —
Прямо на нос к ней садится,
Нос ужалил богатырь:
На носу вскочил волдырь.
И опять пошла тревога: 725
«Помогите, ради бога!
Караул! лови, лови,
Да дави его, дави...
Вот ужо! пожди немножко,
Погоди!..» А шмель в окошко,   730
Да спокойно в свой удел
Через море полетел.

    Князь у синя моря ходит,
С синя моря глаз не сводит;
Глядь — поверх текучих вод   735
Лебедь белая плывет.
«Здравствуй, князь ты мой прекрасный!
Что ж ты тих, как день ненастный?
Опечалился чему?» —
Говорит она ему.   740
Князь Гвидон ей отвечает:
«Грусть-тоска меня съедает:
Люди женятся; гляжу,
Не женат лишь я хожу».
«А кого же на примете   745
Ты имеешь?» — «Да на свете,
Говорят, царевна есть,
Что не можно глаз отвесть.

And to look at she is splendid,
Glides forth like a peacock;   710
And when she holds speech,
[It is] as though a brook were murmuring.
One may say with justice
Talk of marvels, that's a marvel."
The wise merchants are silent: 715
[They] do not want to quarrel with the woman.
Tsar Saltan marvels at the wonder—
And the Prince, although he rages,
Still feels sorry for the eyes
Of his old granny: 720
He buzzes over her, circles—
Settles straight upon her nose,
The hero stung [her in the] nose:
On the nose a bump sprang up.
And again alarm arose: 725
"Help, for God's sake!
Guard! Catch [him], catch,
And swat him, swat . . .
We'll show you! Wait a little,
Hold on! . . ." But the bumblebee through the window,   730
And calmly to his realm
Flew across the sea.

   The Duke walks by the dark-blue sea,
From the dark-blue sea does not turn his eyes;
Behold—atop the streaming seas   735
Swims the white swan.
"Hail, you fairest Prince of mine!
Why are you still, like a dismal day?
Are you grieved at something?"
She says to him.   740
Duke Guidon replies to her:
"Sadness-sorrow gnaws me:
Folk get married; I look,
Only I unmarried go."
"Why, whom do you   745
Have in view?" "Well, in the world,
They say, is a princess
That one cannot take one's eyes off."

Днем свет божий затмевает,
Ночью землю освещает —   750
Месяц под косой блестит,
А во лбу звезда горит.
А сама-то величава,
Выступает, будто пава;
Сладку речь-то говорит,   755
Будто реченька журчит.
Только, полно, правда ль это?»
Князь со страхом ждет ответа.
Лебедь белая молчит
И, подумав, говорит: 760
«Да! такая есть девица.
Но жена не рукавица:
С белой ручки не стряхнешь,
Да за пояс не заткнешь.
Услужу тебе советом —   765
Слушай: обо всем об этом
Пораздумай ты путем,
Не раскаяться б потом».
Князь пред нею стал божиться,
Что пора ему жениться,   770
Что об этом обо всем
Передумал он путем,
Что готов душою страстной
За царевною прекрасной
Он пешком идти отсель   775
Хоть за тридевять земель.
Лебедь тут, вздохнув глубоко,
Молвила: «Зачем далеко?
Знай, близка судьба твоя,
Ведь царевна эта — я».   780
Тут она, взмахнув крылами,
Полетела над волнами
И на берег с высоты
Опустилася в кусты,
Встрепенулась, отряхнулась   785
И царевной обернулась:
Месяц под косой блестит,
А во лбу звезда горит;

By day she dims God's light,
By night lights up the earth,   750
The moon gleams beneath her braid,
And on her brow a star glows.
And to look at she is splendid,
Strides forth like a peacock;
And sweet speech she holds,   755
As if a brook were murmuring.
Enough said—only is this true?"
In fear the Duke awaits the reply.
The white swan is silent
And after some thought, says: 760
"Yes! There is such a maiden.
But a wife is not a mitten:
You don't shake her off [your] white little hand,
And don't tuck her behind the belt.
I will serve you with a piece of advice—   765
Listen: about all this
Deliberate a little on the way,
Not to regret [it] afterward."
The Duke before her started swearing by God,
That it was time for him to get married,   770
That about all this
He had reflected on the way;
That he was ready with impassioned soul
For the fairest princess
To walk on foot from here   775
Even through thrice nine lands.
At this the swan, with a deep sigh,
Spoke: "Wherefore far away?
Know, near is your fate,
This princess, you see—am I."   780
With this, beating her wings,
She flew off above the waves
And to the shore from high up
Dropped down into the bushes,
Ruffled her plumage, shook herself,   785
And turned into a princess:
The moon gleams beneath her braid,
And at her brow a star glows;

А сама-то величава,
Выступает, будто пава;   790
А как речь-то говорит,
Словно реченька журчит.
Князь царевну обнимает,
К белой груди прижимает
И ведет ее скорей   795
К милой матушке своей.
Князь ей в ноги, умоляя:
«Государыня родная!
Выбрал я жену себе,
Дочь послушную тебе.   800
Просим оба разрешенья,
Твоего благословенья:
Ты детей благослови
Жить в совете и любви».
Над главою их покорной   805
Мать с иконой чудотворной
Слезы льет и говорит:
«Бог вас, дети, наградит».
Князь не долго собирался,
На царевне обвенчался;   810
Стали жить да поживать,
Да приплода поджидать.

        Ветер по морю гуляет
И кораблик подгоняет;
Он бежит себе в волнах   815
На раздутых   парусах
Мимо острова   крутого,
Мимо города   большого;
Пушки с пристани палят,
Кораблю пристать велят.   820
Пристают к заставе гости.
Князь Гвидон зовет их в гости,
Он их кормит и поит
И ответ держать велит:
«Чем вы, гости, торг ведете   825
И куда теперь плывете?»
Корабельщики в ответ:
«Мы объехали весь свет,

And to look at she is splendid,
Strides forth like a peacock;   790
And when she holds speech,
[It is] as though a brook were murmuring.
The Duke embraces the princess,
To his white breast presses [her]
And leads her swiftly   795
To his dear mama.
The Duke [falls] to her feet, beseeching:
"Sovereign lady dearest!
I have chosen a wife for myself,
An obedient daughter for you,   800
We both ask consent,
Your blessing:
Bless your children
To live in concord and love."
Over their submissive head[s]   805
The mother with the wonder-working ikon
Sheds tears and says:
"God will reward you, children."
The Duke was not long preparing,
Held his wedding with the princess;   810
They began to live and keep living [together]
And to await offspring.

    The wind roams over the sea
And drives up a little ship;
It runs its course in the waves   815
Under bulging sails
Past the steep-to island,
Past the great city;
Cannons fire from the pier,
Command the ship to put in.   820
The merchants make fast to the breakwater.
Duke Guidon bids them be his guests,
He gives them food and drink
And commands them to give answer:
"What, merchants, do you trade in   825
And whither are you sailing now?"
The sailors in reply:
"We have sailed the whole world round;

Торговали мы не даром
Неуказанным товаром;   830
А лежит нам путь далек:
Восвояси на восток,
Мимо острова Буяна,
В царство славного Салтана»
Князь им вымолвил тогда: 835
«Добрый путь вам, господа,
По морю по Окияну
К славному царю Салтану;
Да напомните ему,
Государю своему: 840
К нам он в гости обещался,
А доселе не собрался —
Шлю ему я свой поклон».
Гости в путь, а князь Гвидон
Дома на сей раз остался   845
И с женою не расстался.

    Ветер весело шумит,
Судно весело бежит
Мимо острова Буяна,
К царству славного Салтана,   850
И знакомая страна
Вот уж издали видна.
Вот на берег вышли гости;
Царь Салтан зовет их в гости.
Гости видят: во дворце   855
Царь сидит в своем венце,
А ткачиха с поварихой,
С сватьей бабой Бабарихой,
Около царя сидят,
Четырьмя все три глядят.   860
Царь Салтан гостей сажает
За свой стол и вопрошает:
«Ой вы, гости-господа,
Долго ль ездили? куда?
Ладно ль за морем, иль худо?   865
И какое в свете чудо?»
Корабельщики в ответ:
«Мы объехали весь свет;

We have traded, not for nothing,
In unspecified wares; 830
But a far journey lies [before] us:
Homeward to the east,
Past the island of Buyan,
To the realm of Tsar Saltan."
The Duke told them then: 835
"A good passage to you, gentlemen,
Over the ocean sea
To the famous Tsar Saltan;
And remind him,
Your sovereign: 840
He has promised us a visit,
But to this day has not set forth—
I send him my greeting."
The merchants [start] on [their] way, but Duke Guidon
For this time stayed at home 845
And did not part from [his] wife.

    The wind rushes merrily,
The vessel runs merrily
Past the island of Buyan
To the realm of famed Saltan, 850
And the familiar land
Here is already in sight from afar.
Now the merchants went ashore,
Tsar Saltan bids them be his guests.
The merchants see: in the palace 855
The Tsar is sitting with his crown on,
And the weaver and cook,
And the broker-woman Babarikha
Sit near the Tsar,
With four [eyes] all three look. 860
Tsar Saltan seats the merchants
At his table and questions:
"Ho, you, merchant gentlemen,
Have you fared long? Whither?
Fair things overseas or foul? 865
And what wonder in the world?"
The sailors in reply:
"We have sailed the whole world round;

За морем житье не худо,
В свете ж вот какое чудо: 870
Остров на море лежит,
Град на острове стоит,
С златоглавыми церквами,
С теремами и садами;
Ель растет перед дворцом,   875
А под ней хрустальный дом;
Белка в нем живет ручная,
Да чудесница какая!
Белка песенки поет
Да орешки всё грызет;   880
А орешки не простые,
Скорлупы-то золотые,
Ядра — чистый изумруд;
Белку холят, берегут.
Там еще другое диво: 885
Море вздуется бурливо,
Закипит, подымет вой,
Хлынет на берег пустой,
Расплеснется в скором беге,
И очутятся на бреге   890
В чешуе, как жар горя,
Тридцать три богатыря,
Все красавцы удалые,
Великаны молодые,
Все равны, как на подбор —   895
С ними дядька Черномор.
И той стражи нет надежней,
Ни храбрее, ни прилежней.
А у князя женка есть,
Что не можно глаз отвесть: 900
Днем свет божий затмевает.
Ночью землю освещает;
Месяц под косой блестит,
А во лбу звезда горит.
Князь Гвидон тот город правит,   905
Всяк его усердно славит;
Он прислал тебе поклон,
Да тебе пеняет он:

Life is fair enough beyond the sea,
And there is this wonder in the world: 870
On the sea an island lies,
On the isle a city stands,
With gold-topped churches,
With donjon chambers and gardens;
A spruce grows in front of the palace,   875
And beneath it a crystal house;
A squirrel in it lives, a tame one,
And what a fable-creature it is!
The squirrel sings songs
And keeps gnawing little nuts;   880
And the little nuts not plain ones,
For the shells are golden,
The kernels—pure emerald;
The squirrel they cherish, tend.
Yet another marvel's there: 885
The sea blusters stormily,
Boils up, raises a roar,
Surges up the empty shore,
Breaks with splashing in swift run,
And there emerge on the beach,   890
In armor, like fire glowing,
Thirty-three heroes,
All handsome spirited lads,
Young giants,
All alike, as for a muster—   895
With them uncle Chernomor.
And than this guard none more trusty,
Nor more valiant, nor more diligent.
And the Duke has a little wife
That one cannot take one's eyes off: 900
By day the light of God she dims,
By night lights up the earth;
The moon gleams beneath her braid,
And a star glows at her brow.
Duke Guidon that city rules,   905
Everyone praises him fervently;
He sent you a greeting,
And complains to you:

К нам-де в гости обещался,
А доселе не собрался».   910

Тут уж царь не утерпел,
Снарядить он флот велел.
А ткачиха с поварихой,
С сватьей бабой Бабарихой,
Не хотят царя пустить   915
Чудный остров навестить.
Но Салтан им не внимает
И как раз их унимает:
«Что я? царь или дитя? —
Говорит он не шутя.—   920
Нынче ж еду!» Тут он топнул,
Вышел вон и дверью хлопнул.

Под окном Гвидон сидит,
Молча на море глядит:
Не шумит оно, не хлещет,   925
Лишь едва, едва трепещет,
И в лазоревой дали
Показались корабли:
По равнинам Окияна
Едет флот царя Салтана.   930
Князь Гвидон тогда вскочил,
Громогласно возопил:
«Матушка моя родная!
Ты, княгиня молодая!
Посмотрите вы туда: 935
Едет батюшка сюда».
Флот уж к острову подходит.
Князь Гвидон трубу наводит:
Царь на палубе стоит
И в трубу на них глядит;   940
С ним ткачиха с поварихой,
С сватьей бабой Бабарихой;
Удивляются оне
Незнакомой стороне.
Разом пушки запалили;   945
В колокольнях зазвонили;

He promised us a visit, he says,
But to this day has not set forth."   910

   At this the Tsar could stand no more,
Commanded the fleet to be made ready.
But the weaver and cook,
And the broker-woman Babarikha
Do not want to let the Tsar   915
Visit the wondrous island.
But Saltan does not listen to them
And for once stops them short:
"What am I? Tsar or babe?"
He says, not in jest: 920
"Straightway I am going." Then he stamped his foot,
Went on out, and slammed the door.

   By the window sits Guidon,
Gazes at the sea in silence:
It does not rush, does not plash,   925
Only barely, barely trembles,
And in the azure distance
Ships came into view:
On the level ocean spaces
Sails the fleet of Tsar Saltan.   930
Duke Guidon started up then,
Shouted in a loud voice:
"Mama, my dearest!
You, young Duchess!
Look thither: 935
Papa is coming here."
The fleet is already coming up to the island.
Duke Guidon aims the spyglass:
The Tsar is standing on the deck
And gazing at them through the spyglass;   940
With him are the weaver and cook,
And the broker-woman Babarikha;
They are astonished
At the unknown country.
At once they fired cannons,   945
Started tolling in the belfries;

К морю сам идет Гвидон;
Там царя встречает он
С поварихой и ткачихой,
С сватьей бабой Бабарихой;   950
В город он повел царя,
Ничего не говоря.

      Все теперь идут в палаты:
У ворот блистают латы,
И стоят в глазах царя   955
Тридцать три богатыря,
Все красавцы молодые,
Великаны удалые,
Все равны, как на подбор,
С ними дядька Черномор.   960
Царь ступил на двор широкой:
Там под елкою высокой
Белка песенку поет,
Золотой орех грызет,
Изумрудец вынимает   965
И в мешочек опускает;
И засеян двор большой
Золотою скорлупой.
Гости дале — торопливо
Смотрят — что ж? княгиня — диво: 970
Под косой луна блестит,
А во лбу звезда горит;
А сама-то величава,
Выступает, будто пава,
И свекровь свою ведет.   975
Царь глядит — и узнает...
В нем взыграло ретивое!
«Что я вижу? что такое?
Как!» — и дух в нем занялся...
Царь слезами залился,   980
Обнимает он царицу,
И сынка, и молодицу,
И садятся все за стол;
И веселый пир пошел.
А ткачиха с поварихой,   985
С сватьей бабой Бабарихой,

To the sea goes Guidon himself;
There he welcomes the Tsar
With the cook and weaver,
And the broker-woman Babarikha;   950
To the city he led the Tsar,
Not saying anything.

   All now go to the state apartments:
At the gate gleams armor plating,
And there stand in the Tsar's sight   955
Thirty-three heroes,
All handsome young lads,
Spirited giants,
All alike, as for a muster,
With them uncle Chernomor.   960
The Tsar entered the broad courtyard:
There under a tall spruce
The squirrel sings a little song,
Gnaws a golden nut,
Takes out an emerald stone   965
And drops [it] into a little bag;
And bestrewn is the big yard
With gold shell.
The guests [go] farther—in haste
Look—what is it? The Duchess—a marvel: 970
Beneath her braid gleams the moon,
And at her brow a star glows;
And to look at she is splendid,
Striding forth like a peacock,
And conducting her mother-in-law.   975
The Tsar gazes—and recognizes . . .
His heart started leaping!
"What do I see? What is this?
How?" And it took his breath away . . .
The Tsar dissolved in tears,   980
He embraces the Queen,
And [his] young son, and the bride,
And all sit down to table;
And a merry feast was held.
But the weaver and cook,   985
And the broker-woman Babarikha,

Разбежались по углам;
Их нашли насилу там.
Тут во всем они признались,
Повинились, разрыдались;   990
Царь для радости такой
Отпустил всех трех домой.
День прошел — царя Салтана
Уложили спать вполпьяна.
Я там был; мед, пиво пил —   995
И усы лишь обмочил.

Scattered into corners;
It took some effort to find them.
Then they confessed to everything,
Admitted guilt, started sobbing;   990
The Tsar for the sake of such a joy
Let all three off home.
The day passed by—Tsar Saltan
They laid to bed half-drunk.
I was there; mead, beer I drank—   995
And merely moistened my whiskers.

МЕДНЫЙ ВСАДНИК: Петербургская повесть [1833]

Происшествие, описанное в сей повести, основано на исти-
не. Подробности наводнения заимствованы из тогдашних
журналов. Любопытные могут справиться с известием,
составленным В. Н. Берхом.

ВСТУПЛЕНИЕ

На берегу пустынных волн
Стоял он, дум великих полн,
И вдаль глядел. Пред ним широко
Река неслася; бедный челн
По ней стремился одиноко.   5
По мшистым, топким берегам
Чернели избы здесь и там,
Приют убогого чухонца;
И лес, неведомый лучам
В тумане спрятанного солнца,   10
Кругом шумел.

И думал он:
Отсель грозить мы будем шведу,
Здесь будет город заложен
Назло надменному соседу.
Природой здесь нам суждено   15
В Европу прорубить окно[1],
Ногою твердой стать при море.
Сюда по новым им волнам
Все флаги в гости будут к нам,
И запируем на просторе.   20

Прошло сто лет, и юный град,
Полнощных стран краса и диво,
Из тьмы лесов, из топи блат
Вознесся пышно, горделиво;
Где прежде финский рыболов,   25
Печальный пасынок природы,
Один у низких берегов
Бросал в неведомые воды

---

[1] Альгаротти где-то сказал: «Pétersbourg est la fenêtre par laquelle
la Russie regarde en Europe».

THE BRONZE HORSEMAN: A Tale of Petersburg   [1833]

The occurrence described in this narrative is based on truth.
The details of the flood are drawn from journals of the time.
The curious may consult the account composed by V. N. Berkh.

INTRODUCTION

Upon a shore of desolate waves
Stood *he,* of lofty musings full,
And gazed afar. Before him broadly
The river rolled; a wretched skiff
Held course on it in solitude.   5
About the mossy, marshy banks
Showed blackly cabins here and there,
The shelters of the lowly Finn;
And forest, alien to the rays
Of the fog-enshrouded sun   10
Murmured all about.

                        And he thought:
From here we shall threaten the Swede,
Here shall a city be founded
To spite the puffed-up neighbor.
By Nature we are destined here   15
To hack a window through to Europe,
To plant a firm foot by the sea.
Here upon billows new to them
All flags will come to visit us,
And we shall revel in open space.   20

A hundred years have passed, and the young city,
Glory and marvel of the midnight lands,
From forest gloom, out of the bog of marshlands,
Has risen splendidly, pridefully;
Where formerly the Finnish fisherman,   25
Sad step-son of Nature,
Alone by the low banks
Used to cast into the unknown waters

Свой ветхий невод, ныне там
По оживленным берегам   30
Громады стройные теснятся
Дворцов и башен; корабли
Толпой со всех концов земли
К богатым пристаням стремятся;
В гранит оделася Нева;   35
Мосты повисли над водами;
Темно-зелеными садами
Ее покрылись острова,
И перед младшею столицей
Померкла старая Москва,   40
Как перед новою царицей
Порфироносная вдова.

    Люблю тебя, Петра творенье,
Люблю твой строгий, стройный вид,
Невы державное теченье,   45
Береговой ее гранит,
Твоих оград узор чугунный,
Твоих задумчивых ночей
Прозрачный сумрак, блеск безлунный,
Когда я в комнате моей   50
Пишу, читаю без лампады,
И ясны спящие громады
Пустынных улиц, и светла
Адмиралтейская игла,
И, не пуская тьму ночную   55
На золотые небеса,
Одна заря сменить другую
Спешит, дав ночи полчаса [2].
Люблю зимы твоей жестокой
Недвижный воздух и мороз,   60
Бег санок вдоль Невы широкой,
Девичьи лица ярче роз,
И блеск, и шум, и говор балов,
А в час пирушки холостой
Шипенье пенистых бокалов   65
И пунша пламень голубой.
Люблю воинственную живость

[2] Смотри стихи князя Вяземского к графине З.

His brittle net, there now
Along the animated banks   30
Are crowded shapely masses
Of palaces and towers; ships
(In a crowd) in squadrons from all corners of the earth
Press toward the opulent docks;
Nevá has been clad in granite;   35
Bridges are suspended over [her] waters;
With dark-green gardens
Are her islands covered,
And before the younger capital
Old Moscow has faded,   40
As before a new empress
The dowager in purple robes.

    I love you, Peter's creation,
I love your austere, comely look,
Nevá's majestic flow,   45
The granite of her banks,
The iron pattern of your railings,
Of your pensive nights
The translucent twilight, the moonless sheen,
When in my room I   50
Write [or] read without a lamp,
And clear there show the slumbering expanses
Of deserted streets, and brightly shines
The needle of the Admiralty [spire],
And barring the gloom of night   55
From the golden skies,
One dawn hurries to relieve the other,
Allowing half-an-hour to night.
I love your harsh winter's
Motionless air and frost,   60
The coursing of sleighs along the broad Nevá,
Girls' faces brighter than roses,
And the glitter and hubbub and chatter of balls,
And at the hour of a bachelors' party,
The hiss of foaming beakers   65
And the punch's blue flame.
I love the warlike verve

Потешных Марсовых полей,
Пехотных ратей и коней
Однообразную красивость,   70
В их стройно зыблемом строю
Лоскутья сих знамен победных,
Сиянье шапок этих медных,
Насквозь простреленных в бою.
Люблю, военная столица,   75
Твоей твердыни дым и гром,
Когда полнощная царица
Дарует сына в царский дом,
Или победу над врагом
Россия снова торжествует,   80
Или, взломав свой синий лед,
Нева к морям его несет
И, чуя вешни дни, ликует.

    Красуйся, град Петров, и стой
Неколебимо, как Россия,   85
Да умирится же с тобой
И побежденная стихия;
Вражду и плен старинный свой
Пусть волны финские забудут
И тщетной злобою не будут   90
Тревожить вечный сон Петра!

    Была ужасная пора,
Об ней свежо воспоминанье...
Об ней, друзья мои, для вас
Начну свое повествованье.   95
Печален будет мой рассказ.

ЧАСТЬ ПЕРВАЯ

    Над омраченным Петроградом
Дышал ноябрь осенним хладом.
Плеская шумною волной
В края своей ограды стройной,   100
Нева металась, как больной
В своей постеле беспокойной.

Of the playgrounds of Mars,[1]
Of troops of infantry and horse
The uniform beauty,   70
In their in-unison-swaying array
The tatters of those victorious standards,
The gleam of those bronze helmets,
Shot right through in battle.
I love, martial capital,   75
Your citadel's smoke and thunder,
When the Empress of the North
Presents a son to the imperial house,
Or Russia once again celebrates
A victory over the foe.   80
Or, having broken her blue ice,
Nevá bears it to the seas,
And scenting vernal days, exults.

    Flaunt your beauty, Peter's city, and stand
Unshakable, like Russia,   85
And may even the conquered element
Make its peace with you;
Would that the Finnish seas forget
[Their] enmity and ancient bondage
And trouble not with empty spite   90
Peter's eternal slumber.

    There was a dreadful time,
Fresh is the memory of it . . .
Of it, my friends, for you
I will begin my narrative.   95
Sorrowful will be my tale.

PART ONE

    Over darkened Petrograd
November breathed autumnal chill.
Splashing with noisy wave
Against the edges of her neat embankment,   100
Nevá was tossing like a sick man
In his unrestful bed.

1 The parade grounds of St. Petersburg are called the Mars Field.

Уж было поздно и темно;
Сердито бился дождь в окно,
И ветер дул, печально воя.   105
В то время из гостей домой
Пришел Евгений молодой...
Мы будем нашего героя
Звать этим именем. Оно
Звучит приятно; с ним давно   110
Мое перо к тому же дружно.
Прозванья нам его не нужно,
Хотя в минувши времена
Оно, быть может, и блистало,
И под пером Карамзина   115
В родных преданьях прозвучало;
Но ныне светом и молвой
Оно забыто. Наш герой
Живет в Коломне; где-то служит,
Дичится знатных и не тужит   120
Ни о почиющей родне,
Ни о забытой старине.

    Итак, домой пришед, Евгений
Стряхнул шинель, разделся, лег.
Но долго он заснуть не мог   125
В волненье разных размышлений.
О чем же думал он? о том,
Что был он беден, что трудом
Он должен был себе доставить
И независимость и честь;   130
Что мог бы бог ему прибавить
Ума и денег. Что ведь есть
Такие праздные счастливцы,
Ума недальнего, ленивцы,
Которым жизнь куда легка!   135
Что служит он всего два года;
Он также думал, что погода
Не унималась; что река
Всё прибывала; что едва ли
С Невы мостов уже не сняли   140
И что с Парашей будет он
Дни на два, на три разлучен.

It was already late and dark;
Angrily the rain beat on the window,
And the wind blew, dismally howling.   105
At that time homeward from a visit
Came young Eugene . . .
We will call our hero
By this name. It has
A pleasant sound; long with it   110
My pen has been on friendly terms, what's more;
His other name we have no need for,
Although in bygone times
It may perhaps have shone
And by the pen of Karamzin[2]   115
Have rung out in [our] native legends;
But nowadays by society and fame
It is forgotten. Our hero
Lives in Kolomna;[3] he works in some office,
Shies away from the eminent and worries his head   120
Neither about buried kin
Nor about forgotten times of yore.

    And so, having come home, Eugene
Flung off his cloak, undressed, lay down.
But for a long time he could not go to sleep   125
In the excitement of diverse trains of thought.
What did he think about, then? About the fact
That he was poor, that by hard work
He had to secure for himself
Independence as well as honor;   130
That God might have granted him
More brains and money; that there were, after all,
Such lucky idlers,
Of limited wits, lazy fellows,
Who had such an easy life of it!   135
That he had been in the service but two years;
He also reflected that the weather
Was not clearing; that the river
Kept rising; that they would hardly
Have failed to take down the Nevá bridges by now,   140
And that Parasha and he would be
Parted for two or three days.

---

[2] Allusion to Karamzin's monumental *History of the Russian State.*
[3] Then an outlying faubourg of St. Petersburg.

Евгений тут вздохнул сердечно
И размечтался, как поэт:

«Жениться? Мне? зачем же нет?   145
Оно и тяжело, конечно;
Но что ж, я молод и здоров,
Трудиться день и ночь готов;
Уж кое-как себе устрою
Приют смиренный и простой   150
И в нем Парашу успокою.
Пройдет, быть может, год-другой —
Местечко получу, Параше
Препоручу семейство наше
И воспитание ребят...   155
И станем жить, и так до гроба
Рука с рукой дойдем мы оба,
И внуки нас похоронят...»

Так он мечтал. И грустно было
Ему в ту ночь, и он желал,   160
Чтоб ветер выл не так уныло
И чтобы дождь в окно стучал
Не так сердито...
        Сонны очи
Он наконец закрыл. И вот
Редеет мгла ненастной ночи   165
И бледный день уж настает...[3]
Ужасный день!
        Нева всю ночь
Рвалася к морю против бури,
Не одолев их буйной дури...
И спорить стало ей невмочь...   170
Поутру над ее брегами
Теснился кучами народ,
Любуясь брызгами, горами
И пеной разъяренных вод.
Но силой ветров от залива   175
Перегражденная Нева
Обратно шла, гневна, бурлива,
И затопляла острова,

[3] Мицкевич прекрасными стихами описал день, предшествовавший петербургскому наводнению, в одном из лучших своих стихотворений Oleszkiewicz. Жаль только, что описание его не точно. Снегу не было — Нева не была покрыта льдом. Наше описание вернее, хотя в нем и нет ярких красок польского поэта.

At this point Eugene gave a feeling sigh
And gave way to his thoughts like a poet.

"Get married? I? Well, why not?   145
It [would be] hard going, certainly;
But what of it, I am young and healthy,
Ready to labor day and night;
Somehow I'll surely manage for myself
A humble and simple refuge,   150
And in it I'll settle Parasha to a peaceful life.
A year or two perhaps will pass,
[And] I'll receive a modest position; to Parasha
I'll entrust our family
And the upbringing of the children . . .   155
And we shall begin our life, and so to the grave
The two of us will go hand in hand,
And [our] grandchildren will bury us . . ."

   Thus he mused. And sad felt
He that night, and he wished   160
The wind would not howl so dismally
Or the rain beat on the window
So angrily—.
                    His sleepy eyes
He closed at last. And here is
The foul night's fog thinning,   165
And pale day already drawing up . . .
[That] day of horror!
                    Nevá all night
Thrust toward the sea against the gales,
Unable to master their boisterous wildness . . .
And could contend no longer . . .   170
In the morning on her banks
People crowded in swarms,
Relishing the spray, the mountains
And foam of the maddened waters.
But by the force of the winds from the gulf   175
Dammed up, Nevá
Turned back, wrathful, tempestuous, .
And swamped the islands;

Погода пуще свирепела,
Нева вздувалась и ревела,   180
Котлом клокоча и клубясь.
И вдруг, как зверь остервенясь,
На город кинулась. Пред нею
Всё побежало, всё вокруг
Вдруг опустело — воды вдруг   185
Втекли в подземные подвалы,
К решеткам хлынули каналы,
И всплыл Петрополь, как Тритон,
По пояс в воду погружен.

        Осада! приступ! злые волны,   190
Как воры, лезут в окна. Челны
С разбега стекла бьют кормой.
Лотки под мокрой пеленой,
Обломки хижин, бревны, кровли,
Товар запасливой торговли,   195
Пожитки бледной нищеты,
Грозой снесенные мосты,
Гроба с размытого кладбища
Плывут по улицам!
                        Народ
Зрит божий гнев и казни ждет.   200
Увы! всё гибнет: кров и пища!
Где будет взять?
                        В тот грозный год
Покойный царь еще Россией
Со славой правил. На балкон,
Печален, смутен, вышел он   205
И молвил: «С божией стихией
Царям не совладеть». Он сел
И в думе скорбными очами
На злое бедствие глядел.
Стояли стогны озерáми,   210
И в них широкими реками
Вливались улицы. Дворец
Казался островом печальным.
Царь молвил — из конца в конец,
По ближним улицам и дальным   215
В опасный путь средь бурных вод

The weather raged more wildly,
Nevá swelled and roared,   180
Gurgling and welling up like a cauldron,
And of a sudden, bristling like a beast,
Rushed on the city. Before her
All fled, all about
Was suddenly deserted—the waters suddenly   185
Flowed into cellars underground,
Up to the grillwork gushed up the canals,
And afloat was Petropolis, like Triton
Steeped to the waist in water.

Beleaguerment! Assault! The angry waves,   190
Like thieves, climb through the windows. Boats
Swooping, smash panes with [their] stern[s].
Pedlar's trays under sodden cover,
Fragments of huts, beams, roofs,
The merchandise of thrifty trading,   195
The chattels of pale beggary,
Bridges carried away by the storm,
Coffins from the flooded cemetery
Float down the streets!
                    The people
Gaze on the wrath of God and bide [their] doom.   200
Woe! All is perishing: shelter and food!
Where turn for them?
                    That dreadful year
The late Tsar still ruled over Russia
With renown. Onto the balcony,
Sorrowful, troubled, he came out   205
And spoke: "Against God's element
There is no prevailing for tsars." He sat down
And thoughtfully, with stricken eyes
Gazed at the grim calamity.
The squares (stood) lay like lakes,   210
And into them like broad rivers
Debouched the streets. The palace
Seemed a desolate island.
The Tsar spoke—[and] from end to end,
Down the streets nearby and far-off   215
Upon [their] hazardous path amid the stormy waters

Его пустились генералы [4]
Спасать и страхом обуялый
И дома тонущий народ.

    Тогда на площади Петровой,   220
Где дом в углу вознесся новый,
Где над возвышенным крыльцом
С подъятой лапой, как живые,
Стоят два льва сторожевые,
На звере мраморном верхом,   225
Без шляпы, руки сжав крестом,
Сидел недвижный, страшно бледный
Евгений. Он страшился, бедный,
Не за себя. Он не слыхал,
Как подымался жадный вал,   230
Ему подошвы подмывая,
Как дождь ему в лицо хлестал,
Как ветер, буйно завывая,
С него и шляпу вдруг сорвал.
Его отчаянные взоры   235
На край один наведены
Недвижно были. Словно горы,
Из возмущенной глубины
Вставали волны там и злились,
Там буря выла, там носились   240
Обломки... Боже, боже! там —
Увы! близехонько к волнам,
Почти у самого залива —
Забор некрашеный, да ива
И ветхий домик: там оне,   245
Вдова и дочь, его Параша,
Его мечта... Или во сне
Он это видит? иль вся наша
И жизнь ничто, как сон пустой,
Насмешка неба над землей?   250

    И он, как будто околдован,
Как будто к мрамору прикован,
Сойти не может! Вкруг него
Вода и больше ничего!

[4] Граф Милорадович и генерал-адъютант Бенкендорф.

Set off his generals
To save the people who were (both) terror-struck
And drowning (at home) in their homes.

    [It was] then [that] on Peter's square,   220
Where in a corner a new house[4] had risen tall,
Where over [its] lofty porch,
Paw[s] upraised, like live [creatures],
Stand two guardian lions,
Astride on the beast of marble,   225
Hatless, arms crossed,
Sat motionless, terribly pale,
Eugene. He was in terror, poor [soul],
Not for himself. He did not sense
The greedy flood mount up,   230
Lapping at his soles from below,
[Or] the rain lash at his face,
[Or] the wind, wildly howling,
Suddenly tear off his hat.
His despairing gaze   235
Upon one distant range
Was fixed unmovingly. Like mountains,
From the stirred-up deeps
Rose up the billows there and raged,
There howled the storm, there drifted   240
Wreckage . . . God, God! there—
Alas, close, very close to the waves,
Almost right on the gulf—
Is an unpainted fence, and a willow,
And a frail little house: there [are] they,   245
The widow and [her] daughter, his Parasha,
His daydream . . . or [is it] in a dream
He sees this? Or is all our
Very life nothing but an idle dream,
A mockery of heaven at earth?   250

    And he, as though bewitched,
As though onto the marble riveted,
Cannot get down! About him
Is water and nothing more!

[4] The new edifice of the Ministry of War.

И обращен к нему спиною   255
В неколебимой вышине,
Над возмущенною Невою
Стоит с простертою рукою
Кумир на бронзовом коне.

ЧАСТЬ ВТОРАЯ

    Но вот, насытясь разрушеньем   260
И наглым буйством утомясь,
Нева обратно повлеклась,
Своим любуясь возмущеньем
И покидая с небреженьем
Свою добычу. Так злодей,   265
С свирепой шайкою своей
В село ворвавшись, ломит, режет,
Крушит и грабит; вопли, скрежет,
Насилье, брань, тревога, вой!..
И грабежом отягощенны,   270
Боясь погони, утомленны,
Спешат разбойники домой,
Добычу на пути роняя.

    Вода сбыла, и мостовая
Открылась, и Евгений мой   275
Спешит, душою замирая,
В надежде, страхе и тоске
К едва смирившейся реке.
Но, торжеством победы полны,
Еще кипели злобно волны,   280
Как бы под ними тлел огонь,
Еще их пена покрывала,
И тяжело Нева дышала,
Как с битвы прибежавший конь.
Евгений смотрит: видит лодку;   285
Он к ней бежит, как на находку;
Он перевозчика зовет —
И перевозчик беззаботный
Его за гривенник охотно
Чрез волны страшные везет.   290

And, with [his] back turned to him,   255
In unshakable eminence,
Over the tumultuous Nevá
Stands with outstretched hand
The Idol on [his] bronze steed.

PART TWO

But now, sated with destruction   260
And wearied by [her] insolent rampage,
Nevá drew back,
Reveling in the turmoil she had made
And abandoning with heedlessness
Her booty. Thus an outlaw   265
With his ruthless gang
Having burst into a village, will shatter, slash,
Smash and loot; shrieks, gnashing,
Rape, cursing, panic, howls!
And [then], with plunder weighed down,   270
Fearing pursuit, exhausted,
The robbers hurry homeward,
Dropping their plunder as they go.

The water had subsided, and the pavement
Was uncovered, and my Eugene   275
Is hastening, his heart wrenched
In hope, terror, and anguish,
Toward the barely calmed-down river.
But full of the triumph of victory,
The waves still seethed angrily,   280
As if beneath them fire were glowing,
Still foam covered them,
And heavily Nevá was breathing,
Like a charger that has galloped up from battle.
Eugene looks: sees a boat;   285
He runs to it as to a god-send,
And calls the ferryman—
And the ferryman, unconcerned,
For a ten-kopeck piece willingly
Takes him through the fearsome waves.   290

И долго с бурными волнами
Боролся опытный гребец,
И скрыться вглубь меж их рядами
Всечасно с дерзкими пловцами
Готов был челн — и наконец   295
Достиг он берега
                    Несчастный
Знакомой улицей бежит
В места знакомые. Глядит,
Узнать не может. Вид ужасный!
Всё перед ним завалено;   300
Что сброшено, что снесено;
Скривились домики, другие
Совсем обрушились, иные
Волнами сдвинуты; кругом,
Как будто в поле боевом,   305
Тела валяются. Евгений
Стремглав, не помня ничего,
Изнемогая от мучений,
Бежит туда, где ждет его
Судьба с неведомым известьем,   310
Как с запечатанным письмом.
И вот бежит уж он предместьем,
И вот залив, и близок дом...
Что ж это?..
            Он остановился.
Пошел назад и воротился.   315
Глядит... идет... еще глядит.
Вот место, где их дом стоит;
Вот ива. Были здесь вороты —
Снесло их, видно. Где же дом?
И, полон сумрачной заботы,   320
Всё ходит, ходит он кругом,
Толкует громко сам с собою —
И вдруг, ударя в лоб рукою,
Захохотал.

            Ночная мгла
На город трепетный сошла;   325

And long with the stormy waves
Struggled the experienced oarsman,
And the skiff was about to sink into the deep
Between their ranks at any time
With its bold sailors—and at last   295
It reached the bank.
                  The luckless man
Runs down the well-known street
To well-known places. He gazes,
Cannot make [anything] out. Terrible sight!
All before him is piled up,   300
One thing flung down, another swept away;
[Some] little houses are askew, others
Are utterly in ruins, others still
Moved from their places by the waves; all around,
As if upon a battlefield,   305
Bodies lie scattered. Eugene
Headlong, not remembering anything,
Breaking down under [his] torments,
Runs where there awaits him
Fate with unknown tidings,   310
As with a sealed letter.
And here he is already running through the suburb,
And here is the Gulf, and nearby the house . . .
But what is this . . . ?
                He stopped.
He went back and turned around.   315
He gazes . . . walks [on] . . . gazes again.
Here is the place where their house stands;
Here is the willow. There was a gate here—
It must have been swept away. But where is the house?
And full of dark alarm,   320
He keeps walking, walking round about,
Argues aloud with himself—
And suddenly, striking his forehead with his hand,
He burst out laughing.

                The mist of night
Came down upon the quaking city;   325

Но долго жители не спали
И меж собою толковали
О дне минувшем.

Утра луч
Из-за усталых, бледных туч
Блеснул над тихою столицей   330
И не нашел уже следов
Беды вчерашней; багряницей
Уже прикрыто было зло.
В порядок прежний всё вошло.
Уже по улицам свободным   335
С своим бесчувствием холодным
Ходил народ. Чиновный люд,
Покинув свой ночной приют,
На службу шел. Торгаш отважный,
Не унывая, открывал   340
Невой ограбленный подвал,
Сбираясь свой убыток важный
На ближнем выместить. С дворов
Свозили лодки.
                Граф Хвостов,
Поэт, любимый небесами,   345
Уж пел бессмертными стихами
Несчастье невских берегов.

Но бедный, бедный мой Евгений...
Увы! его смятенный ум
Против ужасных потрясений   350
Не устоял. Мятежный шум
Невы и ветров раздавался
В его ушах. Ужасных дум
Безмолвно полон, он скитался.
Его терзал какой-то сон.   355
Прошла неделя, месяц — он
К себе домой не возвращался.
Его пустынный уголок
Отдал внаймы, как вышел срок,
Хозяин бедному поэту.   360
Евгений за своим добром

But long the townsmen did not sleep
And talked among themselves
About the day [just] passed.

      The ray of morning
From behind tired, pale clouds
Glinted over the silent capital   330
And found no more traces
Of yesterday's calamity; with purple cape[5]
Already covered was the mischief.
Everything settled [back] into the former order.
Already along the clear streets   335
With their cool indifference
People were walking. Officialdom,
Having left the night's shelter,
Was off to work. The plucky tradesman,
Undaunted, was opening up   340
The cellar looted by Nevá,
Preparing to recoup his grave loss
At his neighbor's cost. Out of the courtyards
Boats were being carted off.
      Count Khvostov,
Poet beloved of the heavens,   345
Already sang in deathless verses
Of the misfortune of the Nevá banks.

 But my poor, poor Eugene . . .
Alas! his turbid mind
Against [those] dreadful shocks   350
Did not stand up. The noisy tumult
Of the Nevá and of the winds resounded
In his ears, of horrid thoughts
Speechlessly full, he roved about.
He was tormented by a kind of dream. 355
There passed a week, a month—he
Did not return to his own place.
His forsaken nook
Was let upon expiry of [his] term
By the landlord to a poor poet.   360
Eugene never came

[5] This is assumed to refer either to imperial charity or to the calm dawn, or ambiguously to both.

Не приходил. Он скоро свету
Стал чужд. Весь день бродил пешком,
А спал на пристани; питался
В окошко поданным куском.   365
Одежда ветхая на нем
Рвалась и тлела. Злые дети
Бросали камни вслед ему.
Нередко кучерские плети
Его стегали, потому   370
Что он не разбирал дороги
Уж никогда; казалось — он
Не примечал. Он оглушен
Был шумом внутренней тревоги.
И так он свой несчастный век   375
Влачил, ни зверь, ни человек,
Ни то, ни се, ни житель света,
Ни призрак мертвый...
                Раз он спал
У невской пристани. Дни лета
Клонились к осени. Дышал   380
Ненастный ветер. Мрачный вал
Плескал на пристань, ропща пени
И бьясь об гладкие ступени,
Как челобитчик у дверей
Ему не внемлющих судей.   385
Бедняк проснулся. Мрачно было:
Дождь капал, ветер выл уныло,
И с ним вдали, во тьме ночной
Перекликался часовой...
Вскочил Евгений; вспомнил живо   390
Он прошлый ужас; торопливо
Он встал; пошел бродить и вдруг
Остановился — и вокруг
Тихонько стал водить очами
С боязнью дикой на лице.   395
Он очутился под столбами
Большого дома. На крыльце,
С подъятой лапой, как живые,
Стояли львы сторожевые,
И прямо в темной вышине   400
Над огражденною скалою

To fetch his goods. Soon to the world he
Became a stranger. All day he wandered on foot,
And slept on the embankment; he fed
On morsel[s] handed him through window[s].   365
The threadbare clothing he wore
Tore and mildewed. Wicked children
Threw stones at his back.
More than once coachmen's whips
Lashed him, because   370
He could make out his way
No longer, ever; [but] it seemed he
Did not notice. He was deafened
By the rushing noise of anxious inner turmoil.
And so his miserable span of life   375
He dragged on, neither beast nor man,
Neither this nor that, neither dweller of the earth
Nor specter of the dead . . .
                       Once he slept
By the Nevá embankment. The days of summer
Inclined to autumn. There was breathing   380
An untoward wind. A sullen tide
Splashed the embankment, muttering plaints
And beating against the smooth steps
Like a petitioner at the door
Of magistrates who do not hearken him.   385
The poor wretch wakened. It was murky:
Rain dripped, the wind was howling mournfully,
And with it in the distance, in the gloom of night,
A watchman traded hails . . .
Eugene jumped up; he vividly recalled   390
The former horror; hastily
He rose, went off to roam, and of a sudden
Came to a halt—and round about
He gingerly allowed his eyes to wander,
Wild apprehension on his face.   395
He found himself beneath the pillars
Of a great house. Upon the portico
With upraised paw, as though alive,
Stood lions sentinel,
And straight, in his dark eminence,   400
Above the railed-in crag

Кумир с простертою рукою
Сидел на бронзовом коне.

  Евгений вздрогнул. Прояснились
В нем страшно мысли. Он узнал   405
И место, где потоп играл,
Где волны хищные толпились,
Бунтуя злобно вкруг него,
И львов, и площадь, и того,
Кто неподвижно возвышался   410
Во мраке медною главой,
Того, чьей волей роковой
Под морем город основался...
Ужасен он в окрестной мгле!
Какая дума на челе!   415
Какая сила в нем сокрыта!
А в сем коне какой огонь!
Куда ты скачешь, гордый конь,
И где опустишь ты копыта?
О мощный властелин судьбы!   420
Не так ли ты над самой бездной,
На высоте, уздой железной
Россию поднял на дыбы? [5]

  Кругом подножия кумира
Безумец бедный обошел   425
И взоры дикие навел
На лик державца полумира.
Стеснилась грудь его. Чело
К решетке хладной прилегло,
Глаза подернулись туманом,   430
По сердцу пламень пробежал,
Вскипела кровь. Он мрачен стал
Пред горделивым истуканом
И, зубы стиснув, пальцы сжав,
Как обуянный силой черной,   435
«Добро, строитель чудотворный! —
Шепнул он, злобно задрожав,—
Ужо тебе!..» И вдруг стремглав
Бежать пустился. Показалось

---

[5] Смотри описание памятника в Мицкевиче. Оно заимствовано из Рубана — как замечает сам Мицкевич.

The Idol with his arm stretched forth
Was seated on [his] steed of bronze.

    Eugene shuddered. Fearfully clear
Became his thoughts. He recognized   405
The place where the flood had sported
Where the preying waves had crowded,
Rioting viciously about him,
And the lions, and the square, and him,
Who motionlessly loomed,   410
His brazen head in the dusk,
Him by whose fateful will
The city by the sea was founded . . .
Awesome [is] he in the surrounding gloom!
What thought upon his brow!   415
What power within him hidden!
And in that steed, what fire!
Whither do you gallop, haughty steed,
And where will you plant your hooves?
Oh, mighty potentate of fate!   420
Was it not thus, aloft hard by the abyss,
That with curb of iron
You reared up Russia?

    Round about the Idol's pedestal
The poor deranged man walked   425
And cast fierce glances
Upon the countenance of the ruler of half the world.
His chest tightened. [His] brow
Was pressed against the chilly railing,
[His] eyes filmed over with dimness,   430
Flame ran over [his] heart,
[His] blood seethed. Scowling he stood
Before the prideful statue
And, teeth clenched, fingers tightened into fists,
As though possessed by [some] black power,   435
"All right then, wonder-working builder!"
He whispered with a shudder of spite,
"I'll [show] you . . . !" And suddenly full tilt
He set off running. It seemed

Ему, что грозного царя,   440
Мгновенно гневом возгоря,
Лицо тихонько обращалось...
И он по площади пустой
Бежит и слышит за собой —
Как будто грома грохотанье —   445
Тяжело-звонкое скаканье
По потрясенной мостовой.
И, озарен луною бледной,
Простерши руку в вышине,
За ним несется Всадник Медный   450
На звонко-скачущем коне;
И во всю ночь безумец бедный,
Куда стопы ни обращал,
За ним повсюду Всадник Медный
С тяжелым топотом скакал.   455

        И с той поры, когда случалось
Идти той площадью ему,
В его лице изображалось
Смятенье. К сердцу своему
Он прижимал поспешно руку,   460
Как бы его смиряя муку,
Картуз изношенный сымал,
Смущенных глаз не подымал
И шел сторонкой.

                Остров малый
На взморье виден. Иногда   465
Причалит с неводом туда
Рыбак, на ловле запоздалый,
И бедный ужин свой варит,
Или чиновник посетит,
Гуляя в лодке в воскресенье,   470
Пустынный остров. Не взросло
Там ни былинки. Наводненье
Туда, играя, занесло
Домишко ветхий. Над водою
Остался он, как черный куст.   475
Его прошедшею весною

To him that the dread Tsar's face,   440
Instantly aflame with wrath,
Was slowly turning . . .
And he runs down the empty square
And hears behind him,
As if it were the rumbling of thunder,   445
A heavily-ringing gallop
Over the quaking pavement.
And twilit by the pallid moon,
Arm reaching forth on high,
There speeds after him the Bronze Horseman   450
Upon the clangorously galloping steed;
And all night, wherever the wretched madman
Might turn his steps,
Behind him everywhere the Bronze Horseman
Was galloping with heavy clatter.   455

    And since that time, whenever he happened
To walk by that square,
His face would express
Confusion. To his heart
He would hastily press [his] hand,   460
As if soothing its agony,
[His] worn cap he would doff,
Would not lift up [his] abashed eyes
And go some other way.

                        A small island
Can be seen offshore. Sometimes   465
There will make fast there with [his] net
A fisherman belated on [his] haul
And cook his frugal supper there,
Or a government clerk will visit,
Out boating on a Sunday,   470
The desolate island. There has grown
No green blade there. The inundation
Thither in its play had swept
A frail little house. At the waterline
It had been left like a black bush;   475
The foregoing spring

Свезли на барке. Был он пуст
И весь разрушен. У порога
Нашли безумца моего,
И тут же хладный труп его
Похоронили ради бога.

They hauled it off on a barge. It was empty
And all in ruin. At the threshold
They came upon my madman,
And on that spot his chill corpse   480
They buried for the love of God.

Избранные Строфы из *Евгения Онегина:*
РОМАН В СТИХАХ

[1823–1831]

I, 1

«Мой дядя самых честных правил,
Когда не в шутку занемог,
Он уважать себя заставил
И лучше выдумать не мог.
Его пример другим наука;   5
Но, боже мой, какая скука
С больным сидеть и день, и ночь,
Не отходя ни шагу прочь!
Какое низкое коварство
Полуживого забавлять,   10
Ему подушки поправлять,
Печально подносить лекарство,
Вздыхать и думать про себя:
«Когда же черт возьмет тебя!»

I, 2

Так думал молодой повеса,
Летя в пыли на почтовых,
Всевышней волею Зевеса
Наследник всех своих родных.—
Друзья Людмилы и Руслана!   5
С героем моего романа
Без предисловий, сей же час
Позвольте познакомить вас:

Selected Stanzas from *Eugene Onegin*
A NOVEL IN VERSE

[1823–1831]

I, 1

"My uncle of most honest principles,[1]
When in good earnest he fell ill,
Compelled [others] to respect him,
And could not have contrived [a] better [way].
His example [is] a lesson to others;   5
But, oh my goodness, what a bore
With a sick man to sit both day and night,
Not going (off) even a step away!
What low cunning
To amuse one half alive,   10
Adjust the pillows for him,
Sadly bring up to him his medicine,
To sigh and think in private:
Come, when will the Devil take you?"

I, 2

Thus mused a young scapegrace,
As he (flew) sped in the dust on post-horses,
By the all-highest will of Zeus
The heir to all his kinsmen.
Friends of Ljudmila and Ruslan![2]   5
With the hero of my novel
Without foreword, right away
Allow me to acquaint you:

[1] To Pushkin's readers, this inevitably brought to mind the start of a well-known fable by Krylov, "An ass of the most honest principles . . ."
[2] See Introduction, page xxx.

Онегин, добрый мой приятель,
Родился на брегах Невы,
Где, может быть, родились вы
Или блистали, мой читатель;
Там некогда гулял и я:
Но вреден север для меня .

10

II, 1

Деревня, где скучал Евгений,
Была прелестный уголок;
Там друг невинных наслаждений
Благословить бы небо мог.
Господский дом уединенный,
Горой от ветров огражденный,
Стоял над речкою. Вдали
Пред ним пестрели и цвели
Луга и нивы золотые,
Мелькали селы; здесь и там
Стада бродили по лугам,
И сени расширял густые
Огромный, запущенный сад,
Приют задумчивых дриад.

5

10

II, 2

Почтенный замок был построен,
Как замки строиться должны:
Отменно прочен и спокоен
Во вкусе умной старины.
Везде высокие покои,
В гостиной штофные обои,
Царей портреты на стенах,
И печи в пестрых изразцах.
Всё это ныне обветшало,
Не знаю, право, почему;

5

10

Onegin, a good friend of mine,
Was born on the banks of Nevá,   10
Where, maybe, you were born
Or shone, my reader;
There at one time strolled I too:
But harmful is the north for me.[3]

_____

II, 1

The estate where Onegin fretted
Was a delightful little spot;
There a friend of innocent enjoyments
Might well have praised Heaven.
The secluded manor house,   5
Shielded by a hill from winds,
Stood on a little river. In the distance
Before him bloomed and shone in motley colors
Meadows and golden cornfields.
Hamlets winked here and there,   10
Herds wandered on the meadows,
And dense shadows were spread
By a vast neglected park,
Haven of pensive dryads.

II, 2

The worthy mansion was constructed
As mansions ought to be built:
Exquisitely solid and calm [it was],
In the taste of a wise antiquity.
Everywhere were high-ceilinged rooms,   5
The drawing room was lined with brocade,
Portraits of tsars[4] [hung] on the walls,
And [there were] stoves of colorful tiles.
All this is out of fashion nowadays,
I don't know really why;   10

[3] Allusion to Pushkin's recent banishment from St. Petersburg for writing subversive poetry.

[4] The manuscripts have either "tsars" or "ancestors" here; presumably it was suspected that the censors might take umbrage at the notion that displaying portraits of tsars was old-fashioned.

Да, впрочем, другу моему
В том нужды было очень мало,
Затем, что он равно зевал
Средь модных и старинных зал.

=====

III, 22

Я знал красавиц недоступных,
Холодных, чистых, как зима,
Неумолимых, неподкупных,
Непостижимых для ума;
Дивился я их спеси модной,   5
Их добродетели природной,
И, признаюсь, от них бежал,
И, мнится, с ужасом читал
Над их бровями надпись ада:
Оставь надежду навсегда.   10
Внушать любовь для них беда,
Пугать людей для них отрада.
Быть может, на брегах Невы
Подобных дам видали вы.

III, 23

Среди поклонников послушных
Других причудниц я видал,
Самолюбиво равнодушных
Для вздохов страстных и похвал.
И что ж нашел я с изумленьем?   5
Они, суровым поведеньем
Пугая робкую любовь,
Ее привлечь умели вновь
По крайней мере сожаленьем,
По крайней мере звук речей   10
Казался иногда нежней,
И с легковерным ослепленьем
Опять любовник молодой
Бежал за милой суетой.

But for that matter, to my friend
This was of very little use,
Because he yawned impartially
In modish and old-fashioned apartments.

———

III, 22

I have known unapproachable beauties,
Frigid, pure as winter,
Inexorable, incorruptible,
Unattainable to the mind;
I marveled at their modish hauteur,   5
Their innate virtue,
And, I confess, fled from them,
And, it would seem, with terror read
Upon their brows the inscription over hell:
Abandon hope forever.   10
To instill love, to them is a misfortune,
To frighten people, to them is a pleasure.
It may be, on the banks of the Nevá
You have met with ladies of this kind.

III, 23

Amid [their] obedient adherents
Other charmers have I seen,
Complacently indifferent
To sighs of passion and to compliments.
And what did I find to my amazement?   5
They, with [their] severe conduct
Scaring bashful love,
Knew how to lure it back
At least with sympathy,
At least, the sound of their speeches   10
Seemed tenderer at times,
And with credulous blindness
Once again the youthful lover
Pursued the dear vain pastime.

III, 25

Кокетка судит хладнокровно,
Татьяна любит не шутя
И предается безусловно
Любви, как милое дитя.
Не говорит она: отложим —   5
Любви мы цену тем умножим,
Вернее в сети заведем;
Сперва тщеславие кольнем
Надеждой, там недоуменьем
Измучим сердце, а потом   10
Ревнивым оживим огнем;
А то, скучая наслажденьем,
Невольник хитрый из оков
Всечасно вырваться готов.

IV, 38, 39

Прогулки, чтенье, сон глубокой,
Лесная тень, журчанье струй,
Порой белянки черноокой
Младой и свежий поцелуй,
Узде послушный конь ретивый,   5
Обед довольно прихотливый,
Бутылка светлого вина,
Уединенье, тишина:
Вот жизнь Онегина святая;
И нечувствительно он ей   10
Предался, красных летних дней
В беспечной неге не считая,
Забыв и город, и друзей,
И скуку праздничных затей.

IV, 40

Но наше северное лето,
Карикатура южных зим,

III, 25

A flirt discriminates cold-bloodedly,
Tatyana loves in good earnest
And gives herself over unreservedly
To love, like a dear young child.
She does not say: let us defer—   5
Love's price with this we multiply,
The more surely lead [the prey] into the nets;
At first we needle vanity
With hope, there with perplexity
We vex the heart, and then   10
Stir it with jealous fire;
Lest, tiring of enjoyment,
The cunning slave be ready
To break at any moment from his bonds.

IV, 38, 39

Outings, reading, deep sleep,
Sylvan shade, the purl of brooks,
At times a white-skinned, black-eyed girl's
Young and fresh kiss,
A spirited horse, to rein obedient,   5
A rather dainty dinner,
A bottle of bright wine,
Seclusion, quietude:
Thus Onegin's saintly life;
And without awareness he to it   10
Gave himself over, the fair summer days
In carefree indulgence not counting,
Forgotten both city and friends,
And the tedium of holiday pursuits.

IV, 40

But our northern summer,
Caricature of southern winters,

Мелькнет и нет: известно это,
Хоть мы признаться не хотим.
Уж небо осенью дышало,   5
Уж реже солнышко блистало,
Короче становился день,
Лесов таинственная сень
С печальным шумом обнажалась,
Ложился на поля туман,   10
Гусей крикливых караван
Тянулся к югу: приближалась
Довольно скучная пора;
Стоял ноябрь уж у двора.

IV, 41

Встает заря во мгле холодной;
На нивах шум работ умолк;
С своей волчихою голодной
Выходит на дорогу волк;
Его почуя, конь дорожный   5
Храпит — и путник осторожный
Несется в гору во весь дух;
На утренней заре пастух
Не гонит уж коров из хлева,
И в час полуденный в кружок   10
Их не зовет его рожок;
В избушке распевая, дева
Прядет, и, зимних друг ночей,
Трещит лучинка перед ней.

IV, 42

И вот уже трещат морозы
И серебрятся средь полей...
(Читатель ждет уж рифмы розы;
На, вот возьми ее скорей!)
Опрятней модного паркета   5
Блистает речка, льдом одета.

Flashes and is over: this is well known,
Though we don't care to admit it.
The sky already breathed autumn,   5
More seldom already the dear sun glittered,
Shorter became the day,
The woods' mysterious shelter
With mournful murmur bared itself,
Mist settled on the fields.   10
A caravan of strident geese
Drew southward: there approached
A rather irksome season;
November stood already at the door.

IV, 41

The dawn arises in cold fog;
On harvest fields the noise of work(s) is stilled;
With his hungry she-wolf
Comes out upon the road the wolf;
Scenting him, the horse on the road   5
Snorts—and the wary traveler
(Soars) rushes uphill in all haste;
The shepherd at the break of day
No longer drives the cows out of the shed,
And at the hour of noon into a circle   10
His horn calls them no more;
Within the little cabin chanting, the maiden
Spins, and, the friend of winter nights,
The pine-flare crackles in front of her.

IV, 42

And here the frosts already crackle
And silver up amid the fields . . .
(The reader already expects the rhyme *roses;*
So take it and have done with it!)
Neater than a modish parquet floor,   5
Gleams the little river, clad in ice.

Мальчишек радостный народ
Коньками звучно режет лед;
На красных лапках гусь тяжелый,
Задумав плыть по лону вод,   10
Ступает бережно на лед,
Скользит и падает; веселый
Мелькает, вьется первый снег,
Звездами падая на брег.

IV, 43

В глуши что делать в эту пору?
Гулять? Деревня той порой
Невольно докучает взору
Однообразной наготой.
Скакать верхом в степи суровой?   5
Но конь, притупленной подковой
Неверный зацепляя лед,
Того и жди, что упадет.
Сиди под кровлею пустынной,
Читай: вот Прадт, вот W. Scott.   10
Не хочешь? — поверяй расход,
Сердись иль пей, и вечер длинный
Кой-как пройдет, а завтра то ж,
И славно зиму проведешь.

V, 1

В тот год осенняя погода
Стояла долго на дворе,
Зимы ждала, ждала природа.
Снег выпал только в январе
На третье в ночь. Проснувшись рано,   5
В окно увидела Татьяна
Поутру побелевший двор,
Куртины, кровли и забор,
На стеклах легкие узоры,
Деревья в зимнем серебре,   10

The merry tribe of little boys
With a-ringing skates cuts the ice;
On [her] red pads a ponderous goose,
Thinking to swim upon the waters' lap,   10
Steps gingerly upon the ice,
Slithers and falls; joyous[ly]
Flashes, whirls the first snow,
Falling in stars upon the bank.

IV, 43

What to do in the backwoods at this time?
Go for a walk? The countryside that time of year
Is bound to irritate the sight
With its monotonous nakedness.
Canter in the bleak steppe?   5
But [your] steed, with blunted shoe
Catching on the treacherous ice,
Just you wait, may have a fall.
Sit under [your] desolate roof,
Read: here is Pradt, here Walter Scott!   10
Don't want to?—verify expenses,
Sulk, or drink, and the long evening
Somehow will pass, and tomorrow the same thing,
And famously you'll pass the winter.

V, 1

That year the autumn weather
Held for a long time out of doors,
Nature waited [and] waited for the winter.
Snow fell only in January
On the night of the second. Having woken early,   5
Through the window Tatyana saw
At morn the yard turned white,
Flower beds, roofs, and fence,
On the windowpanes faint patterns,
The trees in winter silver,   10

Сорок веселых на дворе
И мягко устланные горы
Зимы блистательным ковром.
Все ярко, все бело кругом.

V, 2

Зима!.. Крестьянин торжествуя
На дровнях обновляет путь;
Его лошадка, снег почуя,
Плетется рысью как-нибудь;
Бразды пушистые взрывая,   5
Летит кибитка удалая;
Ямщик сидит на облучке
В тулупе, в красном кушаке.
Вот бегает дворовый мальчик,
В салазки *жучку* посадив,   10
Себя в коня преобразив;
Шалун уж заморозил пальчик:
Ему и больно и смешно,
А мать грозит ему в окно...

V, 11

И снится чудный сон Татьяне.
Ей снится, будто бы она
Идет по снеговой поляне,
Печальной мглой окружена;
В сугробах снежных перед нею   5
Шумит, клубит волной своею
Кипучий, темный и седой
Поток, не скованный зимой;
Две жердочки, склеены льдиной,
Дрожащий, гибельный мосток,   10
Положены через поток:
И пред шумящею пучиной,
Недоумения полна,
Остановилася она.

Merry magpies in the yard,
And the hills softly sheeted
In winter's glistening carpet.
All is bright, all white around.

V, 2

Winter! . . . The peasant, in a festive mood,
On a sledge opens up the track;
His little nag, sensing the snow,
Shuffles along at a kind of trot;
Carving out fluffy furrows,   5
A spirited kibitka[5] flies along;
The coachman sits upon the box
In sheepskin coat, with a red sash.
Here runs a yard-boy,
Having sat his *Zhuchka* in [his] sled   10
And turned himself into the steed;
The scamp already has frozen a finger;
It both hurts him and makes him laugh,
While mother threatens him from the window . . .

V, 11

And Tatyana dreams a wondrous dream.
She dreams that she
Is walking over a snowy clearing,
Surrounded by dreary fog;
In the snowdrifts before her   5
[There] gurgles, swirls with its wave
A churning, dark and grizzled
Torrent, not fettered by winter;
Two saplings, welded together by some ice,
A shaking, hazardous little bridge,   10
Are laid across the torrent:
And before [this] rushing gulf,
Full of perplexity,
She stopped.

    [5] Light cart or sleigh with a hood.

V, 12

Как на досадную разлуку,
Татьяна ропщет на ручей;
Не видит никого, кто руку
С той стороны подал бы ей;
Но вдруг сугроб зашевелился,   5
И кто ж из-под него явился?
Большой, взъерошенный медведь;
Татьяна *ах!* а он реветь,
И лапу с острыми когтями
Ей протянул; она скрепясь   10
Дрожащей ручкой оперлась
И боязливыми шагами
Перебралась через ручей;
Пошла — и что ж? медведь за ней!

V, 13

Она, взглянуть назад не смея,
Поспешный ускоряет шаг;
Но от косматого лакея
Не может убежать никак;
Кряхтя, валит медведь несносный;   5
Пред ними лес; недвижны сосны
В своей нахмуренной красе;
Отягчены их ветви все
Клоками снега; сквозь вершины
Осин, берез и лип нагих   10
Сияет луч светил ночных;
Дороги нет; кусты, стремнины
Метелью все занесены,
Глубоко в снег погружены.

VI, 44

Познал я глас иных желаний,
Познал я новую печаль;

V, 12

As at an irksome separation
Tatyana mutters at the stream;
Sees no one who a hand
From the far side might offer her;
But suddenly a snowdrift stirred,   5
And who is it emerged from under it?
A big shaggy bear;
"Ah!" [cried] Tatyana, and he roared
And a paw with sharp claws
Stretched out to her; she, nerving herself   10
Leaned on it with a trembling little hand
And with timorous steps
Crossed over the stream;
Went on—and what? The bear [came] after her!

V, 13

Not daring to look back, she
Speeds up her hurried pace;
But from the shaggy footman
[She] cannot escape, try as she might;
Grunting, the loathsome bear lumbers on;   5
Before them [lies] a forest; pines [stand] motionless
In their frowning beauty;
Weighed down are all their branches
With clumps of snow; through the crowns
Of naked aspen, beech, and linden   10
Shines the ray of the nocturnal lights;
There is no path; bushes, ravines
[Are] all drifted over by the blizzard,
Deeply buried in snow.

VI, 44

I have come to know the voice of other desires,
Have come to know a new distress;

Для первых нет мне упований,
А старой мне печали жаль.
Мечты! мечты! где ваша сладость?   5
Где, вечная к ней рифма, *младость?*
Ужель и вправду, наконец,
Увял, увял ее венец?
Ужель и впрямь, и в самом деле,
Без элегических затей,   10
Весна моих промчалась дней
(Что я шутя твердил доселе)?
И ей ужель возврата нет?
Ужель мне скоро тридцать лет?

VI, 45

Так, полдень мой настал, и нужно
Мне в том сознаться, вижу я.
Но, так и быть: простимся дружно,
О юность легкая моя!
Благодарю за наслажденья,   5
За грусть, за милые мученья,
За шум, за бури, за пиры,
За все, за все твои дары;
Благодарю тебя. Тобою,
Среди тревог и в тишине,   10
Я насладился... и вполне;
Довольно! С ясною душою
Пускаюсь ныне в новый путь
От жизни прошлой отдохнуть.

VI, 46

Дай оглянусь. Простите ж, сени,
Где дни мои текли в глуши,
Исполнены страстей и лени,
И снов задумчивой души.
А ты, младое вдохновенье,   5
Волнуй мое воображенье,

Of the first I hold no hopes,
And for the old distress I regret.
Dreams, dreams! Where is your sweetness?   5
Where—constant rhyme to it—is *youth?*
Can it be that in truth at last
Its wreath is wilted, wilted?
Can it be that frankly and in actual fact,
Without elegiac conceits   10
The springtime of my days has flashed by
(As I in jest maintained hitherto)?
And can it be there's no return for it?
Can it be true I shall be thirty soon?

VI, 45

Indeed my midday has arrived, and there is need
For me to be aware of this, I see.
Well, so be it: let us take part in friendship,
Oh my nimble youth!
I render thanks for the delights enjoyed,   5
For grief, for torments dear,
For hubbub, for storms, for feasts,
For all, for all your gifts;
I render thanks to you. In you,
Amid alarums and in quiet time,   10
I have delighted . . . and in full measure;
Enough! With clear soul
I now set off upon a novel path
To rest from former life.

VI, 46

Let me glance back. Farewell then, shelters,
Wherein my days flowed on in deep retreat,
Filled with passions and indolence
And musings of the pensive soul.
And as for thee, young inspiration,   5
Stir my imagination,

Дремоту сердца оживляй,
В мой угол чаще прилетай,
Не дай остыть душе поэта,
Ожесточиться, очерстветь,   10
И, наконец, окаменеть
В мертвящем упоенье света,
В сем омуте, где с вами я
Купаюсь, милые друзья!

─────────

VII, 1

Гонимы вешними лучами,
С окрестных гор уже снега
Сбежали мутными ручьями
На потопленные луга.
Улыбкой ясною природа   5
Сквозь сон встречает утро года;
Синея блещут небеса.
Еще прозрачные, леса
Как будто пухом зеленеют.
Пчела за данью полевой   10
Летит из кельи восковой.
Долины сохнут и пестреют;
Стада шумят, и соловей
Уж пел в безмолвии ночей.

VII, 2

Как грустно мне твое явленье,
Весна, весна! пора любви!
Какое томное волненье
В моей душе, в моей крови!
С каким тяжелым умиленьем   5
Я наслаждаюсь дуновеньем
В лицо мне веющей весны
На лоне сельской тишины!
Или мне чуждо наслажденье,
И всё, что радует, живит,   10

The somnolence of the heart enliven,
Come winging oftener to my nook,
Let not the poet's soul grow frigid,
Coarsen, crust over,   10
And in the end be petrified
In the deadening delirium of the world,
In that morass, where you and I
Are bathing, my dear friends!

VII, 1

Chased by the rays of spring,
Down the surrounding hills the snows already
Have run in turbid streams
Onto the flooded meadows.
With a serene smile, nature   5
Greets, only half awake, the morning of the year;
Turning blue, the heavens glisten.
The yet transparent woods
Come out in green as with a down.
The bee bent on the tribute of the fields   10
Flies from the waxen cell.
The lowlands dry and put on colors;
Herds rustle, and the nightingale
Has sung already in the hush of nights.

VII, 2

How sad to me is your appearing,
Spring, spring! season of love!
What languid stir
[Is] in my soul, in my blood!
With what a heavyhearted tenderness   5
I rejoice in the wafting
Of spring as it breathes against my face
In the lap of rural quietude!
Is then enjoyment strange to me,
And all that gladdens, animates,   10

Все, что ликует и блестит,
Наводит скуку и томленье
На душу мертвую давно,
И всё ей кажется темно?

VII, 6

Меж гор, лежащих полукругом,
Пойдем туда, где ручеек
Виясь, бежит зеленым лугом
К реке сквозь липовый лесок.
Там соловей, весны любовник,   5
Всю ночь поет; цветет шиповник,
И слышен говор ключевой,—
Там виден камень гробовой
В тени двух сосен устарелых.
Пришельцу надпись говорит: 10
«Владимир Ленский здесь лежит,
Погибший рано смертью смелых,
В такой-то год, таких-то лет.
Покойся, юноша-поэт!»

VII, 7

На ветви сосны преклоненной,
Бывало, ранний ветерок
Над этой урною смиренной
Качал таинственный венок.
Бывало, в поздние досуги   5
Сюда ходили две подруги,
И на могиле при луне,
Обнявшись, плакали оне.
Но ныне... памятник унылый
Забыт. К нему привычный след   10
Заглох. Венка на ветви нет;
Один под ним, седой и хилый,
Пастух по-прежнему поет
И обувь бедную плетет.

All that exults and glistens,
Brings dullness and languor
Upon a soul long dead,
And all seems dark to it?

VII, 6

'Mid hills lying in a half-circle,
Let us go where a little stream
Runs meandering through a green meadow
To a river, across a linden grove.
There the nightingale, spring's lover,   5
Sings all night; a wild rosebush blooms,
And one can hear the babble of a spring;
There one can see a gravestone
In the shade of two ancient pines.
An inscription tells the visitor: 10
"Vladimir Lensky lies here,
Who early died the death of the bold,
In such-and-such a year, aged so-and-so.
Rest in peace, poet-youth!"

VII, 7

Upon an overhanging pine bough,
It used to be, the morning breeze
Over that humble urn
Sway a mysterious wreath.
It used to be, in [their] late leisure times   5
Two girl friends would be coming here,
And in the moonlight on the grave
They would embrace and weep.
But now . . . the mournful monument,
Is forgotten. To it the wonted track   10
Is overgrown. No wreath is on the bough;
Alone beneath it, gray and frail,
A shepherd sings as before
And his poor footgear plaits.

―――――――――

VIII, 1

В те дни, когда в садах Лицея
Я безмятежно расцветал,
Читал охотно Апулея,
А Цицерона не читал,
В те дни в таинственных долинах,   5
Весной, при кликах лебединых,
Близ вод, сиявших в тишине,
Являться муза стала мне.
Моя студенческая келья
Вдруг озарилась: муза в ней   10
Открыла пир младых затей,
Воспела детские веселья,
И славу нашей старины,
И сердца трепетные сны.

VIII, 2

И свет ее с улыбкой встретил;
Успех нас первый окрылил;
Старик Державин нас заметил
И, в гроб сходя, благословил.

. . . .
. . . .
. . . .
. . . .
. . . .
. . . .
. . . .
. . . .
. . . .
. . . .

VIII, 3

И я, в закон себе вменяя
Страстей единый произвол,

VIII, 1

In the days when in the Lyceum gardens
I blossomed in untroubled ease,
Eagerly read Apuleius,
And I did not read Cicero.
In those days, in mysterious valleys,   5
In springtime, to the cries of swans,
Close by the waters gleaming in the stillness,
The Muse began to appear to me.
My student cell
Was of a sudden lit with radiance: the Muse in it   10
Opened a feast of young conceits,
[And] sang [of] childish merriments,
And of the glory of our ancient times,
And of the heart's tremulous dreams.

VIII, 2

And the world met her with a smile;
Success first gave me wings;
Old Derzhavin noticed us
And as he sank into the grave, gave his blessing.
. . . .
. . . .
. . . .
. . . .
. . . .
. . . .
. . . .
. . . .
. . . .
. . . .

VIII, 3

And I, as law appointing for myself
The arbitrary impulse of passion alone,

С толпою чувства разделяя,
Я музу резвую привел
На шум пиров и буйных споров,   5
Грозы полуночных дозоров;
И к ним в безумные пиры
Она несла свои дары
И, как вакханочка, резвилась,
За чашей пела для гостей,   10
И молодежь минувших дней
За нею буйно волочилась,
А я гордился меж друзей
Подругой ветреной моей.

VIII, 4

Но я отстал от их союза
И вдаль бежал... Она за мной.
Как часто ласковая муза
Мне услаждала путь немой
Волшебством тайного рассказа!   5
Как часто по скалам Кавказа
Она Ленорой, при луне,
Со мной скакала на коне,
Как часто по брегам Тавриды
Она меня во мгле ночной   10
Водила слушать шум морской,
Немолчный шепот Нереиды,
Глубокий, вечный хор валов,
Хвалебный гимн отцу миров.

VIII, 5

И, позабыв столицы дальной
И блеск, и шумные пиры,
В глуши Молдавии печальной
Она смиренные шатры
Племен бродящих посещала,   5
И между ими одичала,

Sharing [my] feelings with the crowd,
I brought [my] lively Muse
To the hubbub of feasts and high-spirited disputes,   5
The threats of midnight watchmen;
And to their wild feasts
She brought her gifts
And frolicked like a little bacchante,
Over the bowl sang for the guests,   10
And the young men of bygone days
Exuberantly courted her,
And I took pride among my friends
In my volatile companion.

VIII, 4

But I dropped out of their league
And fled afar . . . She followed me.
How often did the tender Muse
Make sweet for me [my] silent path
With the witchery of [her] secret storytelling!   5
How often on the crags of the Caucasus
She, like Lenore, in the moonshine
Did gallop with me on a steed!
How often by the shores of Tauris
In the gloom of night   10
She led me to listen to the ocean's roar,
The never-silent murmur of the Nereid,
The deep, eternal chorus of the swells,
The hymn of praise to the Father of the worlds.

VIII, 5

And, having forgotten the far-off capital's
Glitter and noisy feasts,
In sad Moldavia's desolation
She the pacific tents
Of wandering tribes used to visit,   5
And went native among them,

И позабыла речь богов
Для скудных, странных языков,
Для песен степи ей любезной...
Вдруг изменилось всё кругом: 10
И вот она в саду моем
Явилась барышней уездной,
С печальной думою в очах,
С французской книжкою в руках.

And forgot the speech of the gods
For frugal, strange tongues,
For the songs of the steppe that she found pleasing . . .
All of a sudden all was changed about: 10
And lo! in my garden she appeared
In a provincial damsel's guise,
Sorrowful pensiveness in her eyes,
With a little French book in [her] hands.